C000235554

The Manor Houses of Dorset

Above
The stone figure of a winged dragon, or wyvern, at Little Toller Farm.

Following pages
Melbury Bubb Manor and church from Bubb Down.

UNA RUSSELL & AUDREY GRINDROD

COLOUR PHOTOGRAPHS
MERLE AND ALAN GRAHAM

The MANOR HOUSES of DORSET

THE DOVECOTE PRESS

WATERSTON MANOR.
An eighteenth century engraving of the east front. The gabled bay is dated 1586 and is one of Dorset's architectural masterpieces, reflecting the wealth and self-confidence of the Elizabethan age – a period when many of Dorset's manor houses were first built.

First published in 2007 by The Dovecote Press Ltd
Stanbridge, Wimborne Minster, Dorset, BH21 4JD

ISBN 9781904349525

Designed by The Dovecote Press
Printed and bound in Singapore

All papers used by The Dovecote Press are natural, recyclable products
made from wood grown in sustainable, well-managed forests.

A CIP catalogue record for this book is available
from the British Library

1 3 5 7 9 8 6 4 2

Contents

Foreword

MRS ANTHONY PITT-RIVERS

Her Majesty's Lord-Lieutenant of Dorset

I CAME TO live in Dorset in 1970 and have grown to know and love its countryside and the variety of its architecture. Part of the charm of the county is the range of manor houses, usually set naturally in the landscape, in or on the edge of villages bearing their name. Built as the focal point of the village, they were often working farms as several of them still are today and, though retaining their traditional features, they have adapted well to twenty-first century life.

Some continue to be owned and lived in by the families who built them, but greater mobility has brought newcomers who have taken on dilapidated buildings and saved them and their gardens from almost certain destruction. In this book we see a reflection of past and present owners, their tastes, eccentricities and occasional extravagance.

I would love to have joined Audrey Grindrod and Una Russell during the seven years they spent travelling round the county researching and writing this fascinating book. They have produced a scholarly historical record of some of Dorset's loveliest houses and the families who own them and remind us of their durability, celebrating the style and traditions of the past but proving that we have a wonderful heritage for the future.

Valerie Pitt-Rivers

Introduction

Dorset is fortunate in being endowed with a wealth of delightful old manor houses. This is partly because of its geography and partly because it has never been particularly rich. Dorset was far from the centres of fashion and many of its manor houses survived, more or less intact, because they were leased and there was no incentive for either owner or occupier to follow new building trends.

This is not to say that the houses remained entirely unchanged. As owners' fortunes fluctuated and as time went by, they were altered and added to, but many retained parts of the original manor house at their core. It is these, which can trace some substantial part of their fabric back to the centuries when the manorial system flourished, that we have chosen to be the subject of this book.

Although our choice of houses is based on age, mainly determined by architecture, the focus of the book is the history of the people who have owned and/or lived in them. The earliest houses date back to the thirteenth century and still survive due to being built of stone. Moigne Court was built in 1297, Godlingston around 1300, and Woodsford and Quarleston are also fourteenth century. For some houses documentary evidence suggests an even earlier structure on the site, but before the thirteenth century most houses would have been constructed of wood and had a limited life. Later, at the start of the seventeenth century, brick became a fashionable alternative and appears at Bloxworth in 1603 and slightly later at Anderson and Muston, the latter showing some existing stone and flint walling behind the brick frontage. This pattern of change and development continues through the centuries. However, entirely new houses built later than Tudor and Stuart times and which do not include any part of the original house, for example Bryanston, Kingston Lacy and Crichel, were no longer manor houses but 'gentlemen's residences' and are therefore outside the scope of this book.

WOODSFORD CASTLE. The fourteenth century house remains thatched, and still incorporates much of the original stonework.

The flowering of the feudal manors was mainly from the thirteenth to the fifteenth century, although they continued into the seventeenth century, albeit, by this time, peasants were no longer legally bound to their lords and the holding of land in return for labour had ended. By the beginning of the Civil War the old system was extinct, replaced by ownership or rent.

A frequently asked question is 'What exactly was a manor?' Although an exact definition is virtually impossible, it was essentially a unit of land holding. Confusingly, not all villages were wholly within one manor, though many were, and conversely parts of a single manor could be held by different people.

ANDERSON MANOR. The house was started by John Tregonwell of Milton Abbey in 1622 and is one of the earliest uses of brick in Dorset.

Not all manors actually had a manor house, as the lord could live on one of his greater estates and employ bailiffs to oversee his lesser manors. It was basically an agricultural estate, over which lordship was exercised. The lord had legal rights and duties, which regulated his relationship both to his overlord and to his tenants.

The manor was usually in two parts, the demesne and the customary land. The demesne was land over which the lord retained direct control, farming it to produce food for his own consumption or sale, or leasing it to provide an income in cash or kind. The customary land was occupied by tenants. Some of the work on the lord's demesne would be carried out by paid estate labourers or skilled hired workers, such as ploughmen, but a great deal of it was performed by the tenants of the customary land. Essentially, they were paying rent for their holdings by providing labour and capital equipment, such as ploughs, oxen and other tools. There could be manors with large demesnes and few tenants, and vice versa, and money payments could occasionally be substituted for labour services, but generally about one-third of the land was held in demesne and the other two-thirds occupied by the peasants. It was a system of property holding which changed and developed through time until it was no longer a recognisable entity. The church also owned huge numbers of manors, some leased to tenants and others farmed directly by the abbeys for produce for their own consumption or sale. The land farmed directly by the monasteries was outside the manorial system and not held for rents or services and we have therefore excluded it.

Some readers may wonder why have we not included a particular house. Usually the answer is that, over the centuries, many lovely old houses have acquired the word manor in their name, although they were not actually manor houses, Bettiscombe and Woolbridge are examples. Sadly we cannot include them, nor those that were part of monastery demesne land, as were Cerne, Milton Abbas or Forde. Regretfully after much heart searching, we decided to omit the manors of Sandford Orcas, Trent and Poyntington, because they were not within the boundaries of Dorset until 1896 and their manorial history lies within that of Somerset.

Saxon England had agricultural estates both great and small, and some land was held by services to overlords. In south and south-western England, in particular, the roots of the manorial system were already in place in 1066, but the massive expansion and formalisation of the system came after the Norman Conquest. After his victory at Hastings, William established personal ownership of the whole of England. He then parcelled out large areas of land to his chief knights and retainers as reward for their support and to secure their loyalty in

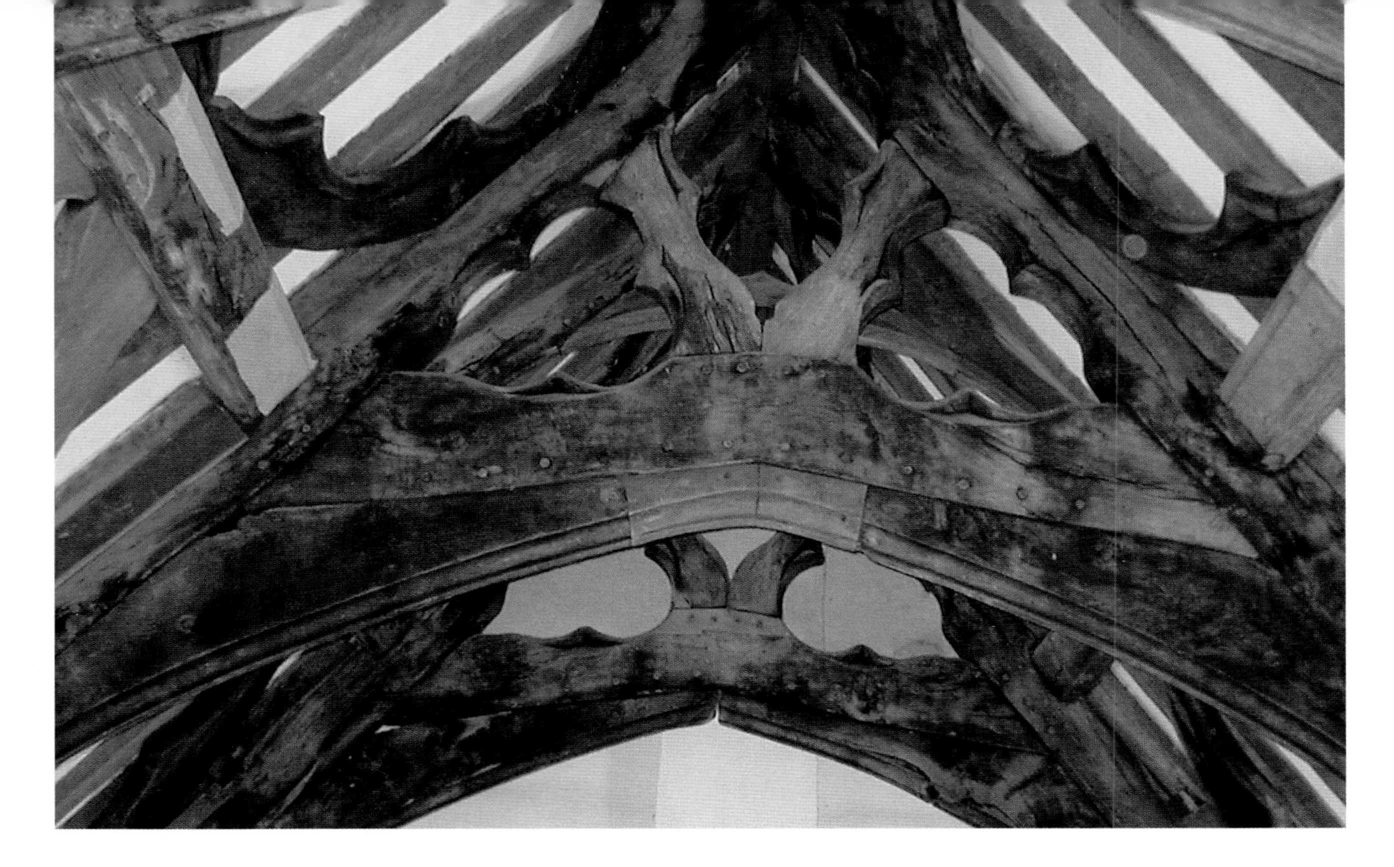

FIDDLEFORD MANOR. The chamfered beams and timber framing are sixteenth century, and the best examples of their kind in Dorset.

future. The service they owed was mainly military, but often included attending the courts of the hundred and county, generally the King's courts, and undertaking other administrative duties. The lords themselves could hold courts on their manors to deal with petty crime, neighbourly disputes and antisocial behaviour. They in turn, granted land on similar terms to their lesser knights and retainers and so on down the social scale, forming a pyramid structure with the king at the top and the peasants at the bottom, who were legally bound to the lord and had little or no personal freedom.

Over the centuries, change was usually gradual, but at times national or world events were such that the pace accelerated and changes were more dramatic. In the mid fourteenth century the cataclysmic event known to us as the Black Death began in Dorset. In July 1348 a ship docked in Melcombe Regis, bringing with it a crew suffering from the plague and also, inevitably, rats, which were carriers of the disease. It raged through Dorset and quickly spread to the rest of the kingdom. The death toll in the county during 1348-49 has been estimated at between a third and a half of the population. Nor was it limited to a single outbreak, the plague recurred at intervals throughout the rest of the century. There are records of buildings being uninhabited and in ruins.

An account of the possessions of the Abbot of Cerne in 1356 lists 'divers buildings in ruin at Radepol, Wyrdesforde, Affepuddle, Blokesworth and Wynfryd' and they were not alone. In 1381 the Abbess of Shaftesbury petitioned the king for relief from taxation because nearly all the tenants on their estates were dead of plague, as well as cattle 'of great number and value'.

Apart from the massive death toll creating dire manpower shortages, many peasants had fled their villages in the hope of escaping the plague. Those that survived had little incentive to return to bondage on their own manors. In the general disruption, they could find employment as free labourers, receiving high wages from other lords, desperate for people to work their land. Efforts were made by parliament to control wages and prices, but increasingly manorial lords had to accept that it was better to pay wages and accept rents rather than to try and enforce poorly performed services from unwilling bondsmen. By the early sixteenth century there were few bondsmen left in Dorset.

The area of cultivated arable land decreased drastically after the Black Death. Much of it was enclosed and used to run sheep, which were less labour intensive. The chalk downs are particularly suited to sheep and their numbers increased until they were the most outstanding feature of the Dorset countryside. This proved profitable to the manorial lords and to the abbeys in particular but it was not until towards the end of the fifteenth century that Dorset really recovered and began to prosper again. Many manor houses began to be extended and refurbished and in many cases rebuilt. Fiddleford Manor was built around this time as was Wolfeton. In the sixteenth century Leland wrote in *The Itinerary* that there were, 'al about great flokkes of sheepe' and at the Dissolution, it was only in Dorset where sheep numbers were listed as part of monastic wealth.

In the sixteenth century Henry VIII's determination to divorce Catherine of Aragon in order to marry Anne Boleyn had far reaching consequences. The Pope's refusal to grant the divorce led to the link with Rome being severed. In 1535, Henry became Supreme Head of the Church in England, forcing clergy and heads of all religious houses to swear an Oath of Supremacy to the monarch.

The monasteries had accumulated enormous wealth by way of gifts and endowments from royalty and gentry. Their land spread right across the county bringing in rents from tenants as well as a huge income from sheep. Henry's royal coffers were invariably empty so the monasteries seemed an ideal source of replenishment. Around 1534, Thomas Cromwell, the Vicar General, carried out a survey to assess the wealth of these religious houses. The report must have satisfied Henry, for just five years later the monasteries were dissolved and their land and property passed to the King.

There was little resistance to the Dissolution in

The effigies of Sir John Horsey and his son, also John, in Sherborne Abbey. Sir John built Clifton Maybank and was typical of the Dorset landowners who took advantage of the Dissolution of the Monasteries to increase their wealth.

Dorset. Knowing that the end was in sight, the more astute abbots set about leasing out parts of their land to family and prospective buyers. This provoked Cromwell into swift action and the larger abbeys were taken over in just under three weeks. The local gentry were quick to take advantage of Henry VIII's need for cash, snapping up monastic land at bargain prices. Sir Giles Strangways bought Abbotsbury from the King, with 2000 acres of land, for £1,096 10s. He demolished the buildings, using the material to build a fine mansion, a pattern repeated around the county. Sir John Horsey of Clifton Maybank was another beneficiary of the break-up of the abbeys. The result of this upheaval allowed for the building of new manor houses, with older ones being extended, renovated, or totally rebuilt.

Nearly one hundred years later Charles I was also in financial difficulties. Ultimately his belief in the Divine Right of Kings brought the country to its knees in a Civil War and cost him his head. The country split into two, the Parliamentarians under Oliver Cromwell and the Royalists. Dissatisfaction with the state of the Church of England had seen the growth of Puritanism, and the Puritans sided with Cromwell.

As in the rest of the country, Dorset towns and families were split in their allegiance between Parliament and the King. Dorchester, Wareham,

CREECH GRANGE. Shown here as a model of Victorian domesticity in this nineteenth century engraving, the home of the Royalist Colonel Robert Lawrence was plundered during the Civil War.

Beaminster, Lyme Regis, Poole and Melcombe Regis declared for Parliament. Amongst the leading Parliamentarians were Colonel John Bingham of Binghams Melcombe, Sir Thomas Trenchard of Wolfeton, and the Sydenhams of Wynford Eagle. The Royalist strongholds were Blandford, Sherborne, Bridport, Corfe Castle, Weymouth and Portland, with Sir John and Lady Bankes at Corfe Castle, the Digby family at Sherborne and Sir John Strangways at Abbotsbury. The first major attack came in 1642, when the Earl of Bedford and Sir Walter Erle of Charborough besieged Sherborne Castle, forcing it to surrender.

Though Dorset saw no major battles, it lay between two Royalist strongholds, Oxford, the King's headquarters, and the Royalist West Country. The suffering of the townspeople, as well as the rural communities was hideous, especially at the hands of the King's nephew, Prince Maurice, who did wanton damage to Cranborne Manor, allowed his army to pillage Dorchester and set fire to Beaminster.

There were numerous skirmishes and sieges in the county, the most famous being the great siege of Corfe Castle, defended by the remarkable Lady Bankes. From time to time some gentry changed sides, depending upon how they felt the war was going. The Earl of Bedford changed over to the Royalists, whilst Gerard Napier of More Crichel and Anthony Ashley-Cooper of Wimborne-St-Giles, joined Cromwell's New Model Army. Ashley-Cooper went on to destroy Abbotsbury House, home of Sir John Strangways and likewise Sir Walter Erle plundered Creech Grange, home of Colonel Robert Lawrence, then Governor of Corfe Castle, and who later also changed sides. By 1645, the Royalists were defeated and much of their land was confiscated to pay for the war. Later, if they had the resources, they paid large sums to Parliament in order to reclaim what had once been their own. After the Restoration many Royalists, despite regaining their property, remained impoverished by their contribution to the war. As a result, many houses changed hands towards the end of the century.

By the eighteenth century the old manorial system had long gone but the landed gentry, often direct descendants of the old manorial lords, were still virtual lords of the manor, now serving as Members

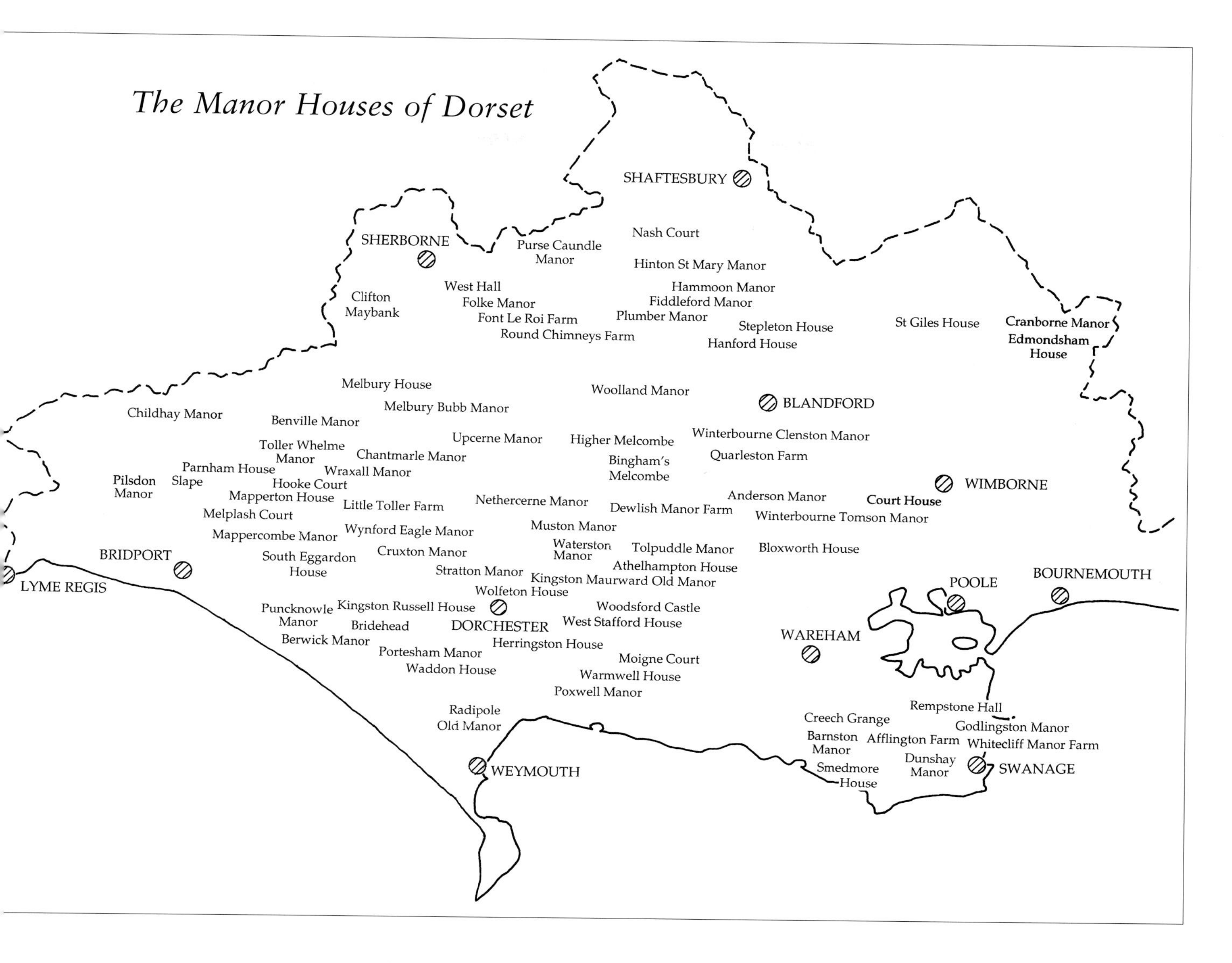

of Parliament, Justices of the Peace and local government officials. They still dominated the class structure, with many families, who had intermarried over generations, creating ties of kinship throughout the county and often forming large estates. Wolfeton, Poxwell and Bloxworth, for example, were united through marriages and inheritance by the Trenchards, who also had family connections with various other manors. Gradually however, their ranks had been infiltrated by wealthy merchants and successful lawyers, who had made their fortunes outside agriculture. One such was Peter Beckford of Stepleton, whose money came from the sugar plantations of Jamaica, while another, Nathaniel Bond of Creech, was a successful lawyer.

These 'nouveau riche' bought up some of the old manors, and either rebuilt the houses or greatly extended and 'modernised' them. By this period some of the smaller manor houses had declined into tenanted farms, yet the eighteenth century was generally one of prosperity for agriculture. The population rose sharply, whilst the Napoleonic wars brought an increased demand for locally grown food due to the naval blockade, which severely limited imports. Prices rose and farmers' profits increased accordingly. Many used this increased prosperity to invest heavily in new leases, stock and equipment, but with the end of the war in 1815 and the resultant imports of European grain, prices dropped. Farmers went out of business and even large landowners felt the pinch. At this time, a number of houses fell into decay and were partially used as farm buildings, for example at Higher Melcombe, Chantmarle and Poxwell.

The nineteenth century as a whole was marked by desperate hardship in the agricultural workforce with an ever widening gap between rich and poor. There was oppression by some landlords but others made valiant efforts to improve the lot of the agricultural workers on their estates, Lord Ilchester at Melbury and the Earl of Shaftesbury at St Giles House for example. Thomas Hardy's descriptions of some of the old manor houses paint a graphic picture of their decay but, although sharply accurate, his romantic vision of life there must have been far from the reality. Victorian taste resulted in many old manor houses being pulled down and rebuilt. Luckily however, by the end of the century, interest in the history of these old houses was developing. During the Edwardian period, new owners often went to great lengths to restore houses sensitively. Waterston, Chantmarle and Anderson all come into this category. Decayed fittings were replaced with contemporary materials brought from houses demolished elsewhere, or local craftsmen created authentic replacements. The first decade of the twentieth century was a time of peace and prosperity and the country houses flourished, but the clouds were gathering and the First World War ushered in another era of major changes.

In the First World War imports of food from the Empire declined drastically due to fear of enemy U-boat attacks. This gave a much needed boost to farming, mainly in milk, pork and potatoes. Land values remained low and some estates were forced to sell a large part of their land to tenants. The Bankes Estates at Corfe Castle and Kingston Lacy parted with over 2,500 acres. Death duties only added to the misery. The fighting itself took its toll on the Dorset gentry, with many of their sons and heirs killed at the front. The young men working on the estates left their jobs to join up and consequently the houses suffered from neglect, and many changed hands after the war.

After a brief respite, the advent of the Second World War temporarily brought a new role to many of the houses. They were occupied by the military, evacuees and refugees and some used as hospitals. For example Anderson Manor was used by the SOE throughout the war and Stafford House became an Officer's Mess for pilots from R.A.F. Warmwell. In the run up to D-Day the Americans flooded into west Dorset, taking over the larger houses and hotels. Parnham House was Headquarters for the US 16th Infantry Regiment, during which time General Eisenhower visited the house. The problems of lack of manpower encountered during the First World War now recurred, with many houses being partially closed up and therefore suffering the effects of damp and decay. Some of the houses requisitioned for the military suffered badly and the cost of repairs was prohibitive.

After the war, domestic staff and farm workers were often unwilling to return to the estates. Death duties became more onerous and during the next two decades many owners, unable to maintain their homes, were forced to sell, with some houses, such as Duntish Court, being demolished. The Old Manor at Kingston Maurward and Bloxworth House were also on the point of being pulled down, but were saved at the eleventh hour. Houses and farms were frequently sold separately, with the houses often being bought by those whose income did not depend on agriculture. New owners, who could invest in restoration and afford the high maintenance costs, brought a renaissance to these ancient houses. This trend continues today, with owners investing capital gained from businesses with no direct link to the countryside into improvements to their houses. The wheel seems to have come full circle, with new money bringing renewed life to these still beautiful houses, as it has in past ages.

Afflington Farm

SITUATED ON THE ancient line of the Purbeck marble quarries, or quarrs as they were called, Afflington Farm is well hidden from the road to Swanage, just west of Corfe. Covering ten acres east of the house, lie remains of the foundations of a hamlet. Henry III granted the inhabitants a market and fair here, indicating a fair sized population at that time, and in 1800 there still remained a community of fifty people.

The present west wing of the farmhouse is the only surviving part of the original house, probably built around 1620 by Giles Green on the site of a previous property. The remainder is a nineteenth century rebuilding in seventeenth century style. The south front of the original wing is least altered, with the original doorway and a two-light stone mullioned window.

AFFLINGTON FARM. The west wing of 1620 is the only surviving part of the original house. It was built by Giles Green, on land leased from Lady Elizabeth Hatton: such agreements between landlord and tenant were once common.

The name comes from the Domesday manor of Alvronetone, held by Aelfrun in the time of Edward the Confessor. Following the Conquest, the manor was held by the Earls of Gloucester and their descendants, the Earls of March.

In 1309 William Baret and his wife Johanna owned land here which passed to Ralph de la Hyde and his wife, Alianor. From then on it moved through several hands until the reign of Henry VIII, when the Marquis of Dorset, Lord Bonvile, sold the manor to Clement Nuce, a London textile dealer who, two years later, sold it to Thomas Hardye, a yeoman farmer and ancestor of Nelson's Admiral Thomas Masterman Hardy.

In 1574, Sir Christopher Hatton purchased Afflington. Knighted for services to Elizabeth I, the queen heaped honours upon him. In 1576 he became Constable of Corfe Castle, Vice-Admiral of Purbeck, Lord Lieutenant of the Island, and guardian of Brownsea Island. He lived mainly in London to be near to the Court, though found the Purbeck appointments lucrative, especially in revenues from piracy. He had a country house in Northamptonshire plus a London house in Holborn, in the neighbourhood now known as Hatton Garden. He died unmarried in 1590 passing his estates to his nephew Sir William Newport of Holdenby, later Sir William Hatton, who married Elizabeth, daughter of Thomas Cecil, Earl of Exeter. Sir Christopher had died leaving huge debts to the crown but the Queen allowed his estates to be leased to William and Francis Tate for twenty-one years or until the debts were paid.

Sir William Hatton also died childless passing on his estate, which included Corfe Castle and Afflington, to his widow, Lady Elizabeth, who leased Afflington in 1620, to Giles Green and it was he who built the manor house. In the lease he promised to 'bestowe twenty pounds at the leaste in new building a farm house near the auncient messuage now standing'. He also promised that 'during the life of Lady Hatton, when she shall have occasion to repaire Corffe Castle, or to erect any new buildings in the island, should allow five carriages yerely with their carters and horses.' Shortly after her husband's death she entered into a mysterious, loveless marriage with Sir Edward Coke, one of the most eminent lawyers in English history, and who as Lord Chief Justice is famed for quotations such as 'a man's house is his castle and where shall a man be safe if it be not in his own home?'

Lady Elizabeth, wealthy in her own right, an arrogant woman, was similar in temperament to her husband. Upon Sir Edward losing favour with James I, she refused to use his name or to live with him, removing furniture and other valuables from their family home at Stoke Poges, Buckinghamshire. They had a daughter, Lady Frances, who lived with her mother, her father taking no interest in her at all, that is, until he could use her for political aims, namely to reinstate himself into royal favour. He abducted his daughter from her mother by force, arranging a marriage between the fourteen-year-old girl and the elderly Sir John Villiers, brother of the favoured Duke of Buckingham. Lady Elizabeth immediately retaliated by arranging for her to marry the Earl of Oxford. For this misdemeanour, Lady Elizabeth was imprisoned. Sir Edward had won the battle. His daughter married Sir John Villiers and was given the title of Lady Purbeck. She hated her husband and her romantic attention to the more dashing Sir Robert Howard, by whom she had a son, brought scandal upon the family.

In 1634, one year after the death of Sir Edward Coke, Lady Elizabeth sold Corfe Castle and her other Purbeck estates to Sir John Bankes. Giles Green then became steward to Sir John and MP for Corfe Castle in 1638, 1640 and 1641 and an Alderman of Melcombe Regis. He is recorded as living at the manor in 1632 and 1654. During the Civil War, a Royalist force plundered Afflington, taking away or killing Giles Green's ewes and lambs. After his death the manor came to the Ettricks of Holt. John Henly of Bristol purchased it in 1731 and through his wife it descended to the Earl of Westmoreland who sold it in 1797 to Edward Balston of Martinstown. In 1822 his daughter sold the estate to Lord Chancellor Eldon of Encombe. It continued as a farm under the ownership of the Scotts of Encombe until 2004.

Anderson Manor

THE HOUSE AT Anderson is less than a mile from the main A31 between Bere Regis and Wimborne, but tucked away in the valley of the Winterborne it seems worlds apart from the rush and bustle of the twenty-first century. It is approached along a country lane from Winterborne Kingston, but the handsome gates and impressive drive to the south front are no longer used. The entrance is now along a short lane, leading past some modern houses and the little church, into a courtyard to the west of the house. The original approach was from the north and curved around the east of the house to the main south entrance.

In *Country Houses of Dorset,* Arthur Oswald described the house as 'one of perhaps a dozen smaller Elizabethan and Jacobean manor houses of England which, by the accomplishment of their design stand in a class by themselves.' He also noted that although the house had been ascribed to Inigo Jones there was no justification for this apart from the obvious quality of its design.

Anderson Manor is three storeys high, of brick with stone dressings, of which every third course of brick is a dark, almost purple shade, giving it a lovely texture. The original house of 1622 was built as an E shape, but in the third quarter of the century a service wing was added at the north-west corner and, soon after, extended further west. The main front faces south and has three gables surmounted by ball finials. The central arm of the E is formed by a half octagonal porch, rising like a turret for the

ANDERSON MANOR. The three gables of the south front, once the main entrance, showing the lovely combination of brick with stone dressings.

John Tregonwell, the builder of Anderson Manor. The house still retains lead rainwater heads and pipes bearing his initials and the date of the house's completion, 1622.

full three storeys. This features lovely mullioned bays to the two storeys above the entrance and has a flat roof with the gable end visible behind it. The whole makes a handsome symmetrical design, whose finishing touch is two lines of four tall chimneys set equidistantly on either side of the central porch.

In front of the house, to the east side, is a delightful formal garden with knots of box enclosing topiary shapes in yew, bounded to the north by a high yew hedge hiding the bowling green. In 1622 when John Tregonwell built his 'faire newe house', as described in Coker's *Survey of Dorsetshire* in about 1625, brick was a comparatively new material in Dorset and it seems strange to consider that his contemporaries would have thought its design extremely modern.

The door in the porch is seventeenth century, studded with nails and with a small spy hole protected by a metal grill. Inside the house, the hall is lined with original oak panelling. Several doorways have moulded surrounds and panelled oak doors with wrought iron hinges.

The oak staircase in the north-west corner of the house has its original wooden dog gate still in situ at the top of the first flight of stairs. The room above the hall on the first floor, which was once the parlour, has an original ceiling with a moulded plaster roundel in the centre. Its design contains roses, thistles, shamrock and a fourth, rather indeterminate plant, which, with a little imagination, could be either a leek or daffodil for Wales.

Anderson has been known by a variety of names over the centuries, the earliest being Winterborne Fyveash, which was recorded in 1294 as held by William de Stokes. The name Five Ash in a variety of spellings persisted for several centuries, but by the beginning of the seventeenth century it was also known as Anderson. There is a reference to it in 1610 as Winterborne Anderson alias Winterborne Fife-Ash. The modern name of Winterborne Anderson is said to derive from the church of St Andrew, although its own little church is dedicated to St Michael.

The Stokes of East Stoke held the manor until the last William de Stokes died childless in 1361 and it was inherited by his two sisters. Only two years later it was in the hands of the Turbervilles, the great landowning family of Bere Regis, and it was theirs at least until 1451. We know that Thomas Morton of Milborne owned it on his death in 1591. There is no clear record of how it came into the Mortons possession, but around the middle of the fifteenth century Richard Morton's wife was Elizabeth Turberville. Their son, also called Richard, married his cousin Edith Turberville, so there is a double connection.

The manor next changed hands in October 1620, when John Tregonwell of Milton Abbey bought it from Sir George Morton as part of a parcel of land which also included the manorial farm of Abbot's Court in Bere Regis. In 1621 John began building his new house at Anderson, which was completed in 1622 and still retains lead rainwater heads and pipes embellished with his initials and that date. His eldest son John married in 1624 and John senior, then 51, retired to live at Anderson leaving his son and new wife to occupy Milton Abbey.

In 1625 Anderson and Abbot's Court were settled on his younger son Thomas when he married Dorothy Ryves. She was a widow and only daughter of Henry Hastings of Woodlands, second son of the 4th Earl of Huntingdon, who lived from 1551 to 1650 and was one of the great personalities of seventeenth century Dorset. Sir Anthony Ashley Cooper, who lived nearby, wrote a humorous account of him in old age. His passion was hunting everything from deer to small birds and his house was full of dogs, hawks and hunting equipment. His floors were strewn with marrow bones, the chairs occupied by litters of cats and the walls hung with skins of foxes and sometimes polecats. His park was well stocked with deer and rabbits and included fishponds and woodland, providing his household with most of its requirements. An exception to this was oysters, which were sent in from Poole, and which he ate morning and evening every day of the year. Perhaps they accounted for his second passion – pursuing the wives and daughters of his neighbours and tenants. Sir Anthony writes, 'there being not a woman in all his walks of the degree of a yeoman's wife or under, and under the age of forty, but it was her own fault if he was not intimately acquainted with her.' These activities notwithstanding, he was a popular man and a generous host with little regard for rank or wealth. He lived to the age of ninety-nine, read and wrote without spectacles to the end of his life and continued stag hunting until he was past eighty.

Anderson was perhaps bought with the intention of it eventually being Thomas's inheritance, although he and Dorothy began their married life at Abbot's Court. It would remain the property of the descendants of Thomas Tregonwell for the next two hundred and eighty years. During the Civil War, John and his eldest son attempted to maintain a neutral stance but Thomas joined the Royalist army, becoming Colonel of a Regiment of Horse, and was fined £600 for taking up arms for the King. In 1645

Henry Hastings of Woodlands, whose daughter Dorothy married Thomas Tregonwell in 1625. Hastings was one of the great eccentrics of seventeenth century Dorset, dying aged ninety-nine.

John senior's property was confiscated, ostensibly because he was Catholic and had left his house, which was forbidden, but he was also accused of lending a sum of £500 to the King and was threatened with 'imprisonment and plundering and that his bones should lie by it' unless he contributed five times that amount to the Parliament. His house, stock and goods were taken away by the Parliamentary forces and in his middle seventies, old and frail, John had to leave his home. In 1646 he paid a fine of £3735 but this was followed almost immediately by a further demand for £1500, which was eventually paid piecemeal over the next few months. After John's death, Thomas and his wife moved to live at Anderson.

Thomas's great, great grandson, born in 1758 and rejoicing in the name of Lewis Dymoke Grosvenor Tregonwell, built the first house at Bournemouth and initiated its growth as a fashionable resort. At

ANDERSON MANOR. An engraving of about 1860.

the age of 23, in 1781, he married Katherine Sydenham, a considerable heiress. Lewis was a spendthrift and by 1787 he had run through Katherine's inheritance and the couple went to France to escape their creditors. He tried to obtain money from his father-in-law, who was feeble-minded, and the following year, on his return from France, Lewis contrived to abduct the elderly Sydenham and persuade him to live with them. He then used the old man's money to buy Cranborne Lodge, which they moved into, letting Anderson to tenants. Katherine had three children, including a son called St Barbe. Katherine died in 1794, by which time the twelve year old St Barbe was already showing signs of suffering from the same mental handicap as his grandfather.

In 1800 Lewis married again, this time to Henrietta Portman, daughter of the extremely wealthy Henry Portman of Bryanston. It was on an outing for a picnic to the little cove and beach at Bourne Mouth in 1810 that Henrietta fell in love with the place and persuaded her husband to build a 'cottage' there as a summer retreat. The 'cottage' was Exeter House, which is now part of the Royal Exeter Hotel and where a small memorial plaque describes Lewis Tregonwell as the 'Founder of Bournemouth'.

Katherine's daughter Helen inherited Anderson, followed by her only surviving son, Edward Sydenham Markland. He and his wife had no children and on his death it passed to his unmarried sister, Sophia. In 1902, she sold it to Mr. H.J.S. Tory of Damory Court, Blandford, who continued to lease it to tenants.

In 1910 the house was sold to Mr. and Mrs. Gordon Gratrix. It was sadly dilapidated by this time, overgrown with ivy and with many windows blocked up, but its exterior was essentially unchanged since its building in 1622. The house found a saviour in Mrs. Gratrix. She carried out repairs and some essential modernisation with great sensitivity, exposing much of the original interior and restoring it to something close to its original plan. She also laid out new gardens based on traces of the old and uncovered the foundations of the original terrace forecourt and garden houses.

In 1913, in spite of the loving care she had lavished on it, Mrs. Gratrix sold the house to Colonel J.C. Tabor of the wonderfully named Eighth Cyclist Battalion of the Essex Regiment. He sold it towards the end of the decade to a Mr.

Hamilton Rivers Pollock who only remained there until 1922. It was then sold to Major R.H. Cholmondeley, who lived there until 1936 when he leased it to Mr. and Mrs. Young, from Dewlish.

In 1942 the house was taken over by the War Ministry and became the headquarters for the Small Scale Raiding Force known as 62 Commando, established on the orders of Winston Churchill, and led by Major Gus March-Phillips. He was a keen amateur sailor and also hunted with the South Dorset. He had lived in Bere Regis before the war and knew Major Cholmondeley and the house and was probably instrumental in its choice as a headquarters. Major March-Phillips was involved in the evacuation from Dunkirk and met Geoffrey Appleyard on the beach, where they talked about the future course of the war and their part in it, and it was there that the seeds of the SSRF were sown.

Back in England, they managed to get their ideas for a small raiding force accepted and, in early 1942, together with a third Army officer, Graham Hayes, set up a small sabotage force under the direct command of Lord Mountbatten and proceeded to recruit and train other volunteers. They found a suitable boat for their purposes in Brixham and requisitioned the trawler *Maid Honour*, entirely on their own authority. They also managed to persuade the owner to accompany them as her skipper. Their earliest exploits were off the coast of West Africa, where one of their raids culminated in the capture of an Italian freighter and a German tanker.

Back in Europe and equipped with Motor Torpedo Boat 344, affectionately christened *The Little Pisser* because of her superior power, 62 Commando were responsible for a number of daring raids across the Channel planned at Anderson. The most famous probably being the raid on a U-boat signalling station based in the Casquettes lighthouse in the Channel Islands, in which they captured all seven German crew and the main U-boat code books. In September 1942 Gus March-Phillips was killed with three of his men during a raid at St Honorine. Graham Hayes escaped and eventually reached neutral Spain but

Major Gus March-Phillips DSO. In 1942 Anderson Manor became the headquarters of the Small Scale Raiding Force, commanded by March-Phillips.

was handed over to the local Gestapo and in 1943 was executed in the notorious Fresnes prison in Paris. Operations continued under the command of Major Appleyard but at the end of the year most of the force was transferred to Algeria and became part of the newly formed SAS Regiment. Geoffrey Appleyard became Second-in-Command of 2 SAS, but was killed in the invasion of Sicily.

The SSRF disbanded in 1943 but Anderson remained in the hands of the SOE as Station 62, used to train undercover agents to operate in occupied territory. During this time there was an outdoor firing range behind the house, an indoor range in the western courtyard and a strenuous obstacle course in the main driveway at the front of the house.

After the war the house was again leased, this time to Lord Chief Justice, Lord Goddard, and then in the early fifties it became empty and neglected and was bought by a consortium, which included Rebbecks Estate Agents. At this time much of the land was sold off in parcels and in 1954 Mr. Eric Bullivant bought the house and lived there until his death in 1973. In 1975 Mr. and Mrs. J.J.B. Isaac bought the house at auction and it once again became a family home.

Athelhampton House

'He who looks at Martyn's ape,
Martyn's ape shall look at him.'

THIS FAMILY motto could be construed as intimidating, but in heraldic language it means 'a martin sejant' or chained ape. In this case, the ape has angel's wings and gazes into a gilded mirror. The 'gilded mirror' could easily be Athelhampton, the beautiful manor house started by the Martyns in the same year as the Battle of Bosworth, 1485, a year generally thought to mark the end of the middle ages and the beginning of the Tudor period.

According to John Hutchins in *The History and Antiquities of the County of Dorset*, many in Dorset traditionally maintained that Athelhampton was the seat of the Saxon kings, with the name Athelhamstan composed of three Saxon words, *athel* meaning noble, *ham* a home, and *stan* implying the highest degree. Again, others say it was the site of the palace of King Athelstan. Unfortunately all this is conjecture. More likely the name comes from Athelhelm, a Saxon Earl of Dorset, who was killed in 837 commanding the Dorsetshire men against the Vikings at Portland. One thing is certain, this was an important place in Saxon times. Situated on the south bank of the River Piddle, the present house lies half a mile south-east of Puddletown. In early times the river, as well as the valley, was called Pidele. In 1066 Aethelric held the manor and in Domesday Book the Bishop of Salisbury held it with Odbold as tenant.

The earliest lords of the manor were the de Londres, from whom it passed to Henry de Pydele in 1280. Around 1350 Sir Richard Martyn of Waterston married the heiress of the Pydele family and thus the Martyn family became Lords of Athelhampton for the next two and a half centuries. The Martyns originally came from Turon, near Bayeaux, arriving in this country with William the Conqueror.

Sir Richard Martyn's grandson, Sir William, built Athelhampton House on the site of an earlier dwelling, inhabited since 1086. He was a London merchant who became Master of the Skinner's Company and held the monopoly of collecting duty on wine in the south of England. He was granted a licence to enclose 160 acres of deer park, part of whose boundary can still be seen south of the church. He also fortified the manor house with walls and crenellated towers. Sir William was Lord Mayor of London in 1493 and knighted by Henry VII in 1494. His tomb is in the Athelhampton Chantry in St Mary's Church, Puddletown.

His house consisted of the porch, the Great Hall, with oriel window and a solar and buttery at opposite ends. The porch, with a room over it, leads into the Great Hall. This magnificent hall rises up to the full height of the open timber roof, which is 50 feet high and ornamented with gilded bosses. Surrounded by windows of armorial glass, many of which are original, this must surely be one of the most beautiful and well-preserved examples of a fifteenth century manor house. The oriel window with its delicate tracery and heraldic glass is delightful. Where the solar was located is now known as the King's Room. Here the manorial court was held. In the Second World War it was used as a gunroom by troops billeted at the house. The State Bedroom has the original fifteenth century Ham stone fireplace showing the crest of the ape of Sir William Martyn's family and the unicorn from the Faringdon crest of his first wife.

Robert Martyn, great grandson of Sir William,

married Elizabeth Kelway of Rockburn, Hampshire. Before 1550 he extended the Great Hall by adding the west wing and a courtyard, bounded by a wall and two-tier gatehouse, both pulled down in 1862. Displayed on the gateway was a cartouche of Martyn quartering Kelway, now preserved in the house. Between 1550 and 1850, the house was extended to the rear with a central court.

Robert's son, Sir Nicholas, married Margaret Wadham, sister of Nicholas Wadham, the founder of Wadham College, Oxford. All three of their sons died young, as did three of their seven daughters. The four remaining daughters inherited equal shares, not only of Athelhampton, but also of the inheritance of their maternal uncle, Nicholas Wadham, a man of great wealth who died childless. As well as the land, the house was also divided into four parts, not returning into single ownership until the 1800s. The eldest daughter, Elizabeth, married Henry Brune a descendant of the Prideaux-Brunes of Cornwall. Their second daughter, Jane, married Chidiock Tichborne, not Henry Tichborne, as claimed by Hutchins. Frances married Thomas White of Fiddleford, and Anne married Anthony

ATHELHAMPTON HOUSE. The south front, showing the porch and oriel window, of the house built by Sir William Martyn towards the end of the fifteenth century.

ATHELHAMPTON HOUSE. The west wing built by Robert Martyn, Sir William's great grandson, in the mid sixteenth century.

ATHELHAMPTON HOUSE. An etching of 1816 by the Dorset artist John Baverstock Knight showing the gatehouse, demolished in 1862.

ATHELHAMPTON HOUSE. An early watercolour by Thomas Hardy, painted in 1859 when Hardy was nineteen and working for the Dorchester architect John Hicks. As with the previous illustration, it includes the soon-to-be demolished gatehouse.

Opposite page ATHELHAMPTON HOUSE. Two views of the gardens created by Francis Inigo Thomas in the Edwardian period.

Floyer, of Floyer's Hays, Devon.

In 1586 Chidiock Tichborne was executed for his part in the Babington Plot to assassinate Elizabeth I and replace her with the Catholic Mary Queen of Scots. The Brunes and the Martins were Catholics and were suspected of assisting Tichborne. Henry Brune was also arrested and imprisoned in the Tower but was luckily released. Jane forfeited her inheritance upon her husband's execution as a traitor, and her share of the estate was divided between her sisters, with the Brunes taking two shares. Sir John Brune, Henry's father, lived for no known reason, in Athelhampton over a long period of time. The Floyers retained their share of Jane's inheritance until 1848. During the Civil War, from 1645-1653 Thomas White's farm here was confiscated and after the war bought by the Brunes.

Henry and Elizabeth Brune's grandson, John, who was a colonel in Cromwell's army, died in 1645 leaving an only daughter, Mary. In 1661 she married Sir Ralph Bankes, the builder of Kingston Lacy. Her inheritance of £1,200 a year was used for the building project, but even so Sir Ralph Bankes was forced to sell Mary's entire inheritance to cover his debts. He sold his wife's share of Athelhampton to Sir Robert Long of Dracot Cerne, Wiltshire.

Sir Robert Long was Secretary to Charles II, member of the Privy Council and Auditor of the Exchequer. Knighted in 1662, he died childless in 1673 and his nephew, Sir James Long of Draycot Cerne, succeeded him. During the Longs' ownership, the house was divided into two separate households and remained so until the nineteenth century. It was occupied by tenant farmers and became run down. Through the Longs, who had little interest in the estate, Athelhampton came into the family of the 4th Earl of Mornington, nephew of the Duke of Wellington.

Around 1840 a farmer, George James Wood, bought the house, with one quarter of it still in the hands of the Floyers until an exchange was agreed with the new owner. Mr. Wood lived here until 1891, during which time he restored much of the house and repaired the hall roof. His builders were members of Thomas Hardy's family.

George Wood demolished the ancient gatehouse and chapel in 1862 along with the enclosing walls of the two front quadrangles. The masonry was used to build the stables. The gatehouse had been in a sad state of repair but he did re-erect its carved oriel into a small building to the west, pulled down

by the next owner, Mr. Alfred Cart de Lafontaine. In 1862 St John's Church was built on the other side of the main road. The building was designed by the Dorchester architect, Hicks, who had the young Thomas Hardy working for him at the time.

Mr. Alfred Cart de Lafontaine purchased the house in 1891. He carefully restored parts of the house, notably the plaster ceiling of the great chamber in 1905. This room had been used as a granary. The library had been partitioned into three bedrooms. He opened them into one room with oak panelling and replaced the plaster ceiling. Perhaps the greatest achievement was his re-creation of the gardens, landscaped by Francis Inigo Thomas. He designed the great court with the pyramid yews, now nearly thirty feet high, along with the Terrace, the Corona, the Private Garden and the Lion's Mouth, all of which give the garden a feeling of opulence. The dovecote, with room for 1,500 birds to nest, was re-roofed in 1971. The cedar lantern has landing stages for forty doves, and among the many names and dates scratched upon it is that of Thomas Hardy.

Mr. George Cochrane became the new owner in 1918. He built the north wing in 1920-21 and reconstructed the rear part of the house. When his wife died he sold the house to the Hon. Mrs. Esmond Harmsworth, then recently separated from her husband, the newspaper tycoon and owner of the *Daily Mail*, later known as Lord Rothermere. Among the many celebrities entertained at the house during her time were Douglas Fairbanks, Noel Coward and the Aga Khan.

Rodney Phillips, who owned the literary periodical *Polemic*, bought the house in 1949. He married Marika Vorobyev, daughter of the Cubist painter Marevna Vorobyev, who often visited the house, and whose work is now permanently exhibited there.

On the break up of the Phillips marriage in 1955, Athelhampton was once again sold. The new owner, Robert Victor Cooke F.R.C.S., though a surgeon by profession, was also a great collector. In 1957 he found Athelhampton the ideal location for his collection. Sadly his wife died in 1964 and, losing interest in his project, he presented the house to his son Robert and future daughter-in-law, Jenifer, on condition that they continued to add to the collection and improve the house and gardens. Sir Robert Cooke was M.P. for Bristol West from 1957 to 1979. He was keenly interested in the Palace of Westminster and Victorian Gothic works of art.

Included in his collection is a delicately carved torchère, or tall floor lamp, made from Coade stone. Eleanor Coade lived in Lyme Regis from 1784 until her death in 1821, although her factory and studio were in Lambeth. The stone to which she gave her name was made from ball clay, crushed flint and finely ground stoneware and glass. It closely resembled natural stone, yet could withstand frost, fire and pollution without losing its fine appearance. This unusual torchère, part of a set of ten, was commissioned for George, Prince of Wales in 1810. Examples of Coade stone are found in many parts of Dorset.

Sir Robert Cooke died in 1987. His widow, Jenifer, married The Rt. Hon. Sir Edward Du Cann in 1990 and she died five years later.

Patrick Cooke and his wife, Andrea, are now the custodians of Athelhampton. Patrick has been instrumental in co-ordinating the restoration of the east wing, severely damaged by fire in 1992. The gardens are constantly changing and become ever more interesting. In 2002 the Elizabethan style Corona was replanted by Andrea with bold regal colours enhancing the beauty of the stone walls of the crown. It is no wonder that these gardens, as well as the house, are a favourite location for films and television programmes. Thomas Hardy, too, found inspiration at Athelhampton for his poetry and his prose. He used the river, hall and gardens in his short, sinister story, *The Waiting Supper*. He also painted a watercolour of the south front, along with the now demolished gatehouse.

The ape, once Martyns's ape, now wearing a Saxon crown and carrying a mace, constitutes the heraldic badge of the Cooke family, a continuing reminder of the fascinating history of Athelhampton spanning over five hundred years.

Barnston Manor

THE PURBECK HILLS enfold several ancient manors, one of which, Barnston, lies well hidden on the north side of the road from Church Knowle. It is believed to be the oldest inhabited manor house in Dorset and its name comes from Bern, a Saxon thane, who held the land in the reign of Edward the Confessor. After the Conquest the land was given to Walter de Clavile, but from the reign of Edward I (1272-1307), until 1426, the Estokes of East Stoke were the owners and it is reasonable to suppose that they built the house.

As the slightly forbidding stone house comes into view, it is the huge eighteenth century barn and stable block which first catches the eye, followed by the towering buttress at the east end of the house. Walking round to the south side, though, the house soon reveals one of its many treasures, a Tudor two-storey bay window which gently softens the ashlar stone facing.

On the north side the walls are thicker, as though built to withstand attack. The buttresses on this wall and an ancient window are probably late thirteenth century. The window is of particular interest with a stone window seat below it and a quatrefoil light above. Before glass panes came into use shutters were used for protection from the elements, and here the hooks upon which the shutters were hung still remain intact, as does the hole in the central mullion through which the shutters were secured.

The interior consisted of the Great Hall with a central hearth and a solar at the western end. A wooden screen would have protected the hall from the outer doorways at the east side of the hall, a remnant of which still survives. During Tudor times the hall was gradually altered. A ceiling was inserted allowing space for bedrooms above, and the central hearth was replaced by the great chimneystack on the south wall. The early wooden staircase, leading from the Great Hall to the solar, was superseded by the present stone one. On this staircase is a doorway, now blocked up, which perhaps marks the original entrance into the solar from the wooden staircase. In this period too, the glorious bay windows would have been added, allowing in much needed light. A wing was added onto the western end, and in the upstairs room there remains the lintel of a doorway which would have led into a long since demolished garderobe. All that survives is a slit window, in the north-west wall, a necessity in a garderobe.

BARNSTON MANOR. The house in the late nineteenth century with the two-storey Tudor bay added by the Clavells before 1550.

Foundations near the east wing could well mark the site of the kitchen, which would have been set slightly away from the house. The south side of the house had a walled courtyard with a gatehouse, removed around 1840. The eighteenth century

outbuildings are worthy of note. In the huge barn there is an old stone corbel in the roof by the south entrance, and outside the stable block is a well worn gargoyle, its origins unknown.

Late in the reign of Henry VI (1421–1471), Barnston returned to the Clavell family when Johanna, heiress of both William Wyot of Smedmore and the Estokes of Barnston, married John Clavell of Leeson. A stone corbel at ceiling level was recently discovered bearing the initials R.C. These could possibly be the initials of Roger Clavell, who died in 1551, and who was the great grandson of John and Johanna Clavell. Little is known of the lives of the Clavells until the time of Roger Clavell's grandsons, John (1541-1609), and William (died 1596). They were well known for their dealings with pirates along the Purbeck coast. As well as Smedmore, they owned Kimmeridge, which their father had bought in 1554, and wrecks from the Purbeck shores provided a lucrative income. They were eventually arrested, along with several others, and sent to London to be examined. Some were sentenced to death, but the Clavell brothers were acquitted, and in 1586 John was appointed M.P. for Corfe. There is a splendid memorial to him and his family in the church of St Peter the Apostle at Church Knowle.

By 1623, Sir William Clavell, John's son, had built Smedmore House. A reckless businessman, he sank into financial difficulties and sold Barnston to William Bond of Blackmanston. It passed down through this family to the Rev. Farr Yeatman, and in 1819 it was sold to George Filliter of Wareham who made various, and not altogether sympathetic, alterations to the house. He divided the Great Hall and removed a dais from the western end. The next purchaser, in 1852, was the Rev. Nathaniel Bond in whose family the house remained until 1968, when it was bought by Mr. Albert Fry of Kimmeridge. He retained the farmland, but sold the house and surrounding buildings to the Mansell-Pleydells, who are descendents of the Clavells. Following in the footsteps of their ancestors, they have repaired and restored the house to much of its original form. It is an achievement to be proud of in a remarkable house which has seen the passing of 700 years.

BARNSTON MANOR. The house was built by the Estokes in the late fourteenth century, and is thought to be the oldest inhabitated manor house in Dorset.

BARNSTON MANOR. A well worn gargoyle on the stable block.

Benville Manor

IN THE MID SEVENTEENTH century two sisters came to Benville to a house bought for them by their father, so that they might 'live quietly'. Benville Manor is still a place where one might live quietly, amidst beautiful Dorset countryside. The village of Benville is small and the house, set a little apart in its garden amongst the trees, is still secluded. Even so it has seen dramatic and frightening events in its long life. It was built early in the seventeenth century and is two storeys, mainly of rubble stone and ashlar with some brick. It was originally designed on an H plan but part of one wing has been pulled down and there are modern additions to the other which obscure the layout. The porch on the south front is modern, but the two storey bay windows on either side of it are seventeenth century. It is a most attractive house, which seems somehow to have a modest and retiring air about it.

It is situated in the parish of Corscombe near Toller Whelme and up until the mid fifteenth century it was also known as Earnley. The name is said to be derived from Earna Legh, or eagles lea, although eagles in Dorset seem a little unlikely! After the Conquest it belonged to Frampton Priory, which William I had added to his Abbey at Caen. In about 1340 a John de Benfeld lived in the neighbourhood and he was possibly the inhabitant of an earlier manor house, which stood some eighty yards north of the present house, where the remains of a rectangular moat can still be seen.

In the second half of the fifteenth century, Gilbert Kymer, Dean of Salisbury, Dean of Wimborne, Chancellor of Oxford University and Physician to

BENVILLE MANOR. The gable end of the house with ascending 5, 4 and 3 light mullioned windows.

Henry VI, was Lord of the Manor of West Chelborough and Benville. The Kymers had owned the manor at West Chelborough from before the fifteenth century and there is a charming seventeenth century tomb to Elizabeth Kymer in the church there.

In 1620 the two sisters, Winifred and Elizabeth Brereton, arrived at Benville. They were the youngest daughters of Thomas Brereton and Jane Hill of Yarde, near Taunton. They were a Catholic family and their father bought Benville for the girls so that they could live quietly with other Catholic families nearby, notably the Arundells at Chideock. This was a time when Catholics were regarded with suspicion and there were even fears that adherents to the Roman Catholic Church might assist any attempted invasion on the Dorset coast.

In 1626 the Breretons were subjected to a terrifying attack by a group of soldiers who had been drinking in the Swan Inn at Evershot and thought that they would find a Catholic priest in the house. They were overheard plotting mischief by a local man called Fookes, who decided to warn the two women of the planned attack, giving them time to lock and bar the doors against the mob. A man called Robert Wareham, who was in the house, tried unsuccessfully to buy off the rioters with £40. Shots were fired and the mob tried to break down the door, making threats to kill everyone in the house. Eventually a terrified Winifred Brereton wrapped three or four pieces of gold in a cloth and threw it out of a window. This seemed to satisfy them and they set off back to Evershot, stopping at another inn on the way to drink their booty.

The next day they were placed under arrest and in due course a warrant was issued for their committal to prison in Dorchester. A constable and twenty-seven musketeers were sent to escort the prisoners to Dorchester but either they were very inefficient or their hearts weren't in it, because en route, some of the prisoners escaped and others were rescued, with only four arriving to be committed to the quarter sessions.

Robert Wareham was a member of a local Catholic family, whose brother John was a priest at Whitchurch Canonicorum. Another brother, George, was an 'agent' for conveying English girls who wished to become nuns to convents in Flanders. Convents accepted young women on the payment of a £300 dowry and for each girl George Wareham delivered he received £50. In due course he escorted Elizabeth Brereton to a convent at Bruges, where she remained for at least eighteen years and probably for the rest of her life. Her elder sister Winifred later married George Arundell, youngest son of John Arundell of Chideock.

After Elizabeth had taken her vows, it was found that all her property, amounting to about £1000 or more, had fallen into the hands of John and George Wareham. Winifred and her husband took out a lawsuit to try and recover it. The evidence given about Wareham's methods reads rather like a modern description of white slave trafficking! He took the girls to London, taking care that they did not meet anyone they knew, and from there they travelled to the Continent. Once abroad, any pleas from the girls to be allowed home again were ignored or met with violence. This treatment had apparently been experienced by two sisters of George Arundell in 1619, but when their father learnt of their distress they were brought home; the convent being willing to release them, providing they retained the girls' £300 dowry. Some witnesses testified that Elizabeth had been visited by English travellers and had always professed a wish to return to England. The Wareham's case was that Elizabeth had made over all her property to them for services rendered. The court found in the Warehams favour and the estate at Benville was divided, half to the Arundells, which included the manor house, and half to the Warehams, who later sold their part to Henry Samways of Waterston.

The descendants of Winifred and George Arundell owned Benville for about the next two hundred and fifty years. Winifred's great grandson, John Arundell, who had no male heirs, bequeathed Benville to a relative, John Hanne of Deviocke in Cornwall, a descendant of Winifred's daughter Mary, who had married John Hanne from Mawgan. It remained the property of the Hannes until the end

BENVIILE MANOR. The manor house with its seventeenth century two storey bay windows, still a peaceful and secluded place.

of the nineteenth century, although it declined into a farmhouse.

In about 1870 the last Miss Arundel Hanne sold the property to Mr. George Troyte-Bullock of Coker House, North Coker (who later added Chafyn-Grove to his surname). He restored it to a manor house and his grandson, Colonel Cecil Troyte-Bullock, was a life tenant. He remained unmarried and when he died in the late 1950s his niece, Elizabeth Grace, daughter of Edward Troyte-Bullock and Grace Batten inherited the manor house. She married twice, firstly to Major Geoffrey Sebag-Montefiore, who died in 1943, and secondly to Brigadier David Block. Her son by her first marriage, Major Peter Sebag-Montefiore, inherited from Mrs. Block in 1975 and he and his wife came to live at Benville in 1977.

Berwick Manor

THIS HOUSE was the childhood home of John Russell, created first Earl of Bedford in 1550. It was probably built in the late fifteenth or early sixteenth century by John Russell's grandfather.

Hutchins knew the house well. He was appointed rector of Holy Trinity, the parish church of Swyre and Berwick in 1729. The church was badly in need of repair and Hutchins spent £40 of his own money repairing the chancel during his tenure. In his *History of Dorset* he describes the house as 'large and ancient and fronted seventy-two feet every way'. In the middle was a small quadrangle and to the north a little court, leading to the principal entrance by a large gateway.

On the east and west sides were the old windows projecting beyond the walls, some as high as the eaves but there were none in the lower part. On the north and east were two turrets projecting six or eight feet beyond the walls containing apertures for arrows or guns. It was a house designed to withstand attack, particularly against the French, who regularly pillaged this coast. Mr. Coker, writing in the 1620s, said the house was ruined in his time, the owners being so harassed by the French pirates that they were forced to flee inland. Hutchins disagreed, finding few signs of any major repairs to the building.

Before the Domesday Survey this land, close to Burton Bradstock, was owned by Toxos, one of the king's bailiffs. He held on to it during the reigns of Edward the Confessor and King Harold. The first record of a Russell connection in Berwick is in 1040, when Hugh de Russell died. John de la Tour, in 1272, also held land in and around Berwick. In 1347 Ralph de Ufford held the manor for the Countess of Sarum while in the early 1400s the Earls of March seem to have been lords of the manor. It is clear that the manor of Berwick had

BERWICK MANOR. Described by John Hutchins as 'large and ancient'.

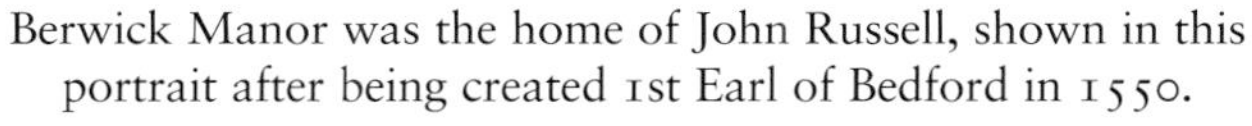

Berwick Manor was the home of John Russell, shown in this portrait after being created 1st Earl of Bedford in 1550.

BERWICK MANOR. A watercolour of the manor and its surrounding farm buildings in the early 1800s by John Baverstock Knight.

been an important manor for over three centuries.

Theobald Russell, of the Kingston Russell family, died in 1340. His second wife was Eleanor de la Tour. Their grandson was known as Henry of Weymouth, who married Elizabeth Frocksmere, and their son, James, married Alice Wyse.

James and Alice's son John was born in 1485 and spent most of his youth overseas. It is thought that John's great-grandfather, Henry of Weymouth, was related to Stephen Russell, a wealthy Weymouth merchant who owned a fleet of ships and who had been MP for Weymouth in 1394-5. He had married Alice, heiress of the Blynchesfields and de la Tour families. In 1422 Alice proved her claim to be the rightful descendant of the de la Tours of Berwick in a court in Dorchester.

As a young man, John Russell ferried pilgrims from Weymouth to Santiago de Compostella, and through his travels learned several languages. His career took a dramatic turn in 1506 when he came to the assistance of Joanna, the daughter of the King and Queen of Castile, and her husband Archduke Philip of Austria. Their ship was forced to seek shelter from a storm in Weymouth. John was called upon to be their interpreter and accompanied them to the court of Henry VII. Thus began his rise to power. He was created Earl of Bedford in 1550 and remained at court until the reign of Mary Tudor (*see* the full story under Wolfeton House).

In the reign of Elizabeth the manor was leased to the Greys of Askerswell, followed by the Holmans and Squibbs in the 1600s. John and Robert Napier of Puncknowle had interests here too. By 1687 the manor was leased to Julius Squibb. His daughter, Mary, married George Gallop of Strode and they too lived at Berwick. George Gallop died in 1729 and was buried at the parish church when John Hutchins was rector.

When the lease ended, the house was rebuilt by the Bedford Estate and scaled down in size. In the hall, which was old, large and lofty, there were formerly stained glass windows displaying the arms of the Russells and de la Tours. They were removed to Woburn Abbey in 1751, severing the last connection of the Russells with Berwick Manor. Around 1794 Berwick was let to the Bryants who were there well into the twentieth century, eventually as owners. Although the interior of the house has been drastically altered in modern times, the exterior of the wing facing the road is still as Hutchins described it. It is interesting to compare the modern photograph with the painting by John Baverstock Knight in the early 1800s. The large barn, south-east of the house was built in the early eighteenth century. Berwick is now part of the Puncknowle Manor estates.

Bingham's Melcombe

TWO STONE EAGLES, with wings poised for flight, stand dramatically upon the gateposts at the entrance to Bingham's Melcombe. The eagle was the crest of the Bingham family who lived here for close on seven hundred years. The manor first belonged to the Turberville family, then in the late thirteenth century, Sir Robert Turberville's daughter and heiress, Lucy, married Robert Bingham of Sutton Bingham in Somerset. Thereafter the Binghams lived here continuously until 1895.

This lovely house, in the parish of Higher Melcombe, nestles in a combe carved through the chalk downland by the Dewlish or Devlish Brook, which flows south towards Puddletown. The driveway leads to the medieval gatehouse on the south side of the manor house and into an irregular shaped courtyard. On the far side, a flight of steps rises to a terrace flanked by hydrangeas – a feature there for at least 150 years.

The house is of many dates from the fifteenth century onwards, built mainly of Purbeck stone with sash windows sitting comfortably next to mullioned windows. From the terrace rises the magnificent two-storey Tudor oriel window. Above the lower half, the achievement-of-arms of the Bingham family is carved in mellow Ham Hill stone and embellished with figures of cherubs in the French Italianate style. On either side ascend slim corner pillars surmounted by eagle crests. The structure is beautifully proportioned and brings to mind the great front of Clifton Maybank, which is now at Montacute.

BINGHAM'S MELCOMBE. The medieval gatehouse.

BINGHAM'S MELCOMBE. The upper photograph shows the Tudor oriel window and achievement-of-arms of the Bingham family. The nineteenth century engraving by Henry James Moule shows how little has changed in the last 150 years.

The porch leads into the hall with access to the oriel through a Purbeck stone archway. This medieval hall, of modest size, was altered in the mid sixteenth century when the oriel and the adjacent stone stairs were built. Just a fragment of its medieval wall remains. The large fireplace with the Bingham crest above was not installed until 1894.

In 1561 Robert Bingham drew up an inventory listing all his personal effects as well as the residential rooms, such as the oriel, hall, parlour wing and first floor rooms in the west range. The furnishings were sparse. He refers to 'andirons in the oryalle' indicating that there was a fireplace in the room, which was unusual for the time. The fireplace is still there, though the surround dates from 1700. There is a similar fireplace on the floor above. The armorial glass in the oriel windows and south windows of the hall is magnificent. Fourteen shields of arms are on display, representing the local gentry. They include Herbert, Earl of Pembroke, and Russell, Earl of Bedford, the Horseys, Basket, Williams and Trenchard, among others who had connections with the Binghams. The arms of Mary Tudor and Philip of Spain, in the south window of the oriel, narrow the date of construction for this part of the house to Queen Mary's brief reign (1553-58).

The parlour wing lies to the west of the hall and was later known as the dining room. Lined with eighteenth century panelling, it contains a mid eighteenth century fire surround surmounted by a superb overmantel from 1600, which includes, among several carvings, the figures of Cain and Abel with Eve, and Adam and Eve. The ceiling, also from 1600, is richly decorated with circles, octagons and lozenges. Upstairs the panelling in the bedrooms ranges from the sixteenth century to the early eighteenth century. The fireplace in the oak bedroom is made from three sixteenth century panels. They are carved with the arms of the

BINGHAM'S MELCOMBE. The courtyard, with the oriel window on the right.

Binghams and embellished with figures and foliage. This west wing of the house fortunately retains many original beams, doorways and windows and the site of a garderobe can still be seen in the north room of the service annexe.

The east wing, across the courtyard and adjacent to the hall, was once a service wing but is now known as the library. In the eighteenth century it was decorated in the style of Queen Anne. The walls are lined with pine panelling and the fireplace is outlined in dark marble with a Vauxhall mirror above. A panel conceals an arched cupboard in the thickness of the wall, predating the decoration of this room. North of the library an elegant staircase and landing, from 1725, leads to a drawing room, completed in 1893-4 when a general restoration of the house took place.

The south range of the courtyard extends west from the ancient gatehouse and has large fireplaces at either end. The hearth at the western end is 11fi feet wide, which indicates that this was the kitchen from very early times. There is an unusual seventeenth century cupboard in the room, with drilled ventilation holes forming patterns in the door, probably an early type of larder. The age of this range has long been a puzzle. Although altered in the eighteenth century and again in 1949, it was not until 1987 that a more accurate date of origin came to light. During restoration work three small windows, each cut from a single stone, were unblocked. The floor in the room above the kitchen, installed around 1700, was in poor condition and a new floor was inserted about 2ins above it. This resulted in a certain loss of headroom, so the ceiling was removed exposing the original smoke blackened timbers. This clearly indicated that at one time the area had been open from floor to roof. English Heritage inspected the work and confirmed that it had been a hall house of around 1450,

BINGHAM'S MELCOMBE. Much of the west front is high quality squared flints alternating with Ham Hill stone.

certainly predating the present house.

Over the gatehouse another handsome bedroom is lined with early seventeenth century panelling, with a magnificent carved fireplace of the same date. To the west of this room, in what is now a bathroom, lies a cleverly concealed priest's hole, just six feet by four feet. Cramped though it was, it would have provided welcome protection in troubled times. During the mid twentieth century, when Lord Southborough lived here, this was the guest wing. On more than one occasion his guests were disturbed by the sounds of children laughing and running through the room. Though the sounds probably emanated from happy Bingham children of past years, Lord Southborough, in order to appease his more nervous guests, invited a priest to exorcise the ghosts, and the sounds were never heard again.

During the fourteenth and fifteenth centuries the Binghams acquired a considerable amount of land in the county, yet none of them seem to have distinguished themselves until the reign of Elizabeth I, when Sir Richard Bingham, Robert Bingham's younger brother, made his name as a soldier. Born in 1528, he fought at the battle of St Quentin in 1557 and then in the Northern Rebellion of 1569. As a mercenary for the Venetians, he fought at the great battles of Candia and Lepanto. War was his life, and Elizabeth made use of his fighting skills in Ireland, where he was made Governor of Connaught. He was a religious man, short of stature and totally fearless. Though respected by some, he was hated by many, especially for his brutality against the rebels in his later years. Two of his brothers, George and John, fought alongside him. Unlike Sir Richard, they settled in Ireland and became the ancestors of the Earls of Lucan and the Barons Clanmorris. Sir Richard returned to England in 1588 to discuss the impending threat of the Spanish Armada, and to marry Mrs. Sarah Higham, by whom he had a daughter. He returned to Ireland in 1593 to a confrontation with McGuire and Gauran, the Primate of Ireland. The Primate was killed in battle and Elizabeth I, in an effort to appease the Pope, as well as the inhabitants of the province, recalled Sir Richard and imprisoned him. Soon, however, another rebellion was brewing, this time led by Tyrone. Once again Bingham's services were required. Now aged seventy, he returned to Ireland as Marshal of Ireland and General of Leinster. He died soon after his arrival and was buried with honours in Westminster Abbey.

Robert Bingham's great grandson was the Cromwellian, Colonel John Bingham, MP for Dorset both during and after the Civil War and Governor of Poole for much of the war. On the outbreak of war in 1642 Bingham's Melcombe became the headquarters of the Parliamentary forces in Dorset. Though considered by Lord Shaftesbury to be an 'honest good man', he was in command at the last siege of Corfe Castle and took away his fair share of loot, which included a large bed, two blankets, a full suit of damask, a single red velvet chair and much more. After the Restoration, in response to a request from Sir Ralph Bankes, he returned several items, but not the bed, the excuse being that 'for 12 years since was opened by a wench at my then house of Bingham's Melcombe when I was in the Isle of Guernsey, and the feathers stolen out and divers other tricks done by her in my being out of the land'. He had been posted to Guernsey and remained as Governor there until 1660.

Colonel John Bingham had no male heirs. For two generations the Binghams had owned, and for some of the time, at least, lived at Quarleston Manor, which they had inherited when Colonel Bingham's grandfather married Anne Chaldicott, heiress to Quarleston. Upon Colonel Binghams' death in 1675, Quarleston went to his daughter Grace, and Bingham's Melcombe passed to his brother Strode, who had been a captain in the Commonwealth army. Strode's son, Richard, married Philadelphia Potenger, and they had thirteen children.

Their sixth son, the Reverend George Bingham, was an eminent scholar, Fellow of All Souls' College, rector of Pimperne and More Crichel, as well as friend of John Hutchins, Dorset's most distinguished historian, rector of Bingham's Melcombe from 1733-1744 and author of *The History and Antiquities of the County of Dorset*. George Bingham enlisted many subscribers to help meet the costs of this publication, as well as modestly contributing his archaeological knowledge of the county to Hutchins' great history. He endured much grief and sadness in his life. First, his wife died aged 36, then his son drowned in the River Itchen while still a student at Winchester College. These tragedies affected him deeply. He died in 1800, aged eighty-five.

Sir George Ridout Bingham (1777-1833) entered the army in 1793 and served with distinction in the Peninsular War from 1809-1812. Afterwards he commanded the troops who accompanied Napoleon to St Helena in 1815, ending his career as Colonel-Commandant of the Rifle Brigade.

In the latter part of the nineteenth century, after extensive and costly alterations to the house, the Binghams' fortunes began to decline. In 1895 George J. Richard Bingham reluctantly sold the manor house and the family moved to Canada. On the eve of the auction he wrote a touching farewell to the house filled with foreboding for its future:

> 'Tonight a part of England passes out. A hearth light lit by a Norman lady and her bridegroom lord dwindles to quenching. The fire burns low. It seems to welcome chill into the Hall. Let it burn low, burn out, and add its ashes to the pallorous gloom . . . Goodnight my home.'

His fears proved unfounded and at a later date he wrote again, this time expressing his relief and delight that the house had been purchased by the naturalist Reginald Bosworth-Smith, author of *Bird Life and Bird Lore*. Reginald Bosworth-Smith died in 1908 and the house passed to his daughter, Lady Ellinor Grogan. During her lifetime much of the Bingham furniture still remained in the house, including an oval table, known as the Armada table, believed, by tradition, to have come from one of the ships of the Spanish Armada. There were also portraits of the Binghams, some of which subsequently went to the National Portrait Gallery.

Lady Grogan died in 1948, and the contents of the house were dispersed. The next owner was Francis Hopwood, later Lord Southborough, chairman of Shell Oil. At that time there were no bathrooms in the house, no central heating, and water was pumped from the river. There was no electricity, only one WC and lighting was by oil lamps. Lord Southborough installed electricity, mains water, central heating and bathrooms. Perhaps his greatest legacy was the magnificent oil fired boiler which provided central heating and hot water continuously for over fifty years. In 1966, when Tyneham House had become ruinous, he brought its entrance porch to Bingham's Melcombe, setting it on the northern side of house where the date of 1583 sits comfortably with the rest of the house. The porch now houses the Queen's Awards for Industry won by the companies owned by the present owner, Mr. John Langham C.B.E.

The grounds of the house are as timeless as the interior. The gardens roll out to the north and west as though through rooms. There is a Ladies' Garden and large vegetable gardens. There are walks between beautifully tended hedges with glimpses of peacocks over a gate, a seventeenth century dovecote with a conical roof, and a cleverly concealed ice-house. To the west stretches the bowling alley, seventy-two yards long, which was there in the reign of Henry VIII. It is sheltered from the northerly winds by the massive yew hedge, twelve feet thick, which is over 500 years old. At the far end of the yew hedge, set into the wall, is a semicircular summerhouse of eighteenth century origin, still with the original seat inside.

Mr. and Mrs. John Langham have lived here since 1980. In that time the house has flourished under their meticulous care. It is now a charming, comfortable home surrounded by the most beautiful gardens, well-tended lawns and immaculate grounds. Standing just south east of the house, the little church of St Andrew, in the parish of Higher Melcombe, was rebuilt by the Binghams in the fourteenth century and is still lovingly cared for. Once there was a hamlet here, long since disappeared. All that is left is a meadow known as Town Hays, yet it still plays a part in the history and romantic setting of Bingham's Melcombe.

BINGHAM'S MELCOMBE. The seventeenth century dovecote.

Bloxworth House

THE VILLAGE OF Bloxworth is about two miles east of Bere Regis on the edge of the conifer woodland that marks the northern rim of the Dorset heathland. It is a small, rather unremarkable place, but Bloxworth House is situated in its own park to the west of the village, completely out of sight. The house faces north with the land falling gently away from it, an outlook enhanced by an ornamental canal. To the rear, beyond a courtyard garden backed by a wall, the land slopes steeply up from the house but has been terraced to accommodate the early seventeenth century brewhouse, a lovely building of similar brickwork to the house.

The house was built of brick on an E shaped plan, probably in 1608, with some limestone dressings and roofed with tiles and stone slates and can claim to be the earliest use of brick in the county. The attractive brickwork uses a combination of red and dark purplish bricks, similar to that used at Anderson a few years later, although in a less formal way. In some places it is banded but in others the patterning is more random.

BLOXWORTH HOUSE. The south west aspect of the house in 1905.

The flanking wings and central porch extend equally but with a small rectangular projection in the easternmost angle containing a staircase. In the middle of the eighteenth century the two re-entrants were enclosed by walls built flush with the front of the porch, giving space for accommodation on two floors. At about the same time a single storey wing was added to the north-east. In the 1970s the infill of the re-entrants was demolished, as were two later extensions to the west and south-east of the house, leaving it much closer to its original plan.

In the first half of the nineteenth century the west wing was remodelled, moving the external wall further out and adding a large two-storey bay window on the north side. Externally, few of the original windows survive and the interior of the house has been extensively, albeit sensitively, modernised.

East of the house is a stable range, probably built in the middle of the seventeenth century, which also uses the combination of red and purple brick to lovely effect. Higher up the slope to the south-east, is a late eighteenth or early nineteenth century icehouse, whilst in the opposite direction, to the north-east of the house is an early eighteenth century walled garden, which has been beautifully restored by the present owners.

The first historical reference to Bloxworth is in a charter of 987, recording that Alfwold gave five dwellings in Blacewerthe to the Abbey of Cerne. The Domesday Book lists Blocheshorde as the property of the Abbot of Cerne. It remained as part of the Abbey's holdings until the Dissolution and seems to have been leased to various lords throughout that time.

BLOXWORTH HOUSE. Looking down on the south front.

In 1547, the last year of his reign, Henry VIII granted the manor, including a house, to Richard Savage of Piddlehinton and Bloxworth and George Strangways. Bloxworth was just one of a larger parcel of properties and it is probable that the two families leased land here from Cerne Abbey before it was dissolved. Ten years later, in 1557, Richard Savage was the sole lessee, so he had presumably bought out the Strangways' interest. Richard's heir was William and by the time he came into his inheritance the family held the freehold.

In 1608 William's son, George, built the present house. George's eldest son, called William after his grandfather, was a London lawyer who, as a supporter of Parliament, played an important part in the county during the Civil War. He was a Justice of the Peace and one of the original members of the Dorset Standing Committee, founded by Parliament in 1644 to co-ordinate raising money for the maintenance of the army. This was mainly achieved by confiscating the estates of Royalist supporters and Roman Catholics and then leasing them to supporters of Parliament. In 1646 William was awarded money for services rendered to Parliament and in 1648 he became High Sheriff of Dorset, dying the following year.

In about 1680 his only son, Sir George Savage, rebuilt the north wall of the church and added a family chapel with seating for his family and friends. The walls were painted with coats of arms of the Rock Savage family, although it seems that George's claim to kinship with this illustrious family was spurious. He amassed huge debts, which he was unable to pay and was eventually arrested. He managed to avoid prison and was kept under arrest at the London house of Henry Glover, Marshall of the Court of Kings Bench, for which he was charged £8 a month for board and lodging. George seemed to feel that his family was in some way to blame for his predicament, writing bitterly about their refusal

Sir John Trenchard inherited Bloxworth from his bachelor uncle in 1694.

to help him pay his debts. In his will, written in custody in 1683, he asks to be buried at Bloxworth, adding, rather poignantly:

> 'My body to be interred in my Isle adjoyning to the parish Church of Bloxworth aforesaid but with as much privacy and as little expense as may decently be.'

When he died in that same year his request was honoured, but his debts became the responsibility of his family and it was clear that the estate would have to be sold.

Six years later his sons, William and George, sold Bloxworth to Henry Trenchard, then a lawyer in the Middle Temple, for £9,200. As Sir George's debts added up to £5,772 they were not left entirely penniless.

When Henry Trenchard died a bachelor in 1694 he left all his property, apart from a few specific bequests, to his elder brother Sir John Trenchard of Lytchett Matravers. Sir John's nephew, Colonel Thomas Trenchard of Wolfeton, had married Elizabeth Henning of Poxwell. When he died in 1702, at the age of 32, he specified in his will that his daughter Mary, who was only eight at the time, should marry one of the sons of his uncle, Sir John Trenchard. She carried out her father's wishes by marrying the eldest son, George, who had inherited on his father's death in 1694, the same year that she was born, thus bringing together the estates of Wolfeton, Bloxworth, Poxwell and Lytchett.

George and Mary had eleven children, six of whom died in infancy. Of their three surviving sons, the two younger remained unmarried and the eldest, George, had no children. The eldest daughter, Henrietta, married Jocelyn Pickard and her father sold Bloxworth to him on their marriage. The younger daughter, Mary, married Richard Cambridge and they had six children, but no surviving grandchildren.

Henrietta inherited her father's estate, which included Wolveton, Lytchett, Bloxworth and Poxwell, and she and Jocelyn had two sons. Thomas, the elder, married Harriet Woodley, daughter of the Governor of the Leeward Isles, but had no children. Their second son, George, was ordained and became rector of Warmwell and Poxwell.

Thomas Pickard succeeded his father in 1789 and when he died in 1830, the property went to his brother George. He was 74 and a widower when he inherited the estate and had been Rector of Warmwell and Poxwell for 50 years.

George had married Frances Payne, whose father was a director of the Bank of England, and they had five sons, one of whom died as a child. The eldest died unmarried, the second died young and so it was their third son, George Pickard Cambridge, who inherited. He had taken the name Cambridge under the terms of the will of his uncle, Charles Cambridge, whose own son had died young and who had no immediate heirs. Their fourth son, John Trenchard Pickard also changed his name under the terms of a will, that of his bachelor great uncle, John Trenchard of Welbeck Street. He discarded Pickard and became John Trenchard Trenchard. The fifth son, Henry joined the Royal Artillery. His son Arthur followed his father into the army and at the age of 22, in 1863, won the Victoria Cross fighting the Maoris at Rangiriri in New Zealand. During an assault on the enemy's position, he and

William Temple, an assistant surgeon, who was also awarded the VC, crossed and re-crossed the entrance to the Maori keep under fierce cross-fire to obtain water for the wounded.

In 1840 George died and his eldest son Edward inherited. He was a bachelor and when he died in 1850 the estate came to his younger brother George Pickard Cambridge. George had followed his father into the Church and married Frances Amelia Whish. George and Frances Amelia had fifteen children, of whom twelve survived. Of their four surviving sons, two went into the Indian Army and two were ordained. Their youngest son Octavius, an ex pupil of William Barnes' School in Dorchester, became Rector of Bloxworth. He later became an eminent naturalist and world authority on spiders, Fellow of the Royal Society and a founder member of the Dorset Natural History and Archaeological

BLOXWORTH HOUSE. The north front in soft early evening light, showing the magnificent canal recently created by Mr. and Mrs. Martin Lane-Fox.

Society. He remained Rector of Bloxworth until his death in 1917 at the age of 92.

George died in 1868, leaving the estate to his eldest son, Henry. Henry had no living children and on his death in 1884 he left the estate to his brother Jocelyn for his lifetime and then to his niece, Mary Ellen Adeline.

In 1880 Mary married Frederick Lane, who was a tea planter in Sri Lanka (then Ceylon). In 1900, when Jocelyn died, they returned to live at Bloxworth. They had six sons and one daughter. Two sons were killed in the First World War and Mary and Frederick built a village hall for Bloxworth as a memorial to them. This was used for many years but has now been replaced.

Frederick died in 1940 and his wife a year later. Their eldest son, Ernest Lane, who was living at Poxwell, inherited the estate. Bloxworth was let to a Mr. Putnam, who owned a company called Putnam's Tents and had become wealthy by supplying tents to the military in the First World War. He and his wife remained there until 1947, when Ernest's younger brother, Lieut. Colonel Philip Lane, came to live there.

Ernest and Jessie Lane had no children and when Ernest died in 1958 he left Bloxworth to his nephew Freddie, Philip's son. By this time the house had become run down and Colonel Lane moved into a smaller house in the village and in 1964 the estate was sold to two businessmen, brothers called McDonald Smith.

They had no interest in the house and wanted to demolish it and rebuild. Dorset County Council prevented them from doing so by issuing preservation and repair orders on the company, which they fiercely argued against. Eventually in 1970 the County Council agreed a compulsory purchase order so that they could carry out rescue repairs before selling the house to private owners for further restoration.

In 1972 Mr. and Mrs. Robin Dulake bought the house and continued the work of repair and restoration. They removed the infill of the re-entrants at the front of the house and the small outer porch, which had been added to the original. Modern extensions to the west and south-east of the house were also demolished, leaving the house closer to its original form. They also undertook considerable restoration and refurbishment to the interior, including replacing the main staircase in the west wing.

In 1997 they sold the house to Mr. and Mrs. Martin Lane Fox, the present owners, who continue to cherish it. Mr. Lane Fox is a notable garden designer with a keen interest in nature conservation. He is a past Vice-Chairman of the Royal Horticultural Society and holder of the Society's highest award, the Victoria Medal of Honour, and has created a magnificent garden to complement the beauty of Bloxworth House.

Bridehead

THE SETTING AT Bridehead must be one of the prettiest in Dorset. The house is secreted in a bowl of hills at the head of the small, steep, Bride Valley. Here the River Bride rises from a spring and fills a small ornamental lake before spilling over a waterfall and continuing on its way down the valley. The house looks south across the lake to the surrounding hills, part wooded, part open grassland and totally beautiful.

The house underwent extensive remodelling and rebuilding in the nineteenth century and now presents a Victorian Gothic façade, creating an attractive picture from across the lake or the surrounding hills.

Remains of the sixteenth century house are incorporated in the east block and on the north side,

BRIDEHEAD. The Victorian east front of the house: a view that is remarkably similar to that of the engraving below.

BRIDEHEAD. A view of the house in the mid nineteenth century.

BRIDEHEAD. Looking from the south across the ornamental lake.

which contained all the Victorian service rooms and where the age of some of the stone flags bears witness to its much earlier origins. The interior of the house is now almost entirely Victorian, with beautifully proportioned rooms with large windows and some spectacular Gothic revival panelling, particularly in the library and an area called the 'Prayer Room' rather than chapel. The many portraits of members of the Williams family, whose lives have been entwined with Bridehead since Robert Williams bought it in 1798, give the history of the house an immediacy often lacking in those that have more frequently changed hands.

The manor of Brydian was given to Cerne Abbey in 987 by Aethelmer and a hundred years later the Domesday Book records that the Abbey farmed half the land directly and that the rest was let in smaller holdings. This arrangement continued, as far as we know, until the Dissolution.

In 1544 the manor was bought by Philip Vanwilder, who resold it forty years later to Robert Freke of Iwerne Courteney. He in turn sold it to John Mellor of Winterborne Came. The origins of the Mellor family are obscure but legend has it that they were millers to the Abbot of Abbotsbury. Little Bredy was settled on John's son Robert, whose second wife was Robert Freke's daughter, so possibly the sale was part of a marriage agreement. It was Robert Mellor who built the first known house on the present site late in the reign of Elizabeth. Hutchins comments sharply on the Mellor family, 'In the reign of Elizabeth they made many purchases of Abbey land, viz. this manor and those of Winterborne Came, Winterborne Faringdon, Upcerne etc. and were remarkable for depopulating most of them'.

Robert died in 1624 leaving as his heir his son John, only child of his first wife, Dorothy Baily. John was knighted the year after his father's death and was heavily fined during the Civil War for his loyalty to the Crown. His eldest son Robert inherited the manor and died at Little Bredy in

Jane Chassereau, daughter of a French Huguenot émigré, matriarch of the Williams of Bridehead.

1655. Robert's widow bequeathed the manor to their only son, Edward.

In 1685, Edward was given permission by Parliament to sell land for the payment of debts. He had no children and retired to Cheneys in Buckinghamshire, having sold off most of his estate. He died in 1699 and was buried at Came, as were all his ancestors. By this time the estate was heavily mortgaged and the house had become a farmhouse.

In 1730 a Mr. Meech of Charminster bought the manor from Edward Mellor's heirs and it remained a tenanted farm throughout the eighteenth century. In about 1798 one of his descendants sold it to Robert Williams of the Herringston family, who named it Bridehead. He was a London banker and shipowner, who later became MP for Dorchester and High Sheriff of Dorset and heralded a new era for the house.

Robert's father was a younger son who was said to have married beneath him, contrary to his father's wishes and was consequently disinherited. He and his wife had four sons who, therefore, had to make their own living. Robert had been apprenticed at the age of fourteen to a cabinet maker in Covent Garden but by the time he was twenty-one he was a partner and later bought the business. In 1764 he married Jane Chassereau, the daughter of a French émigré who had fled from France at the age of fourteen to escape the persecution of the Huguenots.

His elder brother John had been a ship's captain in the East India Company's fleet and had also acquired shares in other ships in the Company. The Company's captains were allowed to carry a proportion of cargo to trade on their own account, which could be very profitable. In 1771 John entered into partnership with Charles Raymond, another retired sea captain and shipowner, and three other men to found a bank, which later became Williams Deacons Bank and later still, Williams and Glyn's Bank. Robert had also invested money in shipping and by the time his brother died in 1774 he was sufficiently wealthy to take his place as a partner and for the next 170 years his descendants were partners or directors of the bank. In 1801 he bought the country estate of Moor Park in Hertfordshire and made it his home.

He died there in 1814 leaving an estate of more than half a million pounds, at that time an enormous fortune. The majority was left to his eldest son, Robert, with £50,000 to his younger son, £10,000 each to his three daughters and a lifetime income for his wife. Robert followed in his father's footsteps and became head of Williams Deacon and Co. Bank. He was Alderman of Cornhill in 1796, Sheriff of London and Middlesex in 1797 and Conservative MP for Dorchester from 1812 to 1835.

In 1825 because of a crisis at the bank he had to retrench and sell Moor Park and the family withdrew to Bridehead, which then became their main home. He embarked on bringing the house 'up to date' and during the first half of the nineteenth century it was largely rebuilt, firstly by P.F. Robinson and with later additions by the Christchurch born architect, Benjamin Ferrey. The Bride was dammed to form the lake and the grounds landscaped. His mother, Jane, lived there until her death in 1841 at the age of 101 and is said to have influenced the development of the estate. One of her descendants wrote, 'She was a fine lady and began, I think, the tradition of Bridehead, thank God carried on to this day, of Christian faith and of Christian life and service'.

Robert died in 1847 and was succeeded by his only son, another Robert, who continued in the family tradition of banking and in his turn became MP for Dorchester and High Sheriff of Dorset in 1856. He was a devout Christian and a friend and correspondent of Cardinal Newman until Newman's conversion to Catholicism caused him to break off the friendship. So appalled was Robert, he was even said to have burnt all of his considerable correspondence with Newman after the rift. He was a strong supporter of the Dorset County Museum, presented the Dorset Natural History and Antiquarian Field Club (as it was then called) with the present site of the Museum and paid the greater part of the cost of erection in 1881. Prior to that the Museum was housed in Judge Jefferies' Lodgings, which was also owned by the Williams family. He had two sons, Robert and John, and three daughters, one of whom died in infancy.

His son Robert was the fourth of that name to inherit the estate. He was an MP for twenty years but devoted a large part of his time to the Church Assembly and the Church Missionary Society, of which he was chairman. He also maintained an interest in the County Museum and was the first President of the combined Museum and Field Club in 1929. In 1915 he was created a baronet. In the same year his eldest son, Nathaniel, was killed at Gallipoli serving with a New Zealand regiment. He was something of a black sheep and had been despatched to New Zealand to keep him out of mischief, perhaps because his sister was married to a bishop there! At the outbreak of war, he enrolled as a private and was killed on the first day of the Gallipoli landings. It was therefore his younger brother, Philip, who inherited the estate and became the 2nd Baronet. Philip will perhaps be known to followers of cricket as P.F.C. Williams, a first class cricketer, who was one time captain of Gloucestershire. The lovely cricket pitch at Bridehead, immortalised in David Inshaw's painting, *The Cricket Match*, is a legacy of his cricketing days.

His son David followed him as the 3rd Baronet. Sir David had wished to join the Royal Navy but was prevented by poor eyesight, he nevertheless served in the RNVR in the Second World War. He also maintained the family interest in the Museum and presented it with the original organ from Little Bredy Church. He was President of the Society in 1965.

Sir David died in 1970 and his elder son, Philip, became the 4th Baronet at the age of 20. His mother, Elizabeth, Lady Williams managed the estate on his behalf until 1985, when he and his wife and family returned to live at Bridehead and took over the running of the estate. They have a son and two daughters.

Chantmarle Manor

TAKE THE TURNING for Chantmarle, off the busy Dorchester to Yeovil road, and within a mile or so it is winding through quiet country lanes with views across valleys and woods, which seem a million miles from the busy twenty-first century. Once across a pretty little bridge there is a first glimpse of the lovely Elizabethan house, set among trees and gardens. It is hard to believe that this secluded house, which owes its name to its medieval owners, the Chantmarle family, was a Police Training Centre belonging to the Home Office for forty years.

The oldest existing part of the house, the west wing, was built in the second half of the fifteenth century and the main part of the present house, between about 1610 and 1620 by the then owner, Sir John Strode. This part was built in a classic Elizabethan E shape, with a central porch and two wings extending eastward at the north and south ends forming the E. The extending wings were later demolished but the site of the former south wing is partly occupied by a twentieth century building and similarly, at the north end of the main front, there is another wing which is probably eighteenth century.

The house is built of golden Ham stone, which, as John Strode records, came from the 'Hamdon and Whetley' quarries. It is two storeys with attics and its roofs are covered with stone slates. The three storey central porch with a lovely oriel window in the second floor is particularly attractive.

The Abbot of Milton Abbas was the first overlord

CHANTMARLE MANOR. The back of the manor house. The wing on the left predates the building of 1612.

CHANTMARLE MANOR. The house was started by a successful lawyer, Sir John Strode, in 1612, and this view shows the three storey central porch and oriel window.

of the manor, but as early as 1212 it was held by Robert Chantmarle. In 1290 one of Robert's descendants married Alice de Estoke, who enriched the estate by inheriting various manors, including East Stoke and Rushton by Bindon, which were then inherited, with Chantmarle, by her son John.

The estate continued to descend to Chantmarle sons until, in 1423, Walter Chantmarle died leaving two daughters, Joan and Christian, as his co-heirs, the estate being divided between them. Joan was married to John Cheverel and her portion included Chantmarle. It then remained the property of the Cheverels for another 170 years and they built the existing west wing in the second half of the fifteenth century.

In 1596 however, the then owner, Christopher Cheverel was in severe financial difficulties and sold the manors of East Stoke and Rushton to John Strode for £1000. This does not seem to have solved his problems, for in 1606 the manors of Chantmarle and Howdon were heavily mortgaged and he allowed the mortgagees to sell them. John Strode was again the purchaser and Christopher Cheverel and his two brothers released all their interests and rights in these manors.

John was a younger son of the Strodes of Parnham and a successful lawyer. He pulled down a large part of the Cheverel house but retained one wing, which adjoins the back of his new building. This contained the original chapel, which Strode described as 'low-rooft, little and dark'. Its situation was identified during restoration work when a piscina and a four light window were discovered blocked up in the east wall of the room, which is now the study. The new chapel he built to replace the original has, sadly, totally disappeared. However he left a diary of the building of it and describes it in loving detail.

He says that he laid the first stone on 2nd April 1612 and his wife, Anne, the second, and that 'the chapel's foundation was first laid and the chapel first finished and covered, before the rest of the dwelling house'. He also says it was finished on the 20th February 1619, providing a useful timescale for the building of the house. His description of the chapel is beautiful:

> 'This chapel hath his outside of Hambledon stone; his inside is plastered white, and fretted over with the sun, moone, starrs, cherubims, doves, grapes, and pomegranates, all supported with 4 angells in the 4 corners of the roofe, which inside was wrought by Eaton of Stoke-gursey or Stowey, in Somersett, and finished 20 Decembris 1615, who for his workmanship had 6 pounds 16 shillings'.

He goes on to say that it was consecrated on 14th September 1619, by the Bishop of Bristol, 'himselfe in person'. It was a long and lavish service and apparently, after dinner, the Bishop returned to the chapel and confirmed '4 or 500 people' before 'being weary, he left some to confirming, and rode hence to Melbury, where he lodged that night with Sir John Strangwayes'. Sadly, by the end of the eighteenth century Hutchins notes 'Mr. Petty, the present tenant, being a dissenter, the chapel is now desecrated and converted into a woodhouse'.

A committed Puritan, Strode deliberately planned his house in the form of an E to represent the word Emmanuel, which, though now almost indecipherable, is carved on the keystone of the porch and dated 1612. However, John Strode and his wife did not live at his lovely new house for long, because in 1628 he inherited Parnham from his brother Robert and Chantmarle became only an occasional residence for the family. Sir John died in his chambers at Lincolns Inn in 1642 at the age of 81.

Thereafter the manor descended with Parnham and eventually, in 1764 when the male line of the Strodes became extinct, was inherited by Sir John Oglander of Nunwell in the Isle of Wight. The link with the Oglanders came through the marriage of Sir John's granddaughter, Elizabeth, to Sir William Oglander in 1699. It remained their property until the death of the last of the Oglanders in 1896, when

Opposite page CHANTMARLE MANOR. Two views of the front of the house, from beyond the canal and the garden.

CHANTMARLE MANOR. An eighteenth century engraving showing the house before the two wings forming the E were demolished.

the Parnham estates were sold, including Chantmarle. By then it had become a farm and the two wings forming the ends of its E shape had been pulled down.

In 1910 it was bought by Mr. F.E. Savile, who restored its country house status. He undertook major restoration work, replacing carved woodwork and ornamented ceilings to replace the lost fittings. It was Mr. Savile who was responsible for building the new staircase wing with its magnificent oak staircase on part of the site of the south wing extension. Much of the interior work carried out by him owes a debt to the Arts and Crafts Movement and sits very happily within its seventeenth century setting. He also re-created the gardens, which were designed and laid out by Francis Thomas, a landscape designer and architect. Thomas was also responsible for the gardens at Athelhampton, and Arthur Oswald suggests that Chantmarle was his finest achievement.

Chantmarle's next owner was Charles St John Hornby, who bought the house from Mr. Savile in 1919. He founded the Ashendene Press in 1895, which, alongside the Kelmscott press and Doves Press, was a leader in the revival of fine English printing. His edition of Dante, printed on vellum and published in 1909, is considered to be on a par with the William Morris edition of Chaucer from

Kelmscott. In 1893, when he joined W.H. Smith, of which he eventually became a director, he spent several months at the firm's printing works learning to set type and pull proofs on a hand press and this, together with a visit to Kelmscott Press, inspired him to take up printing himself. He described the press as 'the absorbing interest of an otherwise busy life' and for many years it was almost entirely worked by him. The press issued forty books, all hand set, between 1895 and 1935. These are now highly sought after collectors' items. His hand press, an archive of his papers and examples of his publications are now in the Bridwell Library of the Southern Methodist University, USA.

Mr. Hornby also left his mark on Chantmarle with some further internal alterations and by extending the gardens. In the study at Chantmarle is a coat of arms for Hornby with the motto 'CREDE CORNU' and the lead rainwater heads at the back of the house carry the horn device for Hornby. In 1951 his son, Michael, sold Chantmarle to the Home Office for use as a Police Training Centre for the south-west. This was a last resort as he had hoped to be able to find a private buyer but was unsuccessful.

Known officially as No.7 Police Training Centre, the police remained in residence until 1995. During that time a range of modern buildings were constructed, but happily they are to the rear and not too obtrusive and the old part of the house seemed to escape relatively unscathed. After the Centre closed, it was purchased by a property developer who hoped to build a complex of houses around it but was unable to obtain the necessary planning permission and resold it a few years later.

Then, in 2002, it was bought by Mr. John Glare. For several years he had been looking for a suitable place to create a Christian Centre that would promote, encourage and teach Christianity. Chantmarle seemed the ideal situation in which to develop his vision of a multi-faceted centre offering a wide range of facilities, from individual quiet retreats to large conferences and seminars, in a beautiful and peaceful place. The manor house itself has been lovingly and sensitively refurbished to provide all the facilities of a luxurious country house hotel, whilst the modern accommodation to the rear provides everything required for a well-equipped conference centre.

Once again Chantmarle has found an owner who will cherish and protect this rather special place.

Childhay Manor

CHILDHAY IS IN the far west of the county, a few miles north-west of Broadwindsor. It sits on a small rise between two streams, the Temple Brook, which rises on the slopes of Pilsdon Hill and joins the River Axe, and another, too small to warrant being named on the Ordnance Survey, which itself joins Temple Brook. The little stream fills a pond to the south of the house and in summer the air is filled with swallows.

The house is built of local rubble stone, faced with ashlar, with slate and tile roofs. It faces south-west and has a two-storey, fifteenth century porch, which is battlemented above a plinth. This displays four magnificent gargoyles, one of which shows two beasts apparently eating a man. The stone-arched doorway contains a handsome ancient oak inner door. To the north of the house there is a superb sixteenth century barn of eight bays, which is faced with ashlar and has two doorways; whilst nearby is the mid seventeenth century dairy, formerly a cottage.

There has been considerable sensitive modernisation of the house, which includes an extension with a new porch at the west end. In the drawing room, which was once the kitchen, there is a lovely Tudor oak-panelled dado with a carved rail. Sadly, the painted wooden panels in the middle room of the main block have not survived.

The name Childhay is not in the Domesday Book

CHILDHAY MANOR. The manor with its fifteenth century battlemented porch.

CHILDHAY MANOR. One gargoyle on the porch shows a man holding a child playing with his mouth. A play on the name of the manor?

but it does appear in the Patent Rolls in 1232. In 1248 it was noted as receiving rent from Poyntington Mill, and in 1334 Forde Abbey Cartulary records a gift of land at Childhay. Hutchins says that in the fourteenth century it came by marriage to John de Crukerne. It remained in the Crukerne family until about 1625, when, inherited by a daughter, it was sold to Thomas Hele of Devon. In 1632 Thomas's son Nicholas sold the manor to Richard Bragge of Sadborrow and Matthew Bragge of Thorncombe. In 1645 the farm at Childhay was sequestered because of Richard Bragge's adherence to the Royalist cause and he died shortly afterwards.

Childhay always seems to have been a manor within the larger manor of Broadwindsor, giving rise to occasional disputes over their respective rights. In 1792 John Bragge of Childhay and Sir William De La Pole of Broadwindsor met at the George Inn in Axminster and hammered out an agreement. This stated that Mr. Bragge would continue to be regarded as Lord of the Manor within the tithing of Childhay but that Sir William, as Lord of the Manor and Liberty of Broadwindsor, would be considered Lord Paramount. This gave him various ancient rights in Childhay, possibly the most significant being equal sporting rights with John Bragge!

In 1809 Sir William sold his rights to the Pinney family, who thus became Lords of the Manor of Broadwindsor and overlords of Childhay. By 1910, Childhay itself was owned by Col. R. J. Pinney. In the 1920s he sold it to William Doble, who farmed there with his brother until 1941, when it was sold to the Cadbury family.

Shortly after the war the Cadburys leased it to Mr. Frost, father of the present owner and in 1981, his son, Mr. Timothy Frost, purchased the estate from the Cadburys. Three generations of the Frost family have developed Childhay into a well regarded organic business consisting of three farms. The home farm at Childhay produces beef and lamb, whilst their pork is bred on a farm near Salisbury and chickens just over the county border in Devon. A family enterprise that ensures that, happily, Childhay Manor is still a working part of the county's agricultural heritage.

Clifton Maybank

THE GREAT MANSION of Clifton Maybank, just two miles south east of Yeovil, was one of the most spectacular houses in Dorset until much of it was brutally demolished in 1786 by its then owner, the Earl of Uxbridge, which explains the rather oddly shaped house we see today. The first view of the house is the south front. Three storeys tall and rather narrow, it still provides a clear picture of the character of the original house, built around 1546 by Sir John Horsey. The mullioned windows, the unequal sized gables, the string-course, and the parapet surmounted by a frieze of lozenges with quatrefoils, are all undoubtedly of the sixteenth century. The west front of the house is wider, having been redesigned after the demolitions of 1786. Here, in the central gable, an oriel window has been reset, and beneath the sill are panels displaying horses' heads (for the Horseys) and Tudor roses. The north and east wings were rebuilt in 1906-7. To date, neither a plan nor a picture of the original house has come to light.

Interestingly, on the eastern side of the house, at a lower level, are the foundations of an even older house, as yet unexcavated, but possibly dating from Saxon times. At the south-east corner of the present house is a detached building of two storeys with cellars. It dates from the sixteenth century with some original windows. A beautiful wooden ceiling in the upper storey is of indeterminate age yet there is no record of the building's original use.

The first mention of the manor was in the 'Saxon Annals' of 1001. The first named owner was Hugo in 1066, followed by William, who held Clifton of the Earl of Chester in the Domesday Book. By the reign of Edward I (1272-1307), Philip Mauban, knight, held land in Dorset. The Maubanks were still there in the fifteenth century when Eleanor, daughter of Philip Maubank, married John Horsey, whose family came from Horsey, near Bridgwater in Somerset.

Over the next two centuries the Horseys increased their land holdings in Dorset and in the latter half of the fifteenth century, the next John Horsey married Elizabeth Turges, of Melcombe Turges, an important Dorset manor, which was renamed Melcombe Horsey. At court John Horsey held the exalted position of Esquire of the Body to Henry VIII, for which he received a fee of 7fi pence per day. Following the Dissolution, the next Sir John Horsey purchased the site of the monastery at Sherborne as well as the manor. At his death in 1546, he owned around 18,000 acres of land in Dorset and

CLIFTON MAYBANK. The Tudor oriel window under the west gable. Little remains of what was once one of the largest houses in Dorset.

CLIFTON MAYBANK. In 1786 the then owner, the Earl of Uxbridge, began vandalizing the house by selling off as much as he could. The top engraving is of the Jacobean gateway sold to Lord Paulet of Hinton St George. The lower illustration shows part of the screen from the façade of the south front, which is now at Montacute.

Somerset. There is a splendid monument to him and his son John in Sherborne Abbey.

John married Edith, daughter of Richard Phelips of Corfe Mullen and a member of the Phelips family of Montacute. During his tenure the house was extended and embellished, and the beautiful façade was added to the south front. The quality of its carvings owes much to the French masons who supposedly worked on it, but sadly the façade itself now graces the west front of Montacute House.

His nephew and heir, Sir Ralph, erected an unusual and ingenious gateway. Inside the main gate was a small door allowing only one person to enter at a time, so avoiding a surprise attack. Sadly Sir Ralph lost money on a scheme to make iron from pit coal, and his son, Sir George, squandered his money on a reckless plan to drain the Fleet at Abbotsbury and ended his life in the debtor's prison. So concluded the long history of the Horseys of Clifton Maybank. (More about their adventures comes under Higher Melcombe.)

In 1635 Charles I granted the estate to John Hele. From him it passed to Michael Harvey of Kingston-upon-Thames, who had business interests in Holland. His influence can be seen in the Dutch tiles around a fireplace, and also in the garden where he introduced the Dutch taste for yew topiary. According to Hutchins, this family, between 1659 and 1747, 'repaired, sashed and otherwise modernised' the house. In 1680 it is recorded that the Duke of Monmouth dined with Mr. Harvey, and after dinner set off on horseback to Longleat, on what, at the time, seemed like a royal tour through the staunchly Exclusionist West Country. Five years later Monmouth was to die on the executioner's block, following his doomed Rebellion. Despite associating with Monmouth, the Harveys were true Royalists, one dying from his wounds in the Rebellion, while in the service of James II at Bridport in 1685.

From the next owner, Peter Walter of Stalbridge, and his heirs, the estate came into the hands of Henry William, the vandalizing Earl of Uxbridge. Tragically Clifton Maybank, in 1786, suffered the fate of many of his other houses. He sold the magnificent south front to the Phelips of Montacute. The unusual gateway was purchased by Lord Paulet for 120 guineas and erected at Hinton St George. Other pieces were scattered around Dorset and Somerset, and scarcely an entire wing of the house was left standing.

CLIFTON MAYBANK. The horses' heads on the gate piers are a reminder of the Horseys who built the house.

Only inside the house is its past carefully preserved. In the east wall of the hall are two sixteenth century doorways with the arms of Horsey, Turgis, Horsey and Maubank in the spandrels. The staircase is of the sixteenth century and there remains eighteenth century deal and oak panelling.

The lawn facing the west front was once a Tudor bowling green. Beyond it, walled paths and fruit trees bear a similarity to the description of the garden as it was in 1648: '. . . of the South West side of the greene court is a large bowling greene, with fower mounted walks about it, all walled about with a battled wall, and sett with all sorts of fruit; and out of it into the fieldes there are large walkes under many tall elmes orderly planted'.

Today, imposing gates with pillars surmounted with horses' heads, again for the Horseys, open into the fields beyond. In the south-west corner of the lawn sits an attractive square gazebo, built around 1700, during the occupancy of Michael Harvey. It is possible that the architect was the artist James Thornhill. He would have known the Harveys, for his drawing of the gatehouse appears in Hutchins entitled 'Mr. Harvey's Lodge'. In recent years this gazebo has been tastefully restored.

The Earl of Uxbridge sold what little remained of the house in 1825 to John Bridge of London, who passed it on to his nephews, John London Bridge and Alfred Charles Bridge. From then until the end of the nineteenth century it was used as a farmhouse and part of the land was sold for the development of the railway.

In 1906 the depleted house came into the kinder hands of Mr. and Mrs. Francis Daniell, a Dorset family. They rebuilt the east wing in what is known as a wrap around effect. They added bathrooms and generally made the house more habitable and comfortable. In 1916 it was sold to Mr. Firth, a master cutler who, in 1925, sold it to Alfred and Greta Turnbull, who, in 1971 passed it to the next purchasers, Professor and Mrs. A.M. Jaffé and her late husband, the legacy of a well-maintained garden and a comfortable home, which has been lovingly cherished to the present day. Despite many turmoils, it is a charming house filled with interesting and varied reminders of its past owners.

Court House

SET BACK FROM the busy main road, opposite St Hubert's Church, Corfe Mullen, lies a manor house in miniature. The size of the original house can only be conjecture, as a large portion was demolished in the nineteenth century. The remaining part lies adjacent to farm buildings but through the small gateway lies a secluded garden, overlooked by a dainty oriel window which lends an aura of tranquillity to the house.

The first name connected with Corfe Mullen is Robert, son of Gerold, who came over with William the Conqueror. Then in 1302, it was listed as the seat of Hubert de la Veille. In 1347, it was divided between Giles de Hardyngton and John de la Veille. There seem to have been three manors in this area, Corfe Nicholas, Corfe Hubert and Corfe Mullen. Corfe Nicholas belonged to the Nicholas Hospital in Salisbury. Thereafter the Erdingtons of Warwickshire held the manor of Corfe Mullen while Corfe Hubert remained with de la Veille. The Erdingtons held their manor until the death of Thomas Erdington in 1436, when it passed through marriage to the Harecourts of Oxfordshire. The Harecourts had the manor until 1538 when, together with Corfe Hubert, it was sold to Richard Phelips of Charborough whose grandson, Edward, later built Montacute House.

Richard Phelips built Court House around 1540. As its name implies, local courts of justice were held here. The Phelips family had long standing connections with Dorset, Richard being deputy controller of wine imports through Lyme and Weymouth. In 1512 he was returned to Parliament as MP for Poole and again in 1529, and in 1533 he attended the Coronation of Henry VIII's second Queen, Anne Boleyn.

Only a small part of the original house survives today, but it is beautifully preserved. The mullion windows still retain their original fittings and the Italianate plaster ceilings in both the lower and upper rooms are remarkable. In the upper room the carvings display the rose of the Phelips crest with stylised fruits. On the south side of the house is a large projecting chimney-breast with lozenge shaped stacks. Hutchins describes in detail the Phelips family's armorial windows in the parlour. Unfortunately, the panes were removed to Montacute House in 1799. We can now only imagine the sunlight filtering through the richly painted glass, filling the elegant room with a myriad of colours.

The manor and house descended through the Phelips' family until the death of William Phelips, the last of the family, in 1747, when it came to Jane, daughter of Edward Phelips of Wimborne Minster, William's second brother. Jane had married the Reverend James Hanham, rector of Winterborne Zelston, who later became Sir James Hanham of Deans Court, Wimborne. During their life time the house was neglected, and when Sir James died in 1806, the estate was divided among his children. Soon Court House was sold to the Hon John Coventry, a local landowner who, after selling one part of the house, converted the rest into a farmhouse. His son Frederick, notorious for his drunkenness, violent moods, and being heavily in debt by the 1850s, pulled down the central and western parts of the house, leaving only the wing we see today. A dairy was later added to the farmhouse by Frederick's son, StJohn, who restored the family's reputation and was High Sheriff of Dorset in 1866.

COURT HOUSE. This delightful little house is all that remains of the manor house built by Richard Phelips in 1540.

By the 1920s the house had several occupants and was listed as tenements but in the 1930s it was restored. It was during this period that the handsome Tudor staircase was installed. It had been saved from an old house condemned to be submerged in the new reservoir at Staines and now sits sturdily and comfortably in the hallway at Court House.

In 1906, the Dorset historian, Sir Frederick Treves gave an account of the house in his book *Highways and Byways of Dorset*. He described it poetically as:

'a little old manor house of faded brick. It is now a farmhouse, standing derelict in a bald waste. Tall chimneys crown a roof burnished with yellow moss, a valiant buttress holds up the sober wall, while a most delicate window looks out over a dismal pond and a rough railing which encloses nothing. The house is like a dainty shoe found on a rubbish heap.'

How different his description would have been today! No longer a derelict farmhouse, now a comfortable family home. Mr. and Mrs. Antony Yeatman have lived here for over two decades. From 1999-2000 Mr. Yeatman was High Sheriff of Dorset and for many years has been a Deputy Lieutenant. Court House is truly a manor house in miniature yet exquisite in every detail. The delicate window now looks out over flourishing gardens, while the rough railing mentioned by Treves seems to have totally disappeared.

Cranborne Manor

CRANBORNE MANOR HOUSE, totally in harmony with its surroundings, must surely be amongst the brightest of jewels in the crown of English manor houses. It is significant not only for being one of the oldest inhabited houses in England, but also for its architecture and remarkable state of preservation. The Jacobean house rises out of a partially ruined thirteenth century hunting lodge, with all the romanticism of the early English Renaissance endowing it with a sense of timelessness.

From Saxon and Norman times Cranborne was important for its Chase, the hunting grounds of kings and lords, and for the Benedictine Monastery founded in 980. It was the largest parish in the county and under the honour of the Earls of Gloucester. After the Conquest, Cranborne belonged to Queen Matilda, eventually passing to her nephew, Robert Fitz-Hamon who rebuilt Tewkesbury Monastery into which the Cranborne Monastery was merged, thus becoming a priory. By the time of the Dissolution, in 1539, only two monks remained in the priory. The present church is probably on the site of the priory church, as fifty yards to the south lay the ruins of the priory buildings, taken down in 1703.

Robert Cecil, 1st Earl of Salisbury.

A keen huntsman, King John visited Cranborne Chase fourteen times during his reign. In 1207-8, Ralph Neville, the chief forester, spent £67.6s.4d 'building the king's houses of Cranborne'. The main hunting lodge stood the test of time, and by the late sixteenth century, although dilapidated, a large part of the building still remained.

Robert Cecil, son of William Cecil, Lord Burghley, the great Tudor statesman, became Secretary of State to Elizabeth in 1596. During the last years of her reign he smoothed the way for the succession of James VI of Scotland to the English throne. Between

CRANBORNE MANOR. John Norden's drawing of King John's hunting lodge in 1605.

CRANBORNE MANOR. The south entrance with two large brick Jacobean lodges.

1599 and 1603 Cecil purchased Cranborne Manor from the Queen, but did not start to rebuild until 1606.

James I, like his predecessor, found the services of Robert Cecil invaluable. Short, barrel-chested and a hunchback, Cecil was a formidable statesman. The king nicknamed him 'My little beagle' on account of his stature and the cunning way in which he tracked down conspiracies, notably the Gunpowder Plot in 1605. He was created Earl of Cranborne in 1604 and Earl of Salisbury the following year. Away from the political scene, he enjoyed building houses. James I exchanged his old palace at Hatfield for Theobalds, Cecil's house in Hertfordshire, which he much preferred. An offer Cecil could hardly refuse! Consequently Robert Cecil built two great houses, Cranborne and Hatfield, with the latter becoming the main seat of the Earls of Salisbury, while Cranborne became the home of the eldest son, Viscount Cranborne. Cecil never lived at Hatfield as he died before it was completed.

In 1605 Cecil, now Earl of Salisbury, commissioned John Norden, the surveyor and cartographer, to draw up a survey of the existing building at Cranborne. Norden described it as 'an ancient house or hall of the manor, in the form of a castle, constructed of white stone, almost demolished'. Details of this early survey still exist at Hatfield House. In the middle ages courts were held here to uphold the Chase laws with the guilty being punished or imprisoned. The walls, for the most part, were strong and sound so Cecil reused them in building his new house. The north-east stairs, seen on the plan, have gone. The fenestration and the floor levels were altered, yet many of the features depicted in Norden's plan can be identified today. In the upper north part of the east elevation, the single pointed window, shown on Norden's plan, has been re-opened, revealing a wide embrasure with a small piscina and recess for an altar with an aumbry. This would almost certainly have been the king's private chapel. On the ground floor the screens-passage leads into the Great Hall with its early seventeenth

CRANBORNE MANOR. The Manor House was built by Sir Robert Cecil in the early 1600s, incorporating parts of the old hunting lodge.

century panelling, magnificent fireplace and stairs leading up to a gallery. The walls are lined with tapestries and the windows on the south side flood the room with light. The ravages of the Civil War have not destroyed the unique atmosphere of this lovely room.

The battlements of the west tower on the south elevation were removed and the tower heightened to accommodate a magnificent Jacobean carved staircase in black oak, a major feature of the interior. A corresponding tower was built to the east of the entrance covering the garderobe turret. The twelve circular recesses on this south front probably held emblems of the zodiac, but only two remain, those of Libra and Virgo.

The king's first visit to Cranborne was in 1607, when the house was scarcely habitable, nor were the alterations complete by the time of his second visit in 1609, but his prime purpose was hunting. He brought a considerable entourage but where they were accommodated is not known.

William Arnold, who supervised the building of Wadham College, Oxford, worked closely with Robert Cecil on the construction of the house. Cecil considered him to be 'the most honest workman in England'. In 1609 Arnold received £5 for 'drawing a plot for Cranborne House' and the following year

CRANBORNE MANOR. Roundels above the south loggia show symbols of Libra and Virgo. The recesses which probably held the remaining signs of the Zodiac can be seen in the photograph above.

he built a 'tarryce and a kitchene'. He continued his work here until 1612 and it is believed that the designs of the beautiful loggias can be attributed to him. Above the window heads to the north east there remain early thirteenth century corbels, while low down on the western side of the north porch is a thirteenth century archers' loophole with two splayed loops, which only came to light in recent years. The decorative buttresses are probably of medieval origin, with seventeenth century facing.

Thomas Fort, a master mason, also produced major plans for the house and garden. They show that the main approach was originally from the north towards the splendid north loggia and terrace, from where there was a panoramic view over the tiny River Crane and across open countryside. The main entrance was later changed to the south side, through the archway between two brick built Jacobean lodges with pointed roofs.

A keen gardener as well as an enthusiastic builder, Robert Cecil took a great interest in the design of his gardens. John Norden had drawn up a map of the garden in 1610, in which the south court was quartered and filled with plants. There were three terraces to the west, two planted with fruit trees, a parterre and an oval known as a mound, which can be seen today in the sundial garden. The famous plantsman, John Tradescant the Elder, worked for Cecil at his other houses, but seems to have mainly planted trees at Cranborne. On the north side of the house is the original layout of the 'Bowling Allee', by Tradescant, stretching along the side of the croquet lawn. Mountain Jennings designed the garden 'plots' which grew into what must have been beautiful ornamental gardens. Long avenues of trees led into the park; once they were elms, but are now plane trees.

Robert Cecil died in 1612. His son and heir, William Cecil, 2nd Earl of Salisbury was a man of few words, except when hunting. Samuel Pepys referred to him as 'my simple Lord Salisbury'. Until 1639 he spent much time and money improving his estates. Accounts at Hatfield show how he continued to furnish Cranborne in an extravagant manner both inside and out. He also built the wall around the garden. King James continued to visit Cranborne, coming five times between 1615 and 1623, always during August. In the early years of Charles I's reign the Earl faithfully supported the king and was made a privy councillor in 1626. As tensions mounted between the king and Parliament in 1640, the Earl began to reconsider his position, with the result that he failed to commit his loyalty to any party and earned a reputation for political inconsistency, not resolved until the outbreak of

CRANBORNE MANOR. As it was in 1800 when divided into two farmhouses.

CRANBORNE MANOR. The west front designed in 1648 by Captain Richard Ryder for the 2nd Earl of Salisbury.

war. After some hesitation he took the side of Parliament, knowing full well what the consequences might be for his estates. From Cranborne, in April 1643, he sent much of his furniture and valuable possessions to Carisbrooke Castle for safe keeping and returned to Hatfield. It was a wise move, for in May 1643, the Marquess of Hertford and Prince Maurice arrived in the village with 4000 Royalist troops. The Marquess 'commended that no hurt should be done to Cranborne House, but, within half an hour, five or six hundred of the Prince's regiment broke in and, on an instant, pulled out iron bars and casements and carried away everything that was portable.' It was said by some that the Prince roasted an ox in the hall to show his contempt for the owner. Others say he slaughtered sheep there.

The house had been plundered and badly damaged. Thomas Fort was summoned from Salisbury to survey the damage. In a letter of around 1645, he describes how the balustrades of the terrace and the gateway of the north court had been 'broken down by ye souldiers' and requested new designs from Captain Richard Ryder, then working at Wilton. He suggested that the west wing, being in such a bad state of repair, should be rebuilt. By 1648 Captain Ryder's elegant new wing was completed and the furniture was returned from Carisbrooke Castle.

From this time the Earl lost interest in the house and it became neglected. The 3rd Earl of Salisbury was a more political figure, a zealous Whig and a supporter of the exclusion of the Duke of York from succeeding to the throne. In 1671 he sold the Chase to the Earl of Shaftesbury and subsequently the house became even more neglected. In 1685, a note from the Earl's steward George Stillingfleet read, 'There is no present tenant of the mansion house, nor hath been for many years past, but it is kept for the immediate use for the now Earl of Salisbury as it was for his ancestors before him'. In 1774

Hutchins wrote that the hall was the only good room left. In 1790 the title of Marquess was accorded to the 7th Earl with his eldest son becoming Viscount Cranborne. Throughout the eighteenth century and until 1860, the house was divided into two farmhouses.

The 2nd Marquess came to the rescue of the neglected house around 1863. His Clerk of Works, Thomas Champion noted, 'We have taken out more than 100 bushels of grass and other seed from between the floors and ceilings'. The Marquess went on to restore the house completely. His son, the 3rd Marquess, who was three times Prime Minister, showed little interest in the house and limited his wife to spending no more than £400 on renovations. Their son, who succeeded in 1903, visited Cranborne twice a year for six weeks and improved many of the cottages on the estate. The 5th Marquess, in 1929, installed electricity and central heating and began work on the garden.

Repairs and improvements continued under the 6th Marquess, whose wife, Lady Mollie Salisbury became an expert on Tudor and Stuart gardens, travelling to Italy to study Renaissance gardens contemporary with those at Hatfield. Before moving to Hatfield, and as Viscountess Cranborne, she lived for thirty years at Cranborne with her husband, and their seven children. During this time she turned the garden into one of the most celebrated gardens in Britain. She also opened the Garden Centre in Cranborne. In 1945 a fire swept through the hall destroying the tapestries and damaging the panelling. At the same time a medieval door by the fireplace was discovered as well as a window on the west side, which had been blocked up.

The present Marquess and Marchioness of Salisbury lived in Cranborne from 1979, moving into the manor house in 1987 when, as Viscount Cranborne, he was M.P. for South Dorset. The estate consists of the village, the manor house, the farm, famous for its herd of White Park cattle, the Garden Centre and also the village shop, which specializes in local produce, including meat from the farm. Now Lord and Lady Salisbury live at Hatfield House and their eldest son, Ned is the present Viscount Cranborne.

CRANBORNE MANOR. The east side of the house framed in an arch of espalier apples.

The love of gardens continued with the present Lady Salisbury who, during the years she lived at Cranborne, planted many interesting specimens of trees, providing a lasting legacy to the gardens. Her enthusiasm is evident all around. In spring the entire garden shimmers with colour, yet each season has its particular charm. In summer the north garden is aglow with white scented flowers, while the Chalk Walk beckons with its double herbaceous borders leading into the herb garden and ever onwards to more delights. All is enchantment. The wild garden to the north leads down to the Crane. Looking back at the house with its elegant north loggia and fanciful buttresses, the mingling of ages, from medieval to Tudor and Stuart gives the house a truly romantic aura. From every angle appears something of interest and beauty. Even the garden is reminiscent still of the style shown on the old plans, brimming with wonderful scents and vistas, culminating in an overall sense of peace and tranquillity.

Creech Grange

THE FIRST tantalising glimpse of Creech Grange is from the Stoborough Road leading to Whiteway Hill. The east side of the house sits proudly at the end of a long driveway, in springtime lined with a carpet of daffodils. As the road continues to climb up the steep Purbeck ridge, it reveals a breathtaking view of the south side of the house, deep in the valley below.

Creech Barrow lies on the north side of the chalk hills in the Purbecks. Extending from Corfe Castle to Tyneham, it is divided into East and West Creech and Creech Grange. At the Conquest it was held by Robert, Earl of Mortain, the brother of William the Conqueror. In 1280 the land here was transferred to Bindon Abbey, a Cistercian monastery lying just a few miles to the north-west. Creech then became a grange or farm for the abbey, also supplying wheat to Corfe Castle.

After the Dissolution of the Monasteries, around 1540, the Grange was given to Sir John Horsey of Clifton Maybank, who immediately sold it to Oliver Lawrence, whose family came from Lancashire. Lawrence must have already known of Creech as he was Collector of Customs in Poole. Lawrence was knighted for his part in the expedition against the Scots in 1547 and married Ann, sister of Thomas Wriothesley, the Lord Chancellor. Through his brother-in-law's influence he gathered together a large fortune, which he invested in land in the Isle of Purbeck as well as Affpuddle and Bloxworth. Between 1540 and his death in 1559 he rebuilt the house at Creech. Remains of this house are found in the writing room, the kitchen, drawing room and library.

His son, Edward (1527-1601), or his grandson, Sir Edward, (1562-1629) extended the house to the north in 1600. Sir Edward married Margaret Denton, sister-in-law of the wealthy William Napier of Middlemarsh Hall. Sir Edward, knighted in

CREECH GRANGE. The east front of the house was rebuilt between 1540 and 1559.

1619, was Sheriff of Dorset in 1622 and MP for Wareham in 1626.

In 1614, Sir Edward's son, yet another Sir Edward (1600-1647), married Grace Brune of Athelhampton. Soon the Civil War engulfed the country and, being a Royalist, his estate was confiscated. He is remembered, though, as a man of peace, who tried hard to persuade the men of Dorchester not to take up arms.

His son, Colonel Robert Lawrence, joined the Royalist army and was appointed Governor of Corfe Castle. His prime duty was to defend Lady Bankes from attack by Sir Walter Erle, the Parliamentarian, who threatened to spare neither women nor children. Such was his reputation for cruelty that Lord Poulett, of Hinton St George, described him as 'the wickedest rogue of them all and one of the Devil's limbs'. Lady Bankes, aided by Colonel Lawrence, proved to be more than a match for Erle. He withdrew, but not before he had plundered and burned Creech Grange, forcing Lady Lawrence to flee to the woods for safety. Lady Bankes went on to hold the castle from 1643 until 1646.

In 1646 the Puritan Governor of Wareham, Colonel Robert Butler, was captured by the Royalists and imprisoned at Corfe Castle. Colonel Lawrence, probably realising that the Royalist cause was finished, helped Butler to escape and went with him onto the side of Parliament. During the Commonwealth, Robert Lawrence rebuilt Creech Grange, entertaining generously when it was finished, doubtless to ingratiate himself with Puritans and Royalists alike. Some said his house was a 'wicked place', but many of the gentry, from both sides of the conflict, did what they could after the war to reconcile the two factions and bring back an air of normality to the country.

Sir Robert Lawrence must have been particularly successful at this reconciliation, for in 1660, at the Restoration, he was made a member of the Knights of the Royal Oak, as a reward from Charles II, given to all who had distinguished themselves by their loyalty (an award later abandoned). Six years later he died and Creech Grange came to his son Captain John Lawrence, who along with several of the estate workers, in 1678, heard the sound of marching feet along the high ridge south of Creech Grange. He immediately rode to London where fears of a Popish invasion were rife and this story added fuel to the fire until proved to be a false alarm. By 1688, due to heavy debts, John Lawrence was forced to sell Creech Grange to Nathaniel Bond of Lutton, though still reserving part of the estate for himself and his wife Mary. In 1691, however, he surrendered these estates to Mr. Bond and moved away towards Stoborough.

The Bonds had settled in Dorset in the mid fifteenth century, when Robert Bond of Hatch Beauchamp, Somerset, married 'the Lutton heiress', Lutton being a village in the Purbecks which belonged to the Bonds until it was requisitioned in the Second World War. Sir Thomas Bond, who came from a younger branch of the family, gave his name to Bond Street in London, which he laid out at his own expense and which turned into a ruinous speculation. Evelyn, in his diary, says he built it 'to his great undoing'.

Nathaniel (1634-1707) was the youngest of four sons. Unlike his brothers, he preferred his studies to amusements and was a successful lawyer. Soon he was able to buy the Lutton Estates from his brothers and went on to buy Creech Grange and Tyneham from the impoverished Lawrences. He was knighted in 1653, MP for Corfe Castle and Dorchester, and lived at Creech Grange for sixteen years, but did little in the way of alterations to the house.

Denis Bond, (1676-1746) Nathaniel's son, renovated the house to a standard fit for a country gentleman. A book of accounts in his handwriting details the spending of £1300 'building about the house' between 1738 and 1741. He changed the staircase on the west side of the hall and remodelled the south front, using stone from Lutton and Winspit, and placed a bust of William III over the main door. His architect and contractor was a Mr. Cartwright – probably Mr. Francis Cartwright of Blandford. At different times he was MP for Poole, Dorchester and Corfe Castle. In 1732, however, he was expelled from Parliament for fraud, yet,

CREECH GRANGE. A portrait of the Reverend Nathaniel Bond and his family by William Beetham. He inherited the house in 1847.

surprisingly, he continued as Recorder of Poole and Wareham and went on to become Treasurer of the Inner Temple.

Denis Bond landscaped the grounds and built the chapel in 1746, primarily to encompass an impressive Norman chancel arch from Holme Priory, which, along with East Stoke, also belonged to the Bonds. He is best remembered, however, for Grange Arch, an eighteenth century 'eye-catcher', better known as 'Bond's Folly'. Set high up on the ridge as a focal point from the house, as well as being a symbol of wealth, it has long intrigued walkers who pause and wonder what it stands for and why it is there. With its surrounding land, it was the first property in Purbeck to be purchased by the National Trust.

Denis died childless, so the Grange passed to his nephew John, then to John's son, another John, followed by yet another John who, in 1840, paid for work on the chapel, converting it into a chapel of ease for the parish of Steeple. He died unmarried in 1844.

In 1847 The Reverend Nathaniel, John's brother, inherited Creech Grange. Nathaniel was rector of Steeple and with his wife and five children lived at Holme. When they moved into Creech Grange, he began a sensitive restoration of the east front of the house, which dated from between 1540 and 1560. The front was carried up into two new gables for windows to a new attic storey; new stone-mullioned windows were put in place, except in the projecting bay at the south end, where the Tudor windows remain. From Holme, he brought a nineteenth century fireplace, now in the library. Around the Norman arch in the chapel of ease he built a larger church, consecrated in 1859.

Their son, Nathaniel, on his marriage to Lady Selina Scott, the sister of the 3rd Earl of Eldon, moved to Holme. They had eleven children and, in 1881, returned to Creech Grange following the death of Nathaniel's mother. The Bonds remained at Creech Grange for seventy-four years. Colonel Ashley Bond, the last member of the Bonds there, served in the Durham Light Infantry during the Second World War, seeing service at Dunkirk and the Normandy landings. After the war he returned home to assist in running the family quarries. In 1967 he sold the estate to English China Clay with a life interest in the house for his own and his wife's lifetime. He died in 1975 and his second wife continued to live there until around 1979.

Mr. Norman Hayward and his late wife, Patricia, bought the house, plus 50 acres of land, in 1979, moving in three years later. Mrs. Hayward was a keen gardener and took on the task of restoring the gardens. She was also instrumental, along with a group of friends, in setting up the first charity shop for Cancer Research in England, based in Wareham. This is still going strong and Cancer Research now has similar shops all over the country.

Then followed restoration of the drawing room, library and hallway, carefully preserving the original parts of the rooms. A glorious achievement has been the refurbishment of the central eighteenth century staircase. In the ceiling a lantern allows daylight to penetrate the stairwell and the decorative carving around the stairs is on wood, not plaster. Unfortunately, all memories of past inhabitants such as portraits and shields were removed from the house prior to it being sold. All, that is, except the armorial glass in the drawing room, which is a delight. The original windows have been retained in the kitchen and a nineteenth

CREECH GRANGE. South front, a view from West Creech Hill.

century kitchen range was found in pieces in a chimney, concealed behind a modern wall. It has been reconstructed by Mr. Hayward and is once again in working order.

In the grounds Mr. Hayward has built an orangery as well as a terrace made from local stone from St Aldhelm's Quarry. He still has many ideas for the gardens, even adopting the designs in old pictures and plans by previous owners. When English China Clay has sold parcels of the surrounding land, Mr. Hayward has bought them, thus gradually restoring the original estate for future generations.

Cruxton Manor

CRUXTON MANOR, sometimes called West Cruxton Manor, lies alongside the River Frome a couple of miles south of Maiden Newton. The road ends here and the pretty little Tudor manor house appears on the right, behind attractive, modern, wrought iron gates and surrounded by its delightful garden. It looks out to the peaceful chalk stream and on across the valley to a low ridge of hills, whilst behind the house rising land provides shelter from north winds in winter. Just past the house are some old farm cottages and to the left is a newly built farmhouse, which is more or less on the site of the old East Cruxton Farm, demolished in the early 1960s because the structure had become dangerous.

CRUXTON MANOR. The east front, built in the early seventeenth century by John Henning.

The manor house is two storeys with attics and tiled roofs, which were once thatched. It was built in the sixteenth century of stone, banded with flint and is a cruciform shape with central three storey gabled wings at the front and rear which form the cross arms. Both wings have original doorways and adjoining the rear wing is a square stone enclosure, which is all that remains of a spiral staircase. The windows are stone mullions of two or three lights. Sadly, some of them have had to be replaced and the stone used is very white in contrast to the lovely mellow Ham stone of the originals. This work was carried out after the Second World War when building materials were scarce, so perhaps there was little choice. Inside the house are some original oak framed doorways with four centred heads and some seventeenth century panelling. Much of the original panelling was removed and destroyed between the wars, but there is still some beautiful plank and muntin panelling on the first floor landing.

In the Domesday Book, Cruxton was referred to simply as Frome. By 1177 it was called Fromma Johannis Croc and in 1195 had become Crocston. In 1278 John De Crokeston held a knight's fee there.

The first indication of a change of ownership comes in 1456. At an Inquisition Post Mortem, it was recorded as belonging to Alice, daughter and heir of Edith and Hugh Deverel of Combe Deverel, Piddlehinton. Alice was the first wife of Robert Frampton of Moreton and her children had all died young. Thomas More was to inherit her estates, possibly from her cousin, John Spencer, who was her direct heir. Thomas came to an agreement with Robert Frampton that he should benefit from the rents of Alice's land for his lifetime but that they should revert to him at Robert's death. The exception to this was Cruxton, from which Thomas would receive 100 shillings a year rent.

Sir Thomas More's only daughter inherited Cruxton and it became the property of her husband, Lord Thomas Pawlett, second son of the Marquis of

Winchester. In 1542 they leased it to Christopher Pawlett for a term of 99 years but the balance of that term was re-assigned to Robert Napier.

In 1592 the manor was divided between Robert Napier and John Henning, the eastern half to Napier and the western half to Henning, but it was not until 1634 that the freehold was assigned to them by Thomas Pawlett. The property included a manor house and a farm and now became known as West Cruxton and East Cruxton.

John Henning was Sheriff of Dorset in 1609 and owned Poxwell Manor. His second son, Robert, was born in 1590 and became the owner of Cruxton, so perhaps it was purchased as his future inheritance. It seems possible that the Hennings built the present house when they acquired their half of Cruxton and that East Cruxton was the older manor house. West Cruxton, or 'Henning's Cruxton' as it was often called, remained in their possession until the late eighteenth century, when it was sold to George Brown of Frampton.

In 1654 Robert Napier sold East Cruxton to Richard Channing, whose family then owned it until the early nineteenth century, when it was sold to Francis John Browne. This reunited the two manors, which became part of the Frampton Estate and remained so until the estate was broken up and sold in the 1930s.

During the 1930's West Cruxton was farmed by George Churchill. After the war, it was owned by Dudley Cunliffe Owen. It was during his tenure that the thatched roof was replaced by tiles. He and his wife were keen hunting people and well known as great party givers.

From the 1950's to the 1970's it was the property of a retired army officer, Michael Foxley-Norris. By the early 1960's, East Cruxton Farm had apparently deteriorated so much that the structure had become dangerous and Mr. Foxley-Norris used his army contacts to arrange for it to be blown up as a training exercise.

The estate was sold to Mr. Willie Forbes in the early 1970's and was run by a farm manager whilst Mr. Forbes continued his career as an insurance broker. In about 1982, the farmland was sold to Mrs. Lipman of Ashley Chase Estates and the house, together with about two and a half acres of land, was bought by Mr. and Mrs. Heapher. Although now widowed, Mrs. Joan Heapher still lives in the manor.

CRUXTON MANOR. The back of the house and garden.

Dewlish Manor Farm

A MOATED HOUSE, referred to in the twelfth century as 'the house of William de Govis at Develisch' may have been on the site of a medieval village, traces of which still remain east of the church at Dewlish. There was, though, mention of this village even earlier, when Brithric the Saxon, in the reign of Edward the Confessor, held the land of Dewlish as part of his manor of Cranborne, which in turn, was part of the honour of Gloucester. He was sent to France to the court of Baldwin, Count of Flanders, with a mission to arrange a marriage between Judith, the Count's eldest daughter, and Tostig, the brother of King Edward's wife, Edith.

While Brithric was in France, the Count's youngest daughter, Matilda, fell in love with him and proposed marriage. He refused her even though her mother was a daughter of the King of France. Spurned and humiliated, she sought revenge. Later she married William, Duke of Normandy and in 1066 became Queen of England. She then had Brithric arrested and thrown into prison where soon the unfortunate man died. His land was confiscated and given to Matilda. After the queen's death Dewlish passed to the king's nephew, Robert Fitzhamon, who donated its tithes to Tewkesbury Abbey.

Robert Fitzhamon had four daughters, one of whom married Robert, Earl of Gloucester, and so Dewlish passed to the Earl of Gloucester. Meanwhile the de Govis family continued to live here. In the late thirteenth century, Johanna, a daughter of a William Govis married Sir John Latimer of Duntish, and in 1299 Dewlish passed to the Latimers in whose family it remained for two hundred years. During these years the village prospered. At the assize roll of 1332, the manor was assessed at 21s 4fld, while Dorchester, Wareham and Bridport were assessed at 20s each.

The last in the male line of Latimers died in 1505. In 1474 their only daughter, Edith, married Sir John Mordaunt, the Speaker of the House of Commons. The Mordaunts then held the manor until 1601, when, upon the death of the third Lord Mordaunt, it was sold to Lawrence Radford of Devon, who was married to a sister of Sir Walter Raleigh.

It seems most likely that Lawrence's grandson, Arthur Radford, built this handsome house around 1630. It is similar in appearance to Wynford Eagle, a house built in the same year near Maiden Newton. The interior has been well preserved, with several of the rooms retaining their plain seventeenth century oak panelling and moulded beading. Other rooms have enriched friezes. In the dining room the fireplace boasts a carved wooden overmantel of three early seventeenth century panels with strapwork in convex curves, and two tapering pilasters between them. The staircase is magnificent, with seventeenth century turned balusters and moulded handrails with newels rising from floor to floor. Well used for nigh on four hundred years, it has strongly withstood the test of time. A window in one bedroom is flanked with Ionic pilasters while another room retains an original door with six moulded panels below a larger carved panel. Shallow cupboards open into the panelling of yet another bedroom. What they were used for is difficult to determine – maybe at one time they were connecting doors to adjacent chambers.

Another mystery, this time in the twentieth century, concerns the discovery of tunnels found when workmen were laying cables. Starting from the house they went towards the church. Sadly they

DEWLISH MANOR FARM. Evening sun on the wisteria surrounding the main entrance.

did not remain open long enough to be fully excavated.

During the Civil War, Colonel Arthur Radford of Dewlish was a Royalist. Unfortunately his neighbours were the Binghams, whose house at Bingham's Melcombe was a Parliamentary headquarters. His land was confiscated, and though he lived long enough to see it returned to him, he died in 1664, shortly after the Restoration.

He had two sons and three daughters. His heir, also called Arthur, married what was known in those days as a 'light woman' or a fickle wife. He himself was thought of as dissolute and of questionable sanity. He died in 1674, age 22, and his brother Thomas succeeded him, but he too died when only 20 years old in 1679. Consequently his sisters became co-heirs of the estate. Grace married Thomas Gundrey and Elizabeth married Wadham Strangways, son of Giles Strangways of Melbury, and Rachel died unmarried, leaving her portion of the estate to her sister Elizabeth. Dewlish therefore passed to the Strangways and later to the Earls of Ilchester. They let the manor house to a succession of tenants and it became known as Manor Farm.

Ernest Debenham bought Manor Farm from the Ilchester Estate in 1928. Using profits from the London store his family had founded, he pioneered modern methods of dairy farming believing that scientific techniques could make farming more profitable and revive the rural economy. He did not live at Dewlish, as the hub of his organisation was at Briantspuddle where he had a laboratory for analysing the purity and fat content of milk as well as for the processing of long-life milk. He went on to own 10,000 acres in the county and was knighted in

DEWLISH MANOR FARM. The west front. The house was built by Arthur Radford around 1630.

1931. He had a dairy in Milborne St Andrew and a poultry farm on the Blandford Road in Dewlish. In the 1920s he piped a supply of mains water to Dewlish from his farm near Milborne Wood. The supply was meagre and it was not until 1956 that mains water was supplied to all the houses in the village.

When Ernest Debenham bought the house, the tenants, Mr. and Mrs. A.H. Legg and their son left. The new tenants, Mr. and Mrs. Victor Frampton came from Beaminster. They took over a manor house with three acres of ground and a 492 acre farm. In Henry Duke's catalogue for the auction on April 6th 1928, is the following paragraph:

'Some years ago the Ancient Gatehouse, architecturally in keeping with the Manor House, was taken down and rebuilt on the opposite side of the road facing the Entrance Gate of the Drive. This building now contains a Garage, Stable of Two Stalls and Loose Box, Harness Room and a light loft over all that could be converted into Chauffeur's or Groom's quarters.'

The round-headed arch, originally over the gateway, is reset over the right hand doorway of this building. It must certainly have been reduced in size as it would have been impossible for a coach and horses to drive through so narrow an archway. Some seventeenth century mullioned windows were also reset into the structure. The building was converted into a village hall and in 1943, given to the village by the then owners, the Bradford Property Trust Ltd.

The Frampton family have lived at Manor Farm since 1928. Victor Frampton and his wife later bought the farm, and in turn were followed by their son Peter and his wife Margaret. Now Peter and Margaret's daughter Vicky Booth and her husband Andrew run the modern computerised dairy farm in this delightful village.

Dunshay Manor

DUNSHAY IS HIDDEN in a fold of the Purbeck hills above Swanage, about a mile and a half north of Worth Matravers. A narrow drive winds down through the woodland, which now blankets the ancient spoil-heaps and Purbeck marble quarry workings until finally it opens onto a courtyard surrounding a pretty duckpond, with a studio and workshops alongside. The entrance is on the right through white picket gates flanked by elegant, classical gateposts, surmounted by tall, pyramid shaped finials. A path then leads down towards the two-storey porch with its arched doorway, lovely first floor mullioned window and handsome parapet. The walk down to the house provides the additional pleasure of passing some of the magnificent sculptures created by Mary Spencer Watson.

The house is built of local rubble stone faced with ashlar, with Purbeck stone tiled roofs. It is set

DUNSHAY MANOR. The entrance to the house with its mounting block and elegant classical gateposts.

DUNSHAY MANOR. Part of the weathered Purbeck stone tiled roof.

DUNSHAY MANOR. The main front of the manor, with one of Mary Spencer Watson's sculptures.

against a backdrop of trees and is beautifully weathered and totally in tune with its setting. On each side of the porch are two-storey gables. The one to the south is original but the northern side was reconstructed in 1906. On either side of the porch are rainwater heads with dates and initials. 'IAD 1642', commemorates John Dolling and the building of the house, and 'MGM 1906', the rebuilding of the north-east gable by Guy Montague Marston.

Dunshay is believed to have been built on the site of the old medieval manor house of Worth Matravers. The Manor of Worth included the old manors of Weston, Dunshay and Woodyhide, which were amalgamated at an early date, but whose boundaries can still be traced by the old hedges running straight up the hillsides.

The Manor of Worth is recorded in the Domesday Book as being held by Roger Arundel. In the late twelfth century it was inherited by Roger's great-great grandson, Roger de Pole. He followed Richard the Lionheart on Crusade and died at Acre around 1190, leaving Dunshay to Alice, his widow, for her lifetime. She remarried and became Alice de Briwere and it is by this name that she is remembered as one of the benefactors of Salisbury Cathedral. Annually for twelve years she made a gift of marble from Dunshay for the building of the cathedral. The Dunshay marble quarries also supplied stone to other churches and abbeys, including Westminster Abbey and Lincoln Cathedral.

Roger de Pole's mother was also widowed and remarried, and her son by her second marriage, Robert Fitzpaine, eventually inherited Worth from his half brother, the Crusader, and it remained the property of the Fitzpaines until the mid fourteenth century

In 1349 the manor was sold to John, Baron

Benjamin Jesty who first discovered vaccination against smallpox and who lived at Dunshay Manor during the 1770s.

DUNSHAY MANOR. The upper drawing shows the house in the 1880s when the north wing was in ruins. The lower illustration is an architect's drawing of 1906 showing the proposed new wing.

Maltravers, from whom the name Worth Matravers derives. John's heir, his grandaughter Alianor, married John Fitzalan, Earl of Arundel, who added the Barony of Maltravers to his titles. Thus the manor once again belonged to the family of Arundel, who held it until the sixteenth century.

Towards the end of the sixteenth or beginning of the seventeenth century, the manor was sold to the Dollings. Their name was already widespread in Dorset and their forebears may have come from Normandy with William the Conqueror. The present house was probably built by John Dolling, who lived from 1611 to 1663, and whose initials are on the rainwater head on the porch. His son and heir, Robert, died childless in 1673, and his three sisters inherited the property. One died unmarried in 1675 and the manor seems to have been divided equally between the two survivors. One sister was married to John Pyke and the other to George Duke and the two halves of the manor were thereafter inherited by their respective descendants.

In 1771 John Pyke and George Duke each sold their half of the estate to John Calcraft of Rempstone, thus re-uniting the manor, and it was his descendant, Guy Marston Montague, who rebuilt the north wing.

In the late 1770s Benjamin Jesty, who pioneered inoculation against smallpox some twenty years before Dr. Jenner, lived at Dunshay and is buried at Worth Matravers. He is often presumed to have

Mary Spencer Watson RA, at 89 still carving her beloved stone.

conducted his research whilst at Dunshay, but in reality it was whilst he was farming near Yetminster. In 1774 Yetminster was decimated by smallpox and Jesty successfully inoculated his wife and sons, enduring ridicule and condemnation from his neighbours in the process. It was their animosity perhaps that encouraged him to move his family to Dunshay.

In 1921 George and Hilda Spencer Watson purchased the house as a family home. George Spencer Watson RA was a successful and highly respected artist in great demand for his portraits. The family already spent holidays in Purbeck and it was on one of these holidays that Hilda fell in love with Downshay and they decided to buy it as a retreat from the pressures of London life. It was she who suggested that, to avoid confusion with Downshay Farm next door, they should return the spelling of the name to its older version of Dunshay.

Their daughter Mary was then about eight and it must have been an idyllic place for a child, free to roam the Purbeck countryside on her pony. Mary became fascinated by the work of the stone masons and was a frequent visitor to the quarries. One of the masons, intrigued by the intense interest of this little girl, lent her tools and showed her how to begin working the stone. From these small beginnings grew a lifetime spent with the stone she loved, creating work which has given much pleasure to many people. In 2004, at the age of 91 and still carving, Mary had a major retrospective exhibition in Salisbury Cathedral, but perhaps her most appropriate accolade came in 2000, when the Friends of Salisbury Cathedral purchased her statue *The Virgin*, which was set on a plinth of Purbeck marble in the cathedral church which Alice de Briwere of Dunshay had helped to build so many centuries before. Mary Spencer Watson died in March 2006.

Edmondsham House

ONCE CALLED Medesham or Edmondsham-Payne, an early manor on this site was owned by a Saxon, named Dodo. He was ousted by William the Conqueror, who gave part of the land to his wife, Queen Matilda. She in turn granted it to one of her favourites, Humphrey the Chamberlain, who in turn leased it to the widow Eddiva. When the Queen died in 1083, according to custom, the land reverted to the King.

Set amidst the open farmland between the eastern edge of Cranborne Chase and the poorer soils of the New Forest, there were four parts to this manor mentioned in the Domesday Book. Robert de Edmondsham and his son Stephen owned the

EDMONDSHAM HOUSE. Harvesting in the fields around the house in 1760. A detail from a naive painting by George Egan.

Above EDMONDSHAM HOUSE. Built in local brick by Thomas Hussey and completed in 1589.

Below EDMONDSHAM HOUSE. Alterations were made to the west front by John Fry Hussey in the mid 1700s when the three projecting bays and Dutch gables were added.

principal manor. Then in 1290 it passed to the family of Elias de Rabayne, followed by Sir Peter Rabayne. In 1330 John Brakenbergh, co-heir and kinsman of Sir Peter Rabayne, passed part of the manor to Henry de Beauboys (Beauboys, meaning Fair Wood, hence the local name of Verwood). The Beauboys died childless and in 1395 bequeathed their estates to David Servington of Wiltshire whose family continued to hold the manor until 1563.

In 1563 Nicholas Servington sold Edmondsham to Thomas Hussey, whose family had owned the lesser manor of Edmondsham Payne since 1316. Thomas's mother, when widowed, leased the principal manor house and land from Nicholas Servington, and here Thomas was brought up. It was from this house that Thomas married his first wife Anne around 1563 and twenty years or so later he began to build the central portion of the grand Tudor house.

The house was constructed of local brick and was built in two stages – the bottom two storeys first, then, in 1589, the top storey with its Dutch style gabling. The date 1589, recording completion of the house, can be seen on the central pinnacle. Thomas died in 1601 and was succeeded by his son Giles, who lived until 1632, followed by his grandson Thomas, aged two.

In documents stored at the house there is an inventory taken after the death of Thomas Hussey (II) in 1684. It lists his goods and chattels and reveals a picture of the interior of the house and the life style of the family. The value of the contents is interesting. Jewels and plate were worth £40, wearing apparel £20, the chests of bed and table linen, obviously considered valuable at £29, while the contents of his lodging chamber and closet with one bed and linen quilt, bolster, two pillows and two blankets, plus the furnishings of the room came to only £16.6s.8d. On the other hand, his livestock was valued at £346. 8s. The Inventory was dated 16th March 1684-85. 'in the six and thirtieth yeare of the reigne of our Sovraigne Lord King Charles the second' (although Charles II came to the throne following the Restoration in 1660, his reign was recognised as beginning in 1649, the year in which his father Charles I was beheaded).

During the Jacobean period, the house was extended to the north and a fine oak staircase was installed with stout oak newel-posts, ball finials, moulded handrails and turned balusters. Some of the original small metal-framed windows still remain on the top storey. The imposing metal-studded front door is also original. Above the porch a stone cartouche displays the arms of Hussey.

The third Thomas Hussey, who was a Serjeant-at-Law and also mayor of Blandford and Shaftesbury, was the last direct male descendant of the Hussey family to live at Edmondsham. He had no children and, in 1745, left his estate to his sister Philadelphia Fry. After her death her son, John Fry, upon the instruction of his late uncle, added Hussey to his name.

Between 1740 and 1750 John Fry Hussey added the two projecting wings with the Dutch or Flemish style gables ornamented with finials. A painting at Edmondsham by T. Young, dated 1780 but copied from an earlier painting of 1760, shows the new additions to the house. The architect may have been Francis Cartwright of Blandford. The interior of the house was extensively altered at this time too. The Great Hall was sub-divided to create an extra room and interior mouldings and panelled doors with heavy pediments also date from this period.

John Fry Hussey died in 1760 and the estate passed, first, to his widowed sister Philadelphia, and then to his niece, another Philadelphia, who had married the Reverend William Bower, rector of Edmondsham church, which stands close to the house. Once again the estate passed to a niece called Philadelphia (altogether six women in the family bore this name).

In 1796 Philadelphia Bower married Lieutenant-General William Hector Monro, later Governor of Trinidad, and they had ten children. He commanded the British forces in Barbados during the Napoleonic War and was later based at Surinam. Their eldest son, Hector William Bower Monro, inherited the estate in 1821. He was named

A Staffordshire figure depicting the death of Hugh Monro while on a tiger hunt in India in 1792. It was based on Tippoo's Tiger, a mechanical model now in the Victoria and Albert Museum, made in 1795 for the amusement of the ruler of Mysore, Tippoo Sultan, who hated the British, but was defeated by them a few years later.

after his godfather, General Sir Hector Monro, whose son, Hugh, was killed by a tiger in India. A china ornament at Edmonsham illustrates this gruesome death! His other son Alexander was killed by a shark, also in India.

In 1825 Hector William Bower Monro married Henrietta Lewina Tregonwell, daughter of Lewis Tregonwell, the founder of Bournemouth. Through this marriage the portraits of the Tregonwell family came to Edmondsham. The Tregonwells originated in Cornwall, and their family had bought Milton Abbey after the Dissolution of the Monasteries, living there for several generations. Lewis Tregonwell served as a Dorset Volunteer protecting the defences of the Dorset coast from possible Napoleonic attack. A fine portrait of him in uniform hangs in the drawing room. In 1837 Hector and Henrietta Lewina made alterations to the dining room (now the library). Windows and gates were altered and the front of the house stuccoed.

When Hector Monro inherited the estate from his father in 1842, he replaced the original stables, which appear in an eighteenth century painting of the house. The new stable block bears the date 1864. He added new outbuildings, including an octagonal dairy with attractive tiles illustrating pastoral scenes. In 1869, he added a nursery-cum-servant wing to the north side of the house connecting the kitchen to the then dining room (now the library). The conservatory, constructed between 1854 and 1858, and now demolished, was a wedding present from his wife's father.

Their eldest son, Hector Edmond, who inherited in 1902, completely overhauled the water supply, which, until then, was supplied by wells. The house was re-roofed, new windows inserted, some ceilings raised and the kitchen area refurbished. The carriage sweep in front of the house was enlarged and, finally, in 1912, the stable block was altered to accommodate his new motorcar. This meant the construction of a mechanics' workshop, complete with an inspection pit and heating.

Hector Richard Monro, who had been a Lieutenant Commander in the Navy, inherited Edmondsham in 1925. Two years later he installed a generator to provide electricity to the house and replaced the antiquated plumbing system. During the Second World War the army requisitioned the house for use by part of the 2nd Searchlight Regiment. When the war ended, once again the house underwent drastic changes. The Victorian nursery was demolished and the materials reused to build a pair of cottages near the village pump. The stone floor of the dining room was moved out to the rear courtyard and replaced by an oak floor using estate timber. Central heating was installed and the kitchen once again altered. The dining room became a library and new fireplaces were installed in several of the rooms.

The house has not been sold since Tudor times, continuing through the same family, sometimes passing through the female line. Documents stored at the house, containing records, deeds and inventories, are remarkable for their number and content. They span from Tudor times to the present, illustrating the life and times of each century. One of particular interest gives a detailed description of the duties of the staff from 1902-1914 when there were eight full-time and two part-time indoor staff and fifteen outdoor staff. The indoor staff included a cook, a kitchen maid, and a charwoman. There was also a lady's maid, known as 'the useful maid' who made clothes, packed trunks and looked after the older members of the family. The three housemaids rose at 6.30 a.m. to dust and lay fires in the ground floor rooms until 9 a.m., when breakfast was served. They then cleaned the two upper floors. The two senior housemaids would usually take the afternoon off, but the junior maid would spend the afternoons mending clothes and linen. Before every meal as well as at bedtime, they carried hot water to the bedrooms. There was a butler who lived in one of the lodges, as well as a footman who also lived on the premises. The footman was usually a young man trained by the butler and employed on a fairly short-term basis. A general male servant was employed for cleaning shoes, carting the washing to the laundry and general odd jobs. The outside staff consisted of four stable staff, two chauffeurs, two carpenters, and one mason.

An interesting story is of a Miss Penny who worked for the Monros from 1867-1912. Employed as a lady's maid to the elderly Mrs. Monro, she came to Edmondsham just before the birth of Tregonwell Monro, known as Jack, and helped with his upbringing. When Mrs. Monro died in 1903, she left Penny a generous bequest but it was not quite enough to allow her to retire. Consequently she took employment with Adah May Monro, known as Auntie May, as her personal maid. Auntie May, instead of paying Penny the standard wage, deducted her mother's bequest from Penny's wages. Furthermore, she did not see fit to tell Penny about Jack's serious illness though she knew of the close ties between them during Jack's childhood. When he died, in 1912, he left Penny a handsome bequest which finally enabled her to retire after working for the Monros for 45 years.

In 1962 Henry Richard Monro handed over responsibility for the house to his nephew Anthony Medlycott, father of the present owner Mrs. Julia Smith. The Medlycotts lived at Sandford Orcas and Anthony was the second son of Sir Hubert Medlycott and his wife Nell, who was Hector

EDMONDSHAM HOUSE. The stables, rebuilt by Hector Monro in 1864.

Richard Monro's sister. Anthony Medlycott was an architect. He modernised several of the village houses and, for his first commission after qualifying in 1935, designed the village pumphead, now a Listed Building. He married Mary Eden and they had four children. Their eldest daughter, Mrs. Julia Smith, now owns Edmondsham and manages the 1500 acres of farm and woodland.

Though practical care for the house still remains a high priority, so too does land management and care of wildlife. Mrs. Julia Smith was accepted into the Countryside Stewardship scheme in 1994, which ensures that the land is farmed with environmental consideration as the first priority. The Woodland Improvement Grant enabled a 22 acre wood to be cleared of rhododendron and replanted with oak.

The same attention is given to the walled garden, which combines fruit, vegetables and flowers in a delightful array, reminiscent of old Victorian and Edwardian gardens. The work involved in maintaining this lovely garden is greatly appreciated by the many people who visit Edmondsham each year.

Fiddleford Manor

THE MANOR HOUSE is a little to the east of Fiddleford beside the River Stour and looks out over the fields to Sturminster Newton. On a summer day it is a gloriously peaceful pastoral scene. The lawn slopes away from the house down to the Stour, flowing gently past between its tree-lined banks. The mill pond lies opposite, behind the iron wheels and cogs controlling the sluice gates and beyond are the lush pastures of the river valley. The oldest part of the building, which is fourteenth century and in the guardianship of English Heritage, is open to the public and gives the clearest sense of what a medieval house was like in Dorset. The north range of the building, which is mainly sixteenth century, is a private house.

The original building was roughly T shaped, lying east/west, with the head of the T at the western end containing the solar. This part is open to the public and its layout is much as it would have been in the fourteenth century, except that the hall itself has been foreshortened. The roof now consists of three bays with an extra truss to support a smoke louvre in the end bay. This would originally have been situated to allow smoke to filter out from a central hearth, so it is reasonable to assume that the hall would then have consisted of five bays.

FIDDLEFORD MANOR. The restored fourteenth century part of Fiddleford Manor with the solar to the left and the foreshortened Hall to the right.

The magnificent timber roofs of the hall and solar are the glory of the building and are considered to be 'of outstanding importance' by the Royal Commission on Historic Monuments. They are a beautiful example of the skill and craftsmanship of the medieval carpenters and were obviously intended to be decorative as well as functional. The north range was added in the sixteenth century and lengthened again in the eighteenth.

The mill belonging to the manor stands to the north-west of the north range and bears the date 1566, with the following dedication carved on two stone blocks reset in the wall.

'Operam dedic 1566 meis sump's alienis
He that wyll have here any thynge don
Let him com friendly he shal be welcom
A frynd to the owner and enemy to no man
Pass all here freely to com when they can
For the tale of trothe I do always professe
Miller be true disgrace not thy vest
If falsehood appere the fault shal be thine
And of sharpe ponishment think me not unkind
Therefore to be true yt shall the behove
[to] please god chefly [that liveth] above.'

The manor belonged to Glastonbury Abbey and in the fourteenth century it was held by John Latimer, who had acquired it by marriage in about 1355. Latimer was Sheriff of Somerset and Dorset in 1374 and 1380 and there is little doubt that the

FIDDLEFORD MANOR. A view across the millpond.

Great Hall and solar were built for him.

By the early sixteenth century it was the property of Thomas White, a merchant of Poole. The initials T A and W, which appear in several places in the house, are most likely those of his son Thomas and his wife Ann Williams. They were probably married around 1515 because, when Thomas died in 1555, their son, another Thomas, was thirty-nine. Their grandson, Thomas (4) married Frances Martyn of Athelhampton. She was one of four daughters of Nicholas Martyn, who died in 1595 and had no sons, leaving his estate to be divided between the daughters. From 1645 to 1653 Thomas White had his farm at Athelhampton confiscated because he was a Catholic. Soon after this the farm was sold to the Brunes, relatives of his wife.

The sixteenth century north range was built by the White family, who owned the property until after the Restoration. It is difficult to ascertain which generation built what, but it is tempting to speculate that perhaps the advantageous marriage by grandson Thomas into the important Martyn family, and his wife's inheritance, allowed the building of the 'new' north wing. The mill, built in 1566 with its poetic dedication, would have been erected or possibly rebuilt in Thomas White (3)'s

FIDDLEFORD MANOR. The medieval part is in the foreground and the later sixteenth century wing beyond.

FIDDLEFORD MANOR.
Above Part of the roof in the fourteenth century solar, with the medieval painting of an angel on the end wall.
Below The restored medieval gallery at the west end of the hall.

time. Legend has it that the mill was a hiding place for contraband liquor which led to 'much disorderly conduct' amongst the workers of Sturminster Newton.

After the Restoration the family sold the manor to Thomas Freke of Shroton, who already owned Sturminster Newton manor. It was inherited by the Pitts of Stratfield Saye and then passed by descent to the Pitt-Rivers.

The fourteenth century part of the building was abandoned and became increasingly derelict. In 1932 a report of a visit to Fiddleford by the Dorset Natural History and Archaeological Society noted that Captain Pitt-Rivers had removed a Tudor plaster ceiling from the building and re-erected it at Hinton St Mary manor house, presumably to preserve it from destruction. A second plaster ceiling remains in situ in the north wing of the house.

The whole building is still owned by the Pitt-Rivers Estate but eventually the medieval part of the building was handed into the guardianship of the then Ministry of Public Buildings and Works, which became English Heritage, who are now responsible for its preservation.

Folke Manor

THE MANOR HOUSE is just opposite the church in the tiny village of Folke, a hamlet just south of Sherborne in a setting of woodland and wide meadows. The house is two storeys with attics and is built of rubble stone with slate covered roofs. Its general plan is L shaped and the earliest part is the east wing, built in the late fifteenth and early sixteenth century. The south wing, with a porch and staircase, was added in the early seventeenth century. At about the same time the west end of the east wing was rebuilt and a low north-east wing was added, which has since been heightened. The exterior of the house appears typically seventeenth century and is substantially the same as the nineteenth century engraving in the third edition of Hutchins *History of Dorset*. The interior has been greatly altered, but the present owners have returned the east wing kitchen to almost its original dimensions, revealing what was probably the original medieval hall with its heavy oak ceiling beams forming sixteen panels.

The manor was originally divided in two halves. The Bishop of Salisbury owned one half and the other belonged, first to a family called Hungerford, and later to the Dean of Salisbury. The Hungerfords owned their half from at least 1442 until 1471, when Margaret, Lady Hungerford, endowed a chantry in Salisbury Cathedral, in memory of her husband, with their half of the manor and the advowson of the church. It then remained the property of the Dean and Chapter of Salisbury until the end of the nineteenth century. The Hungerfords also seem to have held the other half of the manor from the Bishop during the late fourteenth century. They succeeded the Haddons of Stourton Caundel, who were still in possession in 1362. The oldest part of the house is late fifteenth century and was probably built by the Hungerfords. Tragically, the Hungerford Chantry in Salisbury Cathedral, with its superb medieval wall paintings, was destroyed by James Wyatt in 1789 and Lord Hungerford's alabaster effigy now lies in the nave.

FOLKE MANOR. The south wing from the garden.

There is little further information about the manor until the reign of Elizabeth I, when in 1582 it was granted to John Ashley, who was Master of the Jewels. Quite soon after this it became the property of the Chafins, who lived there until they built their new house at Chettle. John Coker says that they built a new house at Folke during his time. Thomas Chafin originally came from Wiltshire and bought Chettle in 1575 but the present house there was not built until 1710. He was appointed Sheriff of Dorset in 1578-79 and again in 1589-90. The Chafins owned Folke until 1788 and branches of the family seem to have lived both here and at Chettle.

FOLKE MANOR. The south wing with the porch and late fifteenth century wing beyond.

The family were staunch Royalists in the Civil War and, according to Hutchins, Bampfield Chafin, Thomas's son and heir, was besieged by a small detachment of the Parliamentary army in his own house at Folke and taken prisoner. It must have been a fierce encounter because Hutchins also states that the dead of both sides are recorded in the parish register of Folke. He was obviously released because in 1644 he was killed fighting at Exeter and buried in Exeter Cathedral. The following year his widow had her property confiscated and his son, Thomas, was taken prisoner when Sherborne Castle fell to the Parliamentary forces and was imprisoned at Poole. He later paid a fine of £900 for raising money for the King's forces and was released on parole. Lord Shaftesbury describes him in his journal as being, 'a personable well-carriaged man of good estate, wanted neither understanding nor value for himself, was an enemy to the Puritan party.'

His son, Thomas, known as Tossey by family and friends, married Anne Penruddock, the daughter of Colonel John Penruddock, who was executed in 1655 as an instigator of the abortive Royalist rising at Salisbury. Their marriage seems to have been a love match and when Tossey raised and commanded a troop of horse against the ill-fated Duke of Monmouth at the Battle of Sedgemoor in 1685, he sent frequent loving letters to his 'dearest deare Nan' and their ten children.

By the late eighteenth century the family had run out of money and in 1788 an Act of Parliament was passed to allow the sale of part of the estates of William Chafin, seemingly for the payment of debts. By this time the Chafins had ceased using Folke as a family home and the manor was sold to the Rev. E. Jacob of Shillingstone. It was later sold on to J.S.W.S. Drax of Charborough, who still owned it at the end of the nineteenth century.

In 1929 Commander Henry Kelsall Mitchell, bought the manor and lived there with his family, farming 400 acres. He had served in submarines in the First World War and commanded the Dorset Yeomanry between the Wars. In the Second World War he was recalled to the Royal Navy and served throughout the hostilities. He also later served as Chairman of Dorset County Council and was High Sheriff of Dorset.

In 1979 he sold the manor and farm and gradually over the next ten years most of the land was sold piecemeal until, in 1986, Mr. and Mrs. David Young bought the house with just 30 acres of land. They have since added another 120 acres to the estate.

Font Le Roi Farm

IT WOULD BE EASY to miss Font Le Roi altogether, because although it is only yards from the A3030, a mile or so west of Caundle Marsh. the house is hardly visible and at first glance it appears to be merely a collection of farm buildings. The estate's original name was Fauntleroy's Marsh. Fauntleroy deriving from Norman French, either from 'Enfaunt le Roy', son of the king, or a contraction of the war cry 'Defendez le Roi'. The names Fauntleroy and Fitzroy have long been believed to denote illegitimate sons of kings and the Fauntleroys claimed this connection. Their coat-of-arms shows the heads of three infants and the motto *Enfans du Roi*.

The house is built of pretty, warm stone with tiled roofs. Its central core is fifteenth century or earlier and was a medieval hall with screens passage but with extensive fifteenth century additions, including the gatehouse range. There are remains of foundations running under the garden to the south-west from the original part of the house and from the end wall of the 'chapel', extending to the south. These are possibly the remnants of an enclosed courtyard.

The approach to the house is through the main arch of the fifteenth century gateway. This has a single massive baulk of timber supporting the stonework above and connects on its western side with the main house and on the eastern side with a small building, which is said to have once been a chapel. This tradition is probably correct because there are consecration marks visible on the jambs of the fifteenth century doorway. These incised marks were cut on the walls of consecrated buildings, usually a simple cross within a circle – as seen here. A record also survives of a marriage in 1602 between William Fauntleroy and Mary Hurd, 'in the chapel in the courtyard at Fauntleroys Marsh'.

At the south-west corner of the house is a gabled bay whose lower room has an elegant, delicate, Italianate plaster ceiling with thin ribs and sprigs of flowers, which bears a strong resemblance to some of the work in nearby Sherborne Castle. The ceiling was restored in 1938. The room is lit by a beautiful six light window which encompasses the bay, although the two side lights are blocked.

The first written records of Fauntleroys in Dorset appear in 1332, when William Fauntleroy is named in the Subsidy Rolls and in 1340, when Adam of Sherborne was a witness at an inquisition post mortem. In 1373 his son, John, was the plaintiff in a court case in Sherborne, and identified himself as the son of Adam and grandson of Walter Fauntleroy and Juliana de Thornhull. This suggests that the

FONT LE ROI FARM. A view from the south east. The house incorporates the original medieval hall, which is fifteenth century or earlier and retains its original doorway.

FONT LE ROI FARM. The back of the house showing the gable end added in the seventeenth century.

family were already established in the area at least as early as the thirteenth century, although the first record of a Fauntleroy at Fauntleroy's Marsh is John Fauntleroy, knight, who died in 1440. Coker says that the manor came to the Fauntleroys through an heir of the Walleys and as John's wife was Johanna, the daughter and heir of John Le Waleys, it would seem that she brought the estate to the Fauntleroys.

John and Johanna were generous benefactors of Sherborne Abbey. In 1437 John gave £20 and 80 loads of timber to help build the Almshouses there and Johanna gave £5 – a substantial gift. In her will, dated 1444, Johanna asked to be buried near her husband's grave in the Conventual Church of Sherborne and left the church 20 shillings to pay for a thousand misereres (Psalm 51 asking for God's mercy) to be said for her soul and that of her husband and her benefactors, plus another 20 marks, for prayers for their souls. A mark was worth 13s.4d.or two thirds of a pound sterling.

John and Joanna had three sons. John, the eldest, inherited Fauntleroys Marsh, William became a priest and Trystram settled in Hampshire. In 1643 one of Trystram's descendants, Moore Fauntleroy, emigrated to Virginia, establishing an American dynasty of Fauntleroys which is still flourishing today. John married twice, having three children by both of his wives. His eldest son, Peter, inherited Font Le Roi and two of his daughters entered religious orders. Bridget, his daughter by his first wife, was a nun at Shaftesbury and Elizabeth, his youngest daughter by his second wife, became Abbess of Amesbury.

Font Le Roi remained in the Fauntleroy family until 1698, when a subsequent John died childless and bequeathed his estate to a Mr. George Cooper. The will was contested by the heirs of his great aunt Mary, who had died in 1630, and those of his uncle James, who had died in Barbados in 1695. The lawsuit dragged on for several years but was eventually dropped and in 1707 George Cooper sold the estate to the trustees of Thomas, Viscount Weymouth, owner of Longleat.

By the middle of the nineteenth century it was part of the Digby estates and a tenanted farm, which it remained until 1986, when the house was separated from the land and sold to Mr. and Mrs. David Edwards.

Godlingston Manor

High above Swanage, facing south over the bay and protected to the north by the rise of Godlingston Hill, lies Godlingston Manor. It shares with Barnston the claim to be the oldest manor house in Purbeck and, with its trees and hedges around it, seems to huddle into the hillside as if quietly keeping the secrets of centuries. The present farm can be traced back until the Saxon period at least. Fragments of Iron Age and Romano-British pottery have been found there, indicating an immensely long period of habitation.

The earliest parts of the present house date from the end of the thirteenth century, although the rounded tower at the west end of the house may be earlier. It is built of local stone with stone tiled roofs and is part single storey with attics and part two storey. The house began life in about 1290 as a medieval hall house, with its defensive tower at the western end. In the early seventeenth century the north wall was rebuilt and an upper floor inserted over the hall, with a stone turret staircase to reach it, whilst at the eastern end of the house a cross wing was built.

About a century and a half later a kitchen wing was added on the north side and subsequently extended to the west. In the late nineteenth century the cross wing and farm buildings to the east were burnt down. At that time the house was in a dilapidated state but plans to demolish it and rebuild had met with strong opposition and there was some suggestion that the fire was deliberate. In the end, the cross wing was rebuilt and the interior of the medieval house was remodelled. The tower is immensely strong, with walls about ten feet thick, and must surely have been for defensive purposes. It is thought that there may have been two linked towers originally, forming a gateway, but so far no archaelogical evidence for this has been found.

GODLINGSTON MANOR. The earliest parts of the house are thirteenth century, and the defensive tower, just visible in the shadows on the left, has walls about 10 feet thick.

However there is evidence to suggest that there was once a moat around the house. An estate map of 1775 shows a watercourse just to the north of the house, which fed two stretches of water to the east and south, and the tithe map of 1839 shows a long pond to the west of the house.

Godlingston is not mentioned by name in the Domesday Book, but it was almost certainly included in the manor of 'Suuanwic', then part of the property of the wife of Hugh fitz Grip. By 1166 Alured Talbot held land here and the Talbot family appears in Godlingston records for the next two hundred years, until they sold it in 1367, after which its ownership becomes somewhat confusing.

There is a fascinating document, written some time between 1413 and 1427, which has been called *The Godlingston Roll*. This is a record of evidence taken in a dispute over ownership of land at Godlingston between John and Amicia Estoke and Robert and Margaret Rempston. It gives details of family relationships, and who had inherited what and from whom, as recollected by various local inhabitants. As may be imagined it is often confusing and sometimes contradictory, but it provides a wonderful vignette of life at the time. For instance, John Chaunterelle and his wife Margaret, known as Grette, had two daughters, Edith and Rose. Edith, the eldest, married Peter Clavile of La Quarre, but went to London and never returned. Rose, her younger sister 'was hairy and unpretty and never had a husband or any other man as far as anyone knew.'

Whatever the complicated trail of inheritance, the next clear evidence of ownership is that in 1560 it belonged John Pole and that he died and left it to his sister Mary, wife of Henry Wells. Mary was not destined to enjoy her inheritance as she died in the same year as her brother, leaving her husband to inherit Godlingston. The Wells family were staunch Catholics and although Henry seems to have kept a fairly low profile, his elder brother Gilbert, who bought Renscombe in 1566 but continued to live at Bambridge in Hampshire, was in and out of prison in London and Winchester in the 1580s. His brother Swithun was a schoolmaster, active in the Catholic underground, and in 1591 was hanged outside his house in Gray's Inn for allegedly harbouring priests. He was later designated Blessed Swithun Wells by the Roman Catholic Church.

In 1595 another brother, Anthony, sailed on the *Delight* with Raleigh on the abortive expedition up the Orinoco to search for El Dorado. Knowing Henry's background, it would be surprising if Godlingston were not to have seen many secret comings and goings during those troubled times. Henry survived to the great age of 91 and died in 1607. During the sixteenth and seventeenth centuries the Wells family was continuously fined for their adherence to the Catholic faith and in the Civil War, as supporters of the king, their estates were confiscated.

Eventually, in 1687, Henry Wells sold it to William Frampton of Moreton and in 1765, James Frampton sold it again, this time to John Bankes of Kingston Lacy whose descendants owned it until the Bankes' Estates were bequeathed to the National Trust in the late twentieth century.

During the two hundred years of Bankes ownership, the house had about ten tenants. The latest, the Bowermans, took over the tenancy in 1949 and the third generation of the family is still farming there. They have also diversified into marketing Godlingston Manor spring water through 'Aquaid', a company supporting Christian Aid in supplying clean water to some of the poorest communities in the world. Although Godlingston now belongs to the National Trust, it is a private house and not open to the public.

GODLINGSTON MANOR. A nineteenth century drawing.

Hammoon Manor

In 1066 Thomas de Mohun of Moyon in Normandy gathered forty-nine knights and their retainers in support of William, Duke of Normandy's, invasion of England. It was a huge gamble, but if William succeeded in seizing the crown that he claimed was his by right, the potential rewards would be immense. He prevailed by the narrowest of margins at the Battle of Hastings and England became his kingdom. Thomas's reward for his loyalty was Dunster Castle, eleven manors in Dorset and fifty-five other manors in Somerset and Devon. One of these was the tiny settlement of Ham, near Sturminster Newton, which would perpetuate his name by becoming Ham Mohun, gradually anglicised to Hammoon and which his descendants would own for the next eight hundred years.

The present delightful little manor house, in this tiny village, is still the centre of a mixed farm, as it has been for centuries. It must be one of the most picturesque houses in Dorset. The house is L shaped and the oldest, western end of the south facing wing was built at the beginning of the sixteenth century and is partly timber framed. It was extended to the east, using stone, around 1560 and it is to this phase of building that its unusual two-storey porch belongs. During the seventeenth century it was further extended to the north and its only addition since then seems to have been a single storey Victorian extension to the rear of the south wing, hardly more than a passageway. Surprisingly, the house is thatched, an unusual feature, which gives it a particularly rustic charm.

In the interior, a great deal of original timberwork survives, including a substantial seventeenth century oak staircase and some beautiful seventeenth century panelling. On the upper floor of the south range, the room at the western end, once used as an apple store, includes some large painted panels on the sloping area of the ceiling. The design is of white stars on a coloured background and the panels were probably alternated red and green, although the green pigment has faded to a brownish hue. These panels have been dated as probably fourteenth or fifteenth century, which, if correct, raises the question of whether they could have been re-used from an earlier house here or brought from elsewhere.

The principal house of the Mohuns was at Dunster Castle and a younger branch of the family held Hammoon. The last of the Mohun name to live at Hammoon, although the property still remained in the family, was John, who died in 1479 at the age of 73. John's wife, Joanna Jurdain, had inherited Wolfeton and their daughter Christian married

HAMMOON MANOR. The manor house from the south. The earliest part of the house is the western end.

HAMMOON MANOR. The house has a charming, eccentric combination of thatched roof and classical porch.

Henry Trenchard of Hordle, in Hampshire. Christian's son, John Trenchard, inherited both Hammoon and Wolfeton from his grandparents.

Sir John Trenchard supported Henry Tudor in his claim to the throne and when Richard III became king in 1483, he was attainted and his estates were confiscated. He was lucky to avoid execution but in 1485 after the Battle of Bosworth, when Henry Tudor won the throne, his estates were restored to him. The Trenchards never lived at Hammoon, but owned it until 1818, when General Sir John Slade of Maunsell House, Somerset, bought the manor. This sale was the first time, apart from the brief interlude under Richard III, that the manor had changed hands other than by inheritance since 1066.

Sir John Slade was a distinguished cavalry officer and had served under Sir John Moore at Corunna and later under the Duke of Wellington. His son, Sir Alfred Slade, a well-known barrister, inherited the estate and it remained the property of the Slade family, as a tenanted farm, until the late nineteenth century when they sold it to Viscount Portman.

In the mid nineteen twenties the Portman Estate sold it to Captain William Percy Browne, MC, MFH. From at least 1841 until just before the First World War the farm was tenanted by three generations of the Coate family, who were followed by William Crouch, whose wife continued to farm it after the war until the late 1920s.

In 1937 Captain Browne sold the farm to the Baptist Union and during the Second World War it was farmed by Mr. Lionel Knight who did considerable restoration and repair work during his tenancy.

In 1946 Mr. and Mrs. Leonard Frampton leased the farm from The Baptist Union until they were able to buy the freehold in 1952, the first time in four centuries that Hammoon Manor had been occupied and farmed by its owners. For two or three years after the war German prisoners of war, awaiting repatriation in a camp at what is now Port Regis School, provided part of the workforce.

In 1983 the Frampton's son George and his wife Sue took over the farm to run a mixed beef, dairy and sheep farm of about 300 acres and bring up their own family.

Hanford House

THE LOVELY, EARLY Jacobean, Hanford House lies in the wooded valley of the Stour between Iwerne Steepleton and Child Okeford, flanked by the heights of Hod and Hambledon hills. The house was built between 1604 and 1623 by Sir Robert Seymer, whose father purchased the manor in 1599. The Seymers had been at Hanford since long before then, certainly since the reign of Edward IV, when the manor belonged to the nunnery at Tarrant Crawford.

The two-storey house with attics and cellars is built of warm, cream stone, which, over the centuries, has acquired shadings of pink, giving a delightful pastel effect. The grounds slope gently away towards the river. It is a house of many gables and chimneys, some of which display the strange fashion for setting them at the apex of the gable, seen also at Wraxall and Bloxworth, except that here they are in pairs. The house was built around an open quadrangle, harking back to the old medieval courtyard house, but with a more regular and formal arrangement similar to an Italian palace.

The main entrance is through an archway below a two storey Classic frontispiece in the centre of the north-west front. This leads into what was the central courtyard. It is surrounded by large windows, and the imposing, two-storey porch with its Ionic pilasters and Seymer arms, originally the entrance to the house, is in the range once opposite the gateway. The north-east front faces out across the lawns and has four gables and at either end, large, five sided bay windows.

In the nineteenth century the interior was extensively remodelled but it still retains two beautiful staircases. An original dog-leg staircase of oak with heavy turned balusters and handsome newel posts and an elegant, early eighteenth century staircase with a moulded handrail and lovely barley-twist balusters. In 1873 the courtyard was

HANFORD HOUSE. Note the unusual pairs of chimneys at the apex of the gables.

HANFORD HOUSE. The original imposing entrance to the house. Once at the rear of the courtyard, covered over in 1873 and now part of the interior.

roofed over, forming a large hall with a wooden gallery along the north side, possibly in place of an earlier one, and in many of the mullioned windows, leaded casements were replaced by sashes.

In 1086, at the time of the Domesday survey, Hanford was held by the Earl of Moriton, but around 1230 half the manor was granted to the abbess of the newly founded nunnery at Tarrant Crawford. It remained their property until the Dissolution of the Monasteries, when it was obtained by John Daccomb of Stepleton. He died in 1572 and in 1599 his son and grandson sold the manor, the farm, the advowson of the church and the rectory to John Seymer, whose family had long been tenants. John Seymer died in 1611 having acquired a great deal of land during his lifetime.

HANFORD HOUSE. The house in the mid nineteenth century.

His son, Robert, married Joan, daughter of William Pitt of Iwerne Stepleton, in 1603 and a year later embarked on the rebuilding of the house. Robert was a courtier who rose to the influential position of Teller of the Exchequer, a lucrative post responsible for payments and receipts of money on behalf of the king. He was knighted in 1619, and in 1623 the house was completed. The event is commemorated in the date and the Seymer arms embossed on the lead rainwater heads on the front of the house. In the same year his son Henry, aged fourteen, married Mary Wellstead and a year later Sir Robert died.

Sir Robert's great-great-grandson, Henry, who inherited the estate in the eighteenth century, was married to the daughter of Archbishop Wake and was a renowned natural history scholar and brilliant artist whose main interests were insects, shells and fossils. He amassed a large collection of specimens and books from around the world, which, after his death in 1785, were sold at auction in London.

His son, Henry junior, followed his father's interests and was also a talented natural historian and artist, working with his father on illustrating the specimens they collected. He also was a notable collector of entomological specimens and exotic trees and shrubs, many of which were planted in his garden. They commissioned travellers to collect for them and many of the specimens they illustrated would have been completely new to Europe at that time. In 1811 the Vice President of the Linnean Society, which was founded in 1788, three years after Henry senior's death, gave an address on his life and work in which he said, 'he procured many rare species in consequence of the celebrated voyage of the immortal Cook, . . . and had some of the finest orange and lemon trees then in the kingdom, planted in the natural ground against the walls with moveable sash-lights before them and which I have often seen loaded with fruits sufficient to supply his

HANFORD HOUSE. The south east front.

Henry Seymer (1714-1785). Natural historian, plant collector and highly talented artist.

table.' Henry's portrait still hangs in the Society's premises at Burlington House.

During their lifetimes they published none of their work but in 1992 a descendant of the Seymers discovered a folder of their paintings amongst family papers. A magnificent book, *The Seymer Legacy*, by Dr. R.I. Vane-Wright and Dr. H.W.D. Hughes, has recently been published about the Seymers and their work, reproducing their superb paintings.

Henry junior married Grace Ker, a granddaughter of George Pitt of Stratfield Saye, and from the next generation the name Ker was added to Seymer. He died in 1800 but his son and grandson, both called Henry Ker-Symer, were Sheriffs of Dorset in their turn. His grandson, Henry, described by a friend as, 'a person who, neither in public nor private was ever heard to say an unfair or unkind thing', was MP for Dorset from 1846 to 1864. When he died in 1864 his daughter Gertrude inherited his estate. She married Harry Clay, who added the name Ker-Seymer to his own. He was High Sheriff of Dorset in 1877 and died in 1899. The house remained the property of the Clay-Ker-Seymer family, but was let for many years.

In 1947 the Reverend and Mrs. Clifford Canning leased the house and founded Hanford School, a preparatory school for girls. Clifford Canning had previously been a housemaster at Marlborough and Headmaster of Canford School. In 1951 they were able to buy the freehold from the Clay-Ker-Seymer family and in 1959 their daughter, Sarah Canning, took over the school from them and owned it until 2004, when it was transferred to a charitable trust, which now runs it. Miss Canning is still very involved with the school and teaches part time.

The setting is idyllic and must be a delightful place to spend schooldays. The girls have always derived great pleasure from climbing the great cedar tree in the grounds, a climb which has become a tradition. A mid nineteenth century engraving of the house shows it as a mature specimen even then, so perhaps this magnificent tree is a living legacy planted by Henry Seymer.

Herringston House

A MILE or so south of Dorchester, Herringston is at the end of an arrow straight drive, flanked by trees, which leads through its gates to join the road to Dorchester. This road appears to be an extension of Herringston's drive and perhaps it once was part of Herringston's land. The house itself is ancient, but its castellated, early nineteenth century frontage is somewhat unprepossessing and belies the beauty which lies inside. In early spring however, it has its moment of glory when the whole drive is lined with a carpet of snowdrops. Among papers at Herringston there is a letter written nearly 200 years ago describing the snowdrops and saying that the people of Dorchester walk out to look at them – as they still do today.

The oldest part of the house is L-shaped and fourteenth century, although much altered, and probably dates from around 1336. In 1513 John Williams of Dorchester bought the manor and his great-grandson, Sir John Williams, was responsible for remodelling and partly rebuilding the house. He transformed it into a courtyard house, which, until the beginning of the nineteenth century, had its entrance through a gabled range on the north side bearing the date 1582. He was also responsible for the magnificent, south facing Jacobean Great Chamber with its glorious carved panelling and remarkable decorated barrel ceiling. The chamber was constructed partly out of the existing hall and partly by extending to the south of the original building.

Photographs suggest that the room might be overpowering but the reality is light and airy, with a huge mullioned window occupying almost all the south wall and similar but smaller windows in the walls to the left and right. It has an elaborate carved fire surround and a dado of oak panelling running

HERRINGSTON HOUSE. A carpet of snowdrops lining the drive.

beneath the windows and rising to the ceiling between them. This is gloriously carved with biblical and allegorical figures, fruit, foliage and animals, within intricate frameworks and arched niches, but all these riches are eclipsed by the incredible plaster ceiling above. This barrel vaulted ceiling rises from a cornice and decorated frieze and is divided by decorated borders into rectangular panels containing birds, animals and fish, both real and legendary, including an angel, the Royal Arms and the Prince of Wales Feathers with the initials CP for Charles Princeps (later Charles I). The enclosed parts of the end walls are also decorated, at the north end with the Williams arms and trees and animals, including a camel, a rhinoceros and an elephant, all amazingly accurately depicted for the time. At the opposite end, in the smaller space above the window, are a lion, an antelope with a chained crown around its neck, a rose tree, a thistle, and a bear and a bull being baited by hounds.

Along the centre of the ceiling are five pendants, the second and fourth ending in decorated finials and the remaining three carrying chandeliers. These three are larger and are open, built up on metal bands. The first and fifth are made up of eight bands, alternately curved and angular with a central pillar. The third and central pendant is delightfully whimsical. This time its central pillar is an apple tree full of fruit with a small boy climbing up to pick the apples. Instead of eight bands it has four curved ones interspersed with four curved pedestals each topped with a figure of a boy eating an apple and at its foot, another boy sitting astride with feet dangling, also munching an apple. The overall impression is of a joyful, exuberant celebration of life in all its infinite variety – a room where it would be impossible to be bored! Sadly Sir John died in 1617 just as it was on the verge of completion. His canopied tomb stands in St Peter's Church, Dorchester.

The next major alteration of the house was carried out at the beginning of the nineteenth century, when Thomas Leverton was commissioned to design a new front. He demolished the old gabled north range and adjoining parts of the east and west

HERRINGSTON HOUSE. Detail of the magnificent plasterwork ceiling of the Great Chamber, completed about 1615.

sides of the courtyard, including the chapel, which was on the west side, and then built across the quadrangle on the north side, thus transforming the house into a solid block. Later in the nineteenth century a porch was built on the north front and in 1899 a new wing was added to the eastern side of the house. Adjoining the west side there is now a conservatory and other outbuildings.

The earliest recorded owners of Herringston were the Beauchamps of Hatch in Somerset and it was originally known as Winterborne Beauchamp. By the thirteenth century it had come into the possession of the Abbot of Bindon who in 1243 made an agreement with Philip Hareng over an exchange of land, in which the Abbot received Hareng's land at Chaldon Herring in exchange for the Abbey's land at Winterborne. After this it became known as Winterborne Herringston.

In 1336 Edward III gave Walter Heryng licence to 'crenellate and fortify with stone walls' his mansions at Langton (Langton Herring) and Winterborne, and the original structure of the house

HERRINGSTON HOUSE. The south front retains some of the original Tudor windows.

probably dates from Walter's time. By 1416 the Heryng's estate, which included Langton Herring and land at Charminster as well as Herringston, was the property of the Filiol's of Woodlands who seem to have inherited it from the Heryng's in default of any direct heirs.

A century later in 1513, William Filiol sold the manor and land at Winterborne Herringston to John Williams, a prosperous Dorchester merchant, and his son, also John. In 1515 John senior died and his son inherited the property. John junior must have become immensely wealthy, because the subsidy rolls of 1524 assessed his personal property as the highest in Dorset. From then on Herringston has descended through the direct line of the Williams family to the present day.

Sir John Williams, John junior's grandson, inherited the property in 1569 and was responsible for remodelling or partly rebuilding the original Heryng house. He was Sheriff of Dorset in 1582 and 1592 and MP for the County in 1603 and perhaps felt that his increased status required a more impressive house. His creation of the beautiful Great Chamber alone certainly provided him with a fitting memorial. In 1644 during the Civil War, his third son, John, a Royalist officer was killed by Francis Sydenham, who believed that John was responsible for shooting his mother Martha during a raid on her home (*see* Wynford Eagle Manor).

After descending father to son for three more generations, for the first and only time, Herringston failed to pass from father to son. Sir John's great grandson, John Williams, who died around 1640, had no children and no brothers, so the estate was inherited by his second cousin Lewis Williams and duly passed to his son Robert and then his grandson John. It should then have passed to his great grandson, another John. Sadly John predeceased his father. He had joined the army and was serving in Spain in 1708 when he was shot and killed by mistake by one of his own sentries whilst checking them at night. He was only twenty-eight but was married with one son, Sydenham, aged seven and named after his mother, Jane Sydenham – no relation to the Sydenhams of Wynford Eagle. There is a family story that John's mother and sister were sitting in the hall together and caught a glimpse of him in the doorway of the room. Delighted at his unexpected return from Spain, they rushed out to greet him but could find no trace of him and nor could the servants who were roused to look for him. Later it was discovered that he had died on the day they believed they had seen him.

Sydenham inherited from his grandfather in 1722 at the age of twenty-one. He became Sheriff of Dorset in 1730 and was Sheriff again and Governor of Portland Castle in 1741. During his tenure at the Castle, the Dutch merchantman *Hope* was wrecked on the Chesil and Sydenham commanded the troops needed to disperse the lawless crowd of looters who had heard rumours of bullion on the ship and gathered on the beach in search of plunder. Sydenham died in 1757 and was succeeded by his son Thomas.

Thomas married Jane Wilmot, who was the daughter of Sir Edward Wilmot, physician to both George II and George III. Their son Edward Wilmot lived in Bath with his wife and children and the house was let for about thirty years. Edward's son, James, became Master of Horse to Earl de Grey, Lord Lieutenant of Ireland, and married Elizabeth Magennis of County Down, grandaughter of the 1st Earl of Enniskillen. They lived at Herringston and it was Elizabeth who wrote to her mother describing the beauty of the snowdrops.

In 1845 James went to London to speak in Parliament on the Bill to construct the railway from Dorchester to Weymouth. The proposed route passed very close to Herringston, virtually through the kitchen garden. James succeeded in persuading Parliament to move the route further away from the house to its present line, but whilst in London he fell ill and died and was buried at Marylebone. It was his son, Edward Wilmot, who inherited from his grandfather in 1854.

Edward married the Hon. Sophia O'Grady and their son Berkeley was grandfather to the present Mr. Raymond Williams, who inherited from his father Alick Williams in 1994.

Incredibly there has been a Williams at Herringston almost continuously since 1513. Even during the Second World War, when part of the house was used as Brigade Headquarters by General Sir Gerald Templar, Commander of the 6th Armoured Division, the family remained in residence. A magnificent record!

Higher Melcombe

NESTLING IN A DEEP hollow of the hills close by the Dorsetshire Gap, lies Higher Melcombe, known for four hundred years as Melcombe Horsey. The first view of the grey stone house in its magnificent setting leaves the visitor in no doubt as to the length and turbulence of its history. The L shape form suggests that the house once covered a much larger area, indeed foundations of a previous dwelling are visible under the lawn.

From Domesday this land, known as Upmelcombe, was involved in several disputes among powerful landowners of the county, including, in 1257, Ralph Basset. From the Law Records of 1288 comes the tale of two servants of Roger Basset, who occupied the manor at that time. They were accused of murdering a certain Roger Bodde. When the King's bailiff arrived, Basset 'closed the gate against the King's bailiff and stood on the defensive with force and arms and made a castle of the said manor and held themselves therein as enemies of the King'. He evaded punishment until 1299, when he was outlawed, a fate tantamount to the death sentence. There is no record of the fate of his servants.

HIGHER MELCOMBE. The chapel from a nineteenth century etching.

Upmelcombe now passed to John de Cerne who, in 1302, built a chapel in a nearby field, now known as Chapel Close. For more than a century this was the home of the de Cernes, until, in 1408, Robert Turgis of Stratfield Turgis in Hampshire, bought Upmelcombe from the widow, Isabella de Cerne. The Turgis family lived in the house, now called Melcombe Turgis, for 98 years, until their heiress Elizabeth Turgis, in 1506, married Sir John Horsey of Clifton Maybank.

The Horseys were already wealthy landowners in Dorset. Around 1570, a later Sir John Horsey, who was then High Sheriff of Dorset, built here an Elizabethan house nearly three times the size of the present building, renaming it Melcombe Horsey. It was a courtyard house with the Horsey arms displayed on the gatehouse. Leland, the sixteenth century antiquarian, described it as 'one of the fairest lordships of Dorset'. Beautiful linenfold panelling from this time still lines some of the walls in the house today. Despite the grandeur of Melcombe Horsey, Clifton Maybank still remained their principal home.

In 1588 the Spanish Armada threatened England. Sir John Horsey, then Deputy Lieutenant of Dorset, was in command of one of the five divisions into which Dorset had been divided to defend the coast, but he died in 1589 without an heir. His nephew, Sir Ralph Horsey, stepped into his shoes, serving in England and Ireland during the Spanish threat. He too became a Deputy Lieutenant of Dorset. Unfortunately Sir Ralph invested unwisely in a scheme to make iron from pit coal. His debts forced

HIGHER MELCOMBE. Part of a larger house built around 1570 by Sir John Horsey known as Melcombe Horsey. On the right is the chapel of 1610 built by Sir Thomas Freke.

him to mortgage the house to Sir Thomas Freke, father-in-law of his son George.

Sir George, like his father before him, did not manage his financial affairs successfully. He became involved in an absurd plan to drain the Fleet at Abbotsbury and turn the land into arable and pasture land, spending £1000 on the doomed venture. Bankruptcy left him languishing in Newgate Prison in 1638. From there he wrote that he 'had had nothing for two days but water and oatmeal and three pennyworth of sprats!' Unable to clear himself of debt, he died in Dorchester gaol.

Sir Thomas Freke then took over the ownership of Melcombe Horsey. He owned several estates, including Fiddleford, Westbrook, and Shroton near Blandford where he built the church. At Melcombe Horsey, around 1610, he installed a beautiful plaster ceiling encrusted with the Rose and Thistle emblems, similar to one in Sherborne Castle, celebrating the union of England and Scotland in 1605. He built the new chapel on its present site in 1610, using materials from John de Cerne's fourteenth century chapel in the nearby field, which had fallen into disuse after the Reformation. The great fireplace and heraldic windows in the drawing room are reminiscent of this important page in the history of this house.

Melcombe Horsey was now one of the greatest houses in Dorset, having 21 hearths (as opposed to just 7 today). Sir Thomas intended to have the chapel consecrated and to be buried there in the vault. In the end, however, he was buried at Shroton and the vault, if it exists, has not yet been located.

In 1698 George Pitt of Shroton and Stratfield Saye inherited the house through marriage, and from 1705 until 1919 it was part of the Pitt-Rivers estate, with the house occupied by a succession of tenant farmers. In the 1770s a large part of the house was pulled down and the stone was used for building Charles Hall's Ansty Brewery in the nearby village

HIGHER MELCOMBE. The commemorative windows to John and Elizabeth Horsey designed by Stephen Bowman and installed in 1988.

of Ansty. The last wedding in the chapel was in 1774. A floor was inserted to divide the chapel, with the upper storey then used either for timber storage or as a cheese loft, while the lower part became a washing and brew house

In 1919 Captain Pitt Rivers sold the estate and Brigadier Charles Woodhouse, whose family had married into the Hall family in 1843, bought part of the land, and later, in 1938, acquired the house, which remains in his family today. He was Colonel of the Dorset Regiment and president of the Dorset County Museum. From 1938 the house entered a happier period. The chapel was restored and turned into a hall with its splendid seventeenth century wagon roof.

The Brigadier's son, Lieutenant Colonel 'Jock' Woodhouse installed a staircase from the hall to the upper chambers, made from elm from the estate, also two exquisite stained glass windows both designed and made by Stephen Bowman. One, installed in 1988, commemorates John and Elizabeth Horsey, the figures based on those on a memorial brass to them in Yetminster. The other, dated 1992, is in memory of Charles Woodhouse, a botanist and a man who truly loved nature. Shown on the window, among the flowers and insects is a badger, the emblem of the family brewery. These windows, spanning over four hundred years of history, are a fitting tribute to a remarkable house.

Hinton St Mary Manor

THE BLACKMORE VALE, Hardy's 'vale of little dairies', has been rich farmland for centuries and Hinton St Mary, a little north of Sturminster Newton, is just one of the many manors it supported. However, the settlement at Hinton St Mary may have been farmed for much longer than we might imagine. In 1963 a large mosaic floor was discovered in a field there, which included in its design a head surmounted with the Christian Chi-Rho symbol and is believed to be a depiction of Christ. Further investigation revealed it to be part of a large Romano British villa built around AD 350, which would make it the earliest representation of Christ found in England. Later research suggests the site is larger than originally thought and was perhaps a substantial Christian settlement.

In 947, some 600 years after the Roman villa was built, the manor, with its present boundaries and some recognisable field names, was the subject of a Royal Grant. In 968 it was granted to Shaftesbury Abbey and the Domesday Book, a century later, records it as consisting of around 250 acres of land, with the principal tenants each holding around 20 acres and the rest divided between smaller cottagers. By the twelfth century it had become a settlement for lay brothers of the Abbey, and remained so until the Dissolution.

The manor today is a lovely Tudor mansion, close beside the church on the edge of the village. It stands on the site of the monastic dormitory and has a succession of later additions, with the walls of a medieval hall, which may date back to the thirteenth century, identifiable as the central part of the south-east range. The south front of the house opens on to a low terrace, and faces across a rectangular pool, with a tall, single jet fountain, to the garden and distant views of the Blackmore Vale. It is built of squared rubble stone and ashlar with stone slate roofs and has mellowed to lovely shades of grey and earthy pink. The five gables covering the two wings, the porch and the attic dormers, all of different sizes, backed by tall chimneys, together with the stone mullioned windows create a most attractive and varied frontage. Inside the house, over the staircase, is a sixteenth century moulded plaster ceiling, with a beautiful geometrical, curvilinear design containing fleur de lys, small decorative bosses and Tudor roses, which was brought from Fiddleford Manor in the early 20th century, by being cut into two feet square sections and re-erected. The plaster ceiling in the drawing room was erected in 1929 to a design copied from the original Fiddleford ceiling.

In 1545 during the reign of Henry VIII, the manor was granted to Sir William Stourton, but in 1557, his son Charles, who had inherited his estates, was convicted of a particularly vicious murder at Stourton Castle and was executed (see Moigne Court). His property reverted to the Crown and Hinton St Mary was granted to Robert Freke, a rising civil servant and a Teller of the Exchequer, who also bought Shroton Manor from the Earl of Pembroke.

When he died in 1592, his eldest son, Sir Thomas Freke, inherited the estate and one of the younger sons, John Freke, lived at Hinton St Mary. This arrangement, of Hinton St Mary being owned by the heir to the estates but lived in by more junior members of the family, would continue for many years. When Sir Thomas died, his son, yet another John, inherited the estates, living at Shroton whilst his younger brother, Thomas, lived at Hinton.

HINTON ST MARY MANOR. Parts of the central section are medieval, possibly dating back to the thirteenth century.

Thomas was married to Mary Doddington and they began rebuilding the house at Hinton. After he died in 1642, Mary continued to live at the manor for another forty-four years, carrying on with the rebuilding.

When Mary died in 1686 she made provision in her will to set up a charity in the parish. She donated a field, the income from which, amounting to £11 a year, was to be allocated on a rolling programme of three years. The first year to the officiating minister, providing he heard the Catechism of the children of the parish, the second year to such poor old widows and poor old maids as had no parish relief and in the third year to bind some poor child to an honest trade. Mary Freke's charity still exists and now provides about £600 a year, which, in the absence of destitute old widows and old maids, is now used for various charitable purposes within the village. Her son, the Reverend

John Freke, Rector of Okeford Fitzpaine, eventually completed the rebuilding of the house in 1695.

Earlier, in about 1663, John Freke had died and his second son, Thomas, became the owner of the estates.

Around a year after the rebuilding was completed, William Freke, a younger son of Thomas Freke and Cicely Hussey, and Reverend Freke's cousin, came to live at Hinton. In 1677 at the age of fourteen, he had gone to Oxford University, later becoming a lawyer. He was highly eccentric and in 1687 he wrote *An Essay towards an union between Divinity and Morality* in eight parts. In 1693 he published *A Dialogue by way of question and answer concerning the Deity, to which is added a clear and brief Confutation of the Doctrine of the Trinity*, which he sent to several Members of Parliament. His writings were considered heretical and he was suspected of being a Quaker. As a consequence, Parliament voted that the writings should be burnt in Palace Yard and William was indicted in the Kings Bench and found guilty. He was fined £500 and ordered to make a recantation in the four courts in Westminster Hall. After this debacle he turned to what might now be called psychology and published *A Dictionary of Dreams* and *A Collection of Dreams*. Hutchins refers to it as 'a medley of folly, obscenity and blasphemy,' and adds 'His understanding was deranged but he acted as a justice of the peace for many years.' William was married to Elizabeth Harris, had a family of nine children and lived at the manor house from 1696 until his death in 1744 at the grand old age of 81.

Thomas and Cicely had only two sons, Thomas, the eldest, and William. Thomas had no children and his father had decided that William was not to be entrusted with the inheritance so he left it to his son's widow, Elizabeth Pile, for life and then to George Pitt of Stratfield Saye, who was her brother-in-law and MP for Wareham.

William's youngest son, John, married Bridget Pitt of Stratfield Saye, a daughter of George Pitt by his second marriage to Lora Grey of Kingston Maurward. Their son, the Reverend John Freke, had no surviving sons and was the last of the Freke name to live at Hinton St Mary.

Subsequently descendants of the Freke family were tenants of the Pitts, who held the title of Lord Rivers. Among the later tenants was Thomas Lane Fox, the youngest son of James Lane Fox and Marcia Lucy Pitt. He was curate of Sturminster Newton at the beginning of the nineteenth century and for many years refused to accept the post of vicar because that would have meant living in the rectory in Sturminster, which he disliked. He was, however, a generous benefactor to the town and

General Augustus Pitt-Rivers. Eminent archaeologist and England's first Inspector of Ancient Monuments.

gave £28,000 to rebuild the church there. Sadly his charitable impulses outstripped his financial acumen and eventually, due to financial difficulties, he had to move from the Manor House to Sturminster. After he died in 1862, Lord Rivers instructed his agent to sort out Thomas's affairs. It wasn't until 1866 that the agent was able to give a final reckoning and inform Lord Rivers that Reverend Lane Fox had left an estate worth 19s.3d.

In 1880, in default of any direct heirs, the title of Lord Rivers became extinct, and General Augustus Lane-Fox inherited the estate from his cousin Horace, the 6th and last Lord Rivers. At this time the estate was over 27,000 acres and General Lane-Fox lived in the main residence at Rushmore and leased Hinton St Mary. He was born in Yorkshire in 1827 and was a descendant of James Fox and Marcia Pitt. When he inherited the estate he changed his name to Lane-Fox Pitt-Rivers. He served with distinction as a soldier from 1845 to 1882 and fought in the Crimean War. However he is far better known for his work in the field of archaeology and anthropology.

General Pitt-Rivers could well be called the father of modern archaeology. The seeds were sown whilst he was still in the army and became interested in the historical development of weapons, but this soon spread to a much wider field. When he began to undertake archaeological excavation, then an entirely amateur occupation, the usual method was to dig up a likely looking site and collect anything interesting that turned up. As a result much important evidence was destroyed.

Inheriting the Cranborne Estate in 1880 provided Augustus with the opportunity and the means to undertake large-scale excavations in an area full of prehistoric sites. His approach was meticulous, recording in detail all the finds on a site, with their contexts and position and complete details of the excavation. He also maintained that the study of rubbish and seemingly trivial details might be crucial in interpreting a site, all of which were revolutionary ideas in his day but which are now the accepted foundations of modern archaeology.

In 1882, after the passing of the Ancient Monuments Act, General Pitt-Rivers became the country's first Inspector of Ancient Monuments. Much of the excavated material from Cranborne Chase can be seen in the gallery devoted to him and his work in the Salisbury and South Wiltshire Museum. The Pitt Rivers Museum in Oxford was founded in 1884, when he donated his collection of 18,000 artefacts to the University. It exhibits many of his collections and is a major museum of archaeology and anthropology.

Some time before the General's death in 1900 it had been decided to build an estate office and lodges at Hinton. The manor house was recovered from the tenant and refurbished and in the 1890s Alexander Henry Pitt-Rivers, the General's son, came to live there. He was an amateur artist and architect and modernised and enlarged the house, laid out the gardens, created the sunken garden, and restored the Tithe Barn.

In 1927 Alexander died and his son, Captain George Pitt-Rivers inherited the estate. He was an anthropologist and took a great interest in the Pitt-

HINTON ST MARY MANOR. The Tithe Barn, restored by George Pitt-Rivers in 1939 and now used for occasional concerts to raise money for charity.

Rivers Museum in Farnham, re-organising it during the 1930's to better display the varied acquisitions. In 1939 he revamped the Tithe Barn, turning it into a theatre. He had served in the Royal Dragoons in the First World War and was badly injured in the first battle of the Somme. During the Second World War his political beliefs led to him being arrested and interned. He was sent to Brixton Prison but was released in 1942, although he was not allowed to return to Dorset until the end of the war. The Manor House was requisitioned for the army during the war and the Tithe Barn turned into a school for girls. George's second wife, Dr. Rosalind Pitt-Rivers, mother of the present owner, was part of a British and American medical team that entered Belsen concentration camp in 1945. During the 1950s she gained international fame for her discovery of T.3, a major thyroid hormone.

In 1966 Captain George Pitt-Rivers died and in 1970 Mr. Anthony Pitt-Rivers, his youngest son, took over the Manor House with approximately 2000 acres. He and his wife Valerie have done a great deal of work on improving the now very beautiful gardens, and both have played a central role in Dorset life for many years. Anthony Pitt Rivers is a Deputy Lieutenant and Mrs. Pitt-Rivers has been involved with many charitable organisations in the county since the 1970s. She was made a Deputy Lieutenant in 1995 and in 2006 was appointed Lord-Lieutenant, becoming the first female Lord-Lieutenant of Dorset.

Hooke Court

On finding Hooke Court in the tiny remote village of Hooke it seems strange that what was obviously once an important house should be so tucked away. In fact, in its heyday, it was situated at an important road junction. In the middle ages the principal road from Maiden Newton to Beaminster went through the village and a drovers' way linked with a further network of lanes over Rampisham Hill. Tracks from earlier ages also passed through or close by Hooke, the Dorset Ridgeway goes through the parish and at least one authority suggests that the Roman military route followed the old Ridgeway.

It is now a lovely house in beautiful lawned grounds set with magnificent mature trees, and the remains of the medieval moat form an ornamental horseshoe lake. However it is still a vibrant place, which for much of the time rings with children's voices. In the course of a year many hundreds of children and young people come to stay at Hooke Court to learn about history and the countryside and experience both at first hand.

In 2006 Channel 4's Time Team carried out an archaeological investigation at Hooke Court. Their findings are based on documentary and surviving physical evidence, the latter established by trenching selected areas of the site.

The main building is an amalgam of a Tudor block, with a Victorian porch and extension to the right. The team dated the left hand end of the building as part of a fifteenth century building, identified as accommodation by the surviving narrow garderobe windows. These medieval remains, to which the Tudor block had been added, are about three-quarters of the present height of the building. The top storey of the main section dates to the mid seventeenth century, when most of the old house was burnt down in the Civil War and the surviving wing rebuilt.

They considered that the surviving medieval structure would have been part of a much bigger manor house, including a gatehouse and Great Hall as well as other ancillary buildings. With the help of surviving photographs of the demolished north wing and some trenching, the team were able to identify this wing as the old gatehouse, which would have been the house's main entrance, leading into a courtyard. They were less successful in finding the Great Hall, and although the remains of a large two storey building were identified, opinions differed as to whether this could be a rare example of a two storey Great Hall or some other building.

The team's investigation of the surviving moat discovered that a large part of it was a Victorian creation. They believed that the water-filled ditches shown on the nineteenth century tithe map had their origins in Saxon times as a defensive structure, protecting the manor from any unwanted approaches along the ridge of high ground. Before the Conquest, the manor was the property of a king's thane, a warrior of high standing, who was given the estate by Edward the Confessor, and the Time Team considered it highly likely that there was a Saxon residence on the site, giving Hooke Court a long history indeed.

As with so many places, the first written record of Hooke appears in the Domesday Book where we learn that before 1066, Aelfric, a Saxon thane, held La Hoc (the name refers to a bend in the river) but by 1086 the Count of Mortain, William the Conqueror's half brother, had become Aelfric's overlord.

HOOKE COURT. The main front of the Tudor building, incorporating part of a fifteenth century predecessor to the right.

By 1281 it was in the possession of John de Cyfrewast and by 1338 the estate must have included a deer park, because Robert Syfrewast made a present of 'a doe in his park' to a witness at the baptism of his grandson in Powerstock Church. Their daughter Elizabeth married Sir John Mautravers (or Maltravers) of the Lytchett family, so perhaps the christening was of her son. In 1344 the king granted a 'licence to crenellate' the manor, in other words, permission to erect defensive walls or battlements, and it was probably at this time that the moat was constructed. It was thought originally to completely surround the house, passing close to the then north wing, which no longer exists. The Time Team evidence puts this into question, although they established that it did pass in front of the old north wing.

Elizabeth's son, John Maltravers, inherited Hooke after his grandmother's death in 1355. He was married to Elizabeth Aumerle and they had two daughters, Matilda, who was eighteen when her father died in 1386, and Elizabeth who was eight.

Elizabeth Aumerle later remarried, becoming the second wife of Sir Humphrey Stafford senior, and in 1407, her daughter Elizabeth married her stepbrother, Humphrey Stafford junior. It was probably this Humphrey Stafford who built the great Hooke Court, where the old Cyfrewast manor once stood.

He became known as 'Humphrey Stafford with the silver hand'. The origin of this nickname is lost in the past, but two suggested theories are that he had an artificial hand, plated silver, or that he was generous with his money. The latter seems more likely as he was one of the five co-founders of the Almshouse of St John at Sherborne. He gave £10 and nine oaks from his park at Hooke and in 1440, Rochell, Master of the St John's Almshouse, rode to

Hooke to choose suitable oak trees, carrying a present of apples and pears for Sir Humphrey. The fine quality timber can still be seen today in the panelling, beams and jointed cruck trusses of the Almshouse. Elizabeth and Humphrey were both in their thirties when they married, which was then regarded as elderly, particularly for women, but they went on to have four children.

Hooke was eventually inherited by Humphrey Stafford, child of their third son, William. Edward IV created him Baron of Southwick and Earl of Devon. In 1469, at the Battle of Edgecombe, Stafford and the Earl of Pembroke were commanding the main part of the King's forces against the rebel Earl of Warwick. Stafford did not commit his troops in support of Pembroke with the result that the battle was lost and the Earl of Pembroke and his brother were caught and executed. Some days later Stafford was captured by the King and beheaded as a traitor at Bridgwater.

He had no children and the estate was inherited by his three female cousins. Elizabeth, wife of Sir John Coleshill, Alianor, wife of Thomas Strangways, and Sir Robert Willoughby, who inherited his mother Ann's portion. Elizabeth and Sir John Coleshill had no children and after her death Hooke passed to Sir Robert Willoughby, Lord Brooke, who died in 1522, leaving his estate to his two daughters by his second wife, Dorothy Grey, daughter of Thomas Grey, Marquis of Dorset.

The eldest daughter married John Paulet, Marquis of Winchester, and the younger married Charles Blount, Lord Mountjoy. For several generations the Willoughby's part of the estate was shared between the Blounts and the Paulets. In 1609 Charles Blount, Earl of Devon, died without lawful heirs and his half of the estate devolved to the Paulets, who then possessed the whole estate. The surviving, early seventeenth century part of the south wing was probably built by William Paulet.

During the Civil War, John Paulet, 5th Marquess of Winchester, was committed to the Tower and his estates were confiscated. Lady Winchester later joined her husband in the Tower and Parliament ordered a weekly sum of £10, afterwards increased to £15, to be paid to her for the support of herself and her children – provided that the latter were educated as Protestants.

In 1647 the house was badly damaged by fire and almost destroyed. Contemporary accounts list the ten shillings paid to a mason sent to Hooke to dig for lead among the rubbish after the house was burnt, and the receipt of £5 for fifteen hundredweight of burnt lead from Hooke. After the Restoration, Winchester's lands were restored. He later became the 1st Duke of Bolton and rebuilt Hooke Court, but he never succeeded in obtaining any recompense for his heavy losses and damages. In 1747 considerable repairs were carried out by the 3rd Duke of Bolton, who lived there.

By the beginning of the nineteenth century Hooke Court had become a farmhouse and by 1864 was the property of the Duke of Cleveland and the Earl of Sandwich as representatives of the last Duke of Bolton. (They were the descendants of two daughters of the Duke of Bolton, Mary and Katherine, who were married to the 5th Earl of Sandwich and the 1st Duke of Cleveland respectively.) Around 1880, the house was refurbished and became a shooting box, whose guests included the then Prince of Wales, later Edward VII, and his mistress, the actress Lillie Langtry, who stayed in a house at Hillfield, which also belonged to the Earl of Sandwich. The present owners have copies of the original plans submitted by the architects, Crickmays, in 1876.

A report of a nine day shooting party in 1896, hosted by the Earl of Sandwich, records that they bagged 4237 pheasants and rabbits and also one of the guns! A Colonel Papillon was hit by a blast of shotgun pellets, one of which entered the corner of his eye socket and passed out behind his nose. It is reported that he suffered no serious consequences!

In 1891 the Duke of Cleveland died without heirs and his title became extinct. In 1916 the unmarried Earl of Sandwich died and his estates and title went to a nephew. In 1919 Hooke Court was sold to Sir Thomas Salt of the Staffordshire banking family. He apparently suffered from asthma and felt that the Dorset air would improve his health.

HOOKE COURT. The house from across the lake, once part of the medieval moat. A recent 'Time Team' investigation at Hooke Court suggests that a manor has stood on the site since Saxon times.

The Salt family lived at Hooke Court until 1945. Sir Thomas died in 1940 and is buried in Beaminster. His daughter-in-law, who was married in 1943, often visited Hooke Court between the wars and remembered that when the family moved in, there were six servants in the house, three gardeners and two farm workers.

In 1945 the family sold the estate to a local farmer, who then sold it to the Church and in 1946 it became St Francis School, run by the Anglican Franciscan Brothers from Hillfield Friary. It was run as a residential school providing a second chance for boys who had got into trouble through difficulties at home or school. Boys came from London, the Home Counties, Kent and the South West. To begin with, attempts were made to run the 150 acre farm, purchased with the Court, with a farm manager and part time work by the boys, but it was never a really viable proposition and in 1973 the land and stock were sold. In 1964 new buildings had been erected and in 1966 the old north wing was pulled down. About five hundred boys passed through the school before it closed in 1992 due to lack of funds.

In 1994 Hooke Court was purchased by Peter and Mandy Cooper, and is now a residential study centre catering for schools and colleges and a conference venue.

Kingston Maurward Old Manor

THIS ELEGANT Elizabethan manor house, now surrounded by the beautiful grounds of Kingston Maurward Park, was built in a perfect E plan at the end of the sixteenth century by Christopher Grey. Despite many changes of use down the centuries, it is still in fine condition, which, combined with its parkland setting, makes it one of the county's most attractive manor houses.

Kingston Maurward was once a hamlet. The first lords were the Maurwards, but little is known about them or where they came from. In about 1406, Sir Thomas Maurward's daughter Joan brought the manor to the Greys by marrying Robert Grey, whose family was descended from the Barons of Codnor, and Robert's side of the family came from Charleton in Somerset. They are recorded as having land in Askerswell, Bridport, Beaminster and finally Kingston Maurward. In 1567, Thomas Grey died and was succeeded by his young son Christopher. It is quite possible that there was a more modest house on the site of the present one, but, to date, the remains have not been found.

KINGSTON MAURWARD OLD MANOR. The shield of Grey impaling Stawell over the porch recalling the marriage of Katherine Stawell to Angel Grey around 1630.

In Hutchins time there was armorial glass in the windows of the house and the date 1591 was under a coat-of-arms in a window in the hall. This may have recorded the year of completion of the house, though 1597 has also been suggested. Both of these dates suggest that Christopher Grey built the house. When he died in 1607, his wife, Mary, promptly married Jasper Miller of Stratton and went to live there. Christopher's two younger sons and three of his six daughters died young. One daughter married Joseph Long of Frome Billet (now Stafford House) in 1605. George, Christopher's eldest son, married Joan, daughter of Angel Smith of Stratton in 1601. They were married just over a year when he too died. In due course their son, Angel, married Katherine, daughter of Sir John Stawel of Cothelston about 1630. The shield of Grey impaling Stawell remains over the doorway in the porch.

The projecting wings had windows on the sides facing towards the porch. These were blocked up in the first half of the seventeenth century to allow for the insertion of fireplaces and the house was divided into smaller rooms. When Angel Grey added an east wing around 1630 he re-used these discarded mullion windows with their unusual moulded bases, similar to those at Wolfeton, and probably made by the same mason. Fragments of a Jacobean moulded plaster frieze can still be seen in what would have

KINGSTON MAURWARD OLD MANOR. The house was built in 1591 by Christopher Grey.

been the new parlour. A stone fireplace arch in the first floor chamber is also of the same period. Outside, the raised terrace at the front of the house is also the original, though the balustrades have disappeared.

Lora Grey, Angel's grand-daughter, married George Pitt, uncle of William Pitt the Elder, Earl of Chatham, both of whom were part of a wealthy family from Stratfield Saye in Hampshire. George Pitt built the stately Kingston Maurward House across the park within view of the old manor house. Lora was a woman of exceptional qualities, helping many charities, always kind, a tender wife, indulgent parent, and sincere friend. In 1748, at her suggestion, and in memory of her husband, Grey's Bridge was built over the River Frome, just east of Dorchester. In 1698 Lora sold the manor house to John Saunders of Honily, and it became a farmhouse.

By 1866, nearly 200 years later, it had become a home for poor widows, but then fell into neglect. In 1947 it was eventually bought by Dorset County Council and divided into five dwellings for council tenants. By the late 1950s it was derelict once again and the County Council decided to demolish it. It was saved at the eleventh hour by Mr. Rohan Sturdy, a cousin of the Sturdy family of Trigon, Wareham. In 1962 he took over the house for a peppercorn rent, offering to restore it at his own expense. The building was in a sorry state. The floors had fallen in, there was no glass in the windows and it was riddled with death-watch beetle. Rohan Sturdy worked tirelessly, restoring panelling and removing plaster to reveal the old

KINGSTON MAURWARD OLD MANOR. The house owes its survival to Rohan Sturdy, who took it over in the late 1950s when Dorset County Council wished to demolish it.

Tudor fireplace. He felt strongly that there must have been a stairway tower between the original house and Angel Grey's extension. Foundations were found and he rebuilt the stairway using stones from a demolished Tudor house in Weymouth. From the first floor the unusual spiral stairway, said to be cut from a single oak from the Trigon estate, twists upwards to the once deserted attics where some of the eight great 'A' frames still show the numbers scratched on them by Tudor workmen.

Entering the house through the middle arm of the 'E,' in the west front, into what would have been the screens passage, there is now a handsome staircase brought from Little Haddon Hall in Suffolk. To the left would have been the kitchens, now used as a dining room. After six years, and with the house's future finally secure, the County Council granted the freehold to Rohan Sturdy as a token of their gratitude.

All the modern comforts incorporated into the restoration have not hidden the age and beauty of the old house. It is a credit to Rohan Sturdy. Ironically, he never lived there. He passed it to his son Christopher who sold it in 1977. It was then sold again in 1998 to Mr. and Mrs. Andrew Thompson, who happily share their enthusiasm for the house with their visitors. Thomas Hardy used it as the setting for *Desperate Remedies*, and surely the name of Angel Clare in *Tess of the D'Urbervilles* must have come from Angel Grey, whose epitaph in Stinsford Church he would certainly have read – a fitting tribute to a lovely house.

Kingston Russell House

HIDDEN AWAY IN THE Bride Valley, and just skirting Long Bredy, stands Kingston Russell House, built by the Michels early in the seventeenth century. At least three centuries earlier the Russells also had a house near by, just south of the river. The history of the two houses is so closely entwined that it is worth tracing the origin of both these families as well as of the manor itself.

In 987 the eastern side of the Bride Valley belonged to the Saxon Earldom of Cornwall. Earl Aethelmaer gave Little Bredy and part of Long Bredy to Cerne Abbey. Perhaps in order to restrain the wealth and power of Cerne Abbey, a strip of land between Little Bredy and Long Bredy was retained by the king and known as the King's ton. Similarly, on the western side, lay the manor of Dowerfield, which also was retained by the king separating Long Bredy from Baglake. Dowerfield remained crown land under the Duchy of Cornwall until recent times.

Though the Bride Valley was well documented in the Domesday Survey, no mention was made of Kingston or Dowerfield. Then in 1212 it was recorded that John Russell held Kingston 'of the King'. The Russells came from Normandy. It seems likely, therefore, that William the Conqueror gave the manor to John Russell's ancestors. For the privilege of holding this manor, they performed the ancient service of serjeanty, normally an honorary but menial task that had to be undertaken annually

KINGSTON RUSSELL HOUSE. The east front showing the tall double-transomed windows in the galleries added in 1675-80 by John Michel.

KINGSTON RUSSELL HOUSE. The west front.

at Court. John Russell, in King John's reign, was 'Marshall of the King's Buttery' and in charge of the King's Pantry from Christmas until Whitsun. Nearly a century later, in 1306, William Russell was both Keeper of the King's Pantry Door, and his Cup-Bearer, serving the monarch with a cup of beer on the four principal feasts of the year. By 1330 the service also included 'counting the king's chessmen and putting them away when he has finished'.

In 1281 William Russell was granted a fair, market and free court on all his lands in Somerset, Wiltshire and Gloucestershire as well as Kingston Russell. By that time Kingston Russell was an important settlement. The manor house was situated on the south side of the river close to a chapel known as the Free Chapel of St James. In 1341 Eleanor Russell was granted one-third of the manor of Kingston, including 'a high chamber towards the chapel'. This description helps to locate the site of the manor house. Today nothing remains of either the house or the chapel, though Hutchins, in the eighteenth century, saw a few poor people living within the ruins. John Baverstock Knight, the Duke of Bedford's agent, noted that in 1811 a small part of the chapel ruins survived within a milking parlour.

In 1432 Thomas Russell died without a male heir. The manor was divided between his two sisters, who had married into Gloucestershire families. They lost interest in the village and it was neglected for nigh on a hundred years. Both the church and house fell into decay. In 1560, Francis, 2nd Earl of Bedford, bought a large part of the manor in the belief that he was buying back his ancestral home. In fact, his side of the family came from Berwick near Swyre.

John Michel of Dalwood, near Axminster, was an attorney at Clement's Inn. About 1600 he acquired land in Long Bredy, Kingston Russell and Baglake, as well as a scattering of smallholdings in the area. He died in 1639, and his will describes him as holding a share of the manor and farm of Long Bredy as part of 'his manor of Kingston Russell'.

121 / KINGSTON RUSSELL HOUSE

Captain Sir Thomas Masterman Hardy (1769-1839). Hardy was born at Kingston Russell House, and the nearby Hardy Monument commemorates his part in the Battle of Trafalgar. As Nelson's captain on HMS *Victory* it was to Hardy that Nelson whispered his dying words. In this portrait, painted in 1809, Hardy is shown wearing his Trafalgar Medal.

The puzzle here is why the Bedfords, within one generation of repurchasing the manor, should relinquish its title to the Michels. It was upon one of the smaller plots of land, flanked on both sides by Bedford land, that John Michel built an L-shaped house close to the boundary of Long Bredy. The house was only one room deep. The gardens and outbuildings encroached onto Bedford land, causing intermittent conflict between the two families until, in 1769 an agreement was finally drawn up. By the middle of the eighteenth century the Michels owned 1272 acres.

The L-shaped design of the house provided a courtyard access to the old medieval road. There was no approach road from the west as there is today. This was due to the Hurdings, who were lords of the manor of Long Bredy, owning a crucial strip of land along the edge of the Michel's land and Long Bredy. In 1756 the Michels did in fact buy this strip of land but shortly after, in 1760, they moved to Dewlish.

The second John Michel, who died in 1670, had eight sons and five daughters. His first son, John, who died in 1717, married Penelope, daughter and co-heiress of John Bingham of Bingham's Melcombe and Quarleston. Penelope's sister, Grace, married Thomas Skinner, who inherited property at Dewlish. Their son, another Thomas, died childless in 1756, leaving his house and estate at Dewlish to David Robert Michel, Colonel of the Dorset Militia and grandson of John and Penelope. He took up residence in Dewlish in 1760.

Around 1675-80 in John and Penelope's time, the east front of Kingston Russell was rebuilt and galleries were added, allowing easier access to the rooms while still retaining the inner walls of the original house. The tall, double-transomed windows which light the galleries are of an unusual design and not found anywhere else in Dorset. The tinted glass is quite beautiful. Maybe the west front was similar, but between 1717 and 1739 John Michel made alterations to the main entrance and the west front, according to the fashion of the time. The entire house was faced with Portland stone.

Following the departure of the Michels in 1760, the house was let three years later to Thomas Masterman. He and his wife Mary were the parents of Nanny, who married Joseph Hardy of Portesham in 1755. After the death of Nanny's parents the young Hardys moved into Kingston Russell House and their son, Thomas Masterman Hardy, Nelson's captain of HMS *Victory* at Trafalgar, was born there in 1769. Soon afterwards they all returned to Portesham.

In 1862 the Bedford Estate bought the house with all the Michel land, and the house was then let to Algernon Brinsley Sheridan. His wife was the daughter of the historian John Lethrop Motley, the United States ambassador to this country, who died at Kingston Russell House in 1877. Following the departure of the Sheridans the house was sadly

KINGSTON RUSSELL HOUSE. The house when virtually derelict and smothered in ivy in about 1910. George Gribble added the two short flanking wings after buying the house in 1913.

neglected. Stones from part of the old east wing were used for building new houses in the village. The house remained overgrown with ivy and in a ruinous state until 1913 when it was sold by the Duke of Bedford, along with 124 acres of land, to Mr. George Gribble of Henlow Grange, Bedfordshire.

Mr. Gribble set about a grand restoration. He demolished what remained of the old low east wing, which had been used as offices and was probably a survival of the original house, and extended the north and south ends of the main block, giving the house its present day appearance. Panelling had been removed when the house was derelict but Mr. Gribble recovered it and had it re-instated. To his time can be attributed the formal yew gardens, the lawns and the approach road to the west. He had two sons, Philip and Julian. Philip bought around 800 acres of the surrounding farmland and later, in the Second World War, became a war correspondent. Julian was a Captain in the Royal Warwickshire Regiment and won the Victoria Cross in 1918 whilst delaying the German advance at Hermies Ridge in France. He was taken prisoner, sadly dying from his wounds and Spanish Influenza whilst still in German hands just a fortnight after the Armistice in November 1918.

Captain C.J. Kane purchased the house in the 1930s but sold it in 1939 to Mr. and Mrs. William Vestey. Mrs. Tops Vestey modernised the house with flair. She decorated the north dining room with sumptuous nineteenth century Chinese wallpaper designed by Eugene Ehrmann and George Zipelins and produced by the firm of Zuber of Rixheim in 1832. The wallpaper depicts scenes from Chinese life and is still in remarkably good condition. Originally it was not large enough for the room, so an ornamental frieze of tassels was added or painted onto the wall. Other additions included extra bathrooms, a heated swimming pool and the plaster columns in the lower gallery. The garden, too, benefited from her attention to detail.

Following three more owners, the house came into the possession of Mr. Harold Carter in 1984 and once again this lovely house became a family home. The gardens have matured and the yew hedges are magnificent. Time and change move slowly in the Bride Valley and the beautiful landscape remains blissfully unspoilt.

Little Toller Farm

THE INTRIGUING NAMES of Toller Fratrum and Toller Porcorum certainly catch your attention when glimpsed on the small signposts near Maiden Newton. In the reign of Edward the Confessor (1042-1066), Tolre was held by the knight Alward. Porcorum means 'of the pigs', whilst Fratrum, or 'of the brothers', indicates that this was the site of a monastery or friary on the banks of the River Toller. It was connected to the Priory of Buckland in Somerset, whose nuns were subject to the Knights Hospitallers of St John of Jerusalem from the early fourteenth century until the Dissolution. There was possibly a Preceptory here but little is known about the lives of the brethren save that they were farmers.

The tiny parish church of St Basil lies just east of the house. It was rebuilt in the nineteenth century but still contains a font and wall carving from the early part of the eleventh century. The carving depicts part of the figure of St Mary Magdalene wiping the feet of Christ with her hair. These two

LITTLE TOLLER FARM. The figure of an ape breaking his chain is seated between two chimneystacks.

LITTLE TOLLER FARM. A view from the north showing the back of the house.

relics form an interesting link with the years prior to the arrival of the Knights Hospitallers.

An exquisite stone manor house remains today, now called Little Toller Farm. Flanked on the eastern side by a thatched outbuilding, long used as a stable, it was traditionally thought to have been a refectory as a large chimney is still intact in the north gable. Some of the original roof trusses, with collar-beams, still survive. The west front has a string-course above the windows which supports

LITTLE TOLLER FARM. The house was built by John Samways, a Dorchester merchant, some time after 1540 on the site of a monastic grange.

two carvings, one of a boy holding bagpipes, or maybe a leather bottle, the other of the initials of John Samways, 'I.S', either side of his crest which consists of an eagle's claw on a wreath holding a mallet. All of this gives substance to the idea that John Samways rebuilt this wing.

John Samways of Winterborne Martin was a Dorchester merchant. He bought the manor in 1540, including a large amount of the surrounding area, which had belonged to Buckland Priory. The main range, which is of two storeys, may well be on the site of the former grange. The walls are of rubble and the roofs are of slate. The west wing of the house is of a later date. The south front has a moulded string-course with an octagonal shaft in one corner supporting a stone winged dragon or wyvern.

The carvings are remarkable. Above the eighteenth century porch sits a figure of a lion holding a shield of the Tudor arms while in the centre of the main front a chimneybreast supports a pair of barley twist chimneystacks. On the gable sits the figure of a chained monkey holding a hammer. His chain is broken, which perhaps indicates that he has escaped from his shackles. Inside the house is a collar-beam roof with arched braces going the whole length of the house, though a flat ceiling has now been inserted below it. During the nineteenth century the interior was modernised.

John Samways died in 1586 and his eldest son, Robert, who lived until his eightieth year, succeeded him, dying in 1621. Longevity was obviously a Samway's trait, for his younger brother, Bernard, who then inherited the estate, lived to be ninety-six. His two daughters subsequently shared the inheritance. Ann, who married Sir Francis Ashley, inherited Winterborne St Martin, and Elizabeth, wife of Sir Francis Fulford, inherited Toller Fratrum. Sir Francis Fulford was a wealthy landowner from Devon, whose principal seat was at

LITTLE TOLLER FARM. The thatched stable, possibly once used as a refectory.

Dunford, near Exeter.

During the Civil War Sir Francis Fulford supported the Royalists. It was probably Sir Francis who built the west wing of the main house. He left his Dorset estates to his fifth son, George, in 1664, who in due course became Toller Fratrum's rector and married Susanna, daughter of John Browne of Frampton. They had no children and, ten years after her husband's death in 1685, Susanna married John Sydenham of Wynford Eagle.

The estate continued in the Fulford family through Francis Fulford (1688-1730) whose father only appears as George Fulford of London. From this time on the Fulfords took little interest in Toller Fratrum, preferring to live on their Devon estates. In 1762 the estate was sold to George Browne of Frampton whose only surviving son, Francis Browne, passed it to his relative Thomas Fleming of Stoneham Park in Hampshire. By 1867, it had been sold to Lord Wynford. For many years it has been a farm and, in 1975, Lord Wynford sold the farm to the tenant, Mr. Joe Yeates and ownership has continued in this family to the present day.

Mappercombe Manor

THE SETTING OF Mappercombe must surely be one of the prettiest in the county. Built of lovely mellow, golden limestone with weathered tiled roofs, it is situated almost at the head of a little combe. It is protected from the north by the hillside behind and looks south across its delightful garden, falling away from the house in a series of terraces, with a magnificent view across the valley to the hills beyond.

The house consists of three adjoining blocks. The earliest part is the eastern end, dating from the fifteenth century, which has a Perpendicular arched window and a trefoil headed recess in a small room in its upper storey. It is possible that this room was once a chapel. The early seventeenth century main block, set slightly forward of the other two, is the largest. Its central porch was replaced at the beginning of the twentieth century by modern windows in Tudor style with five lights, instead of the three and four lights still seen on the rest of the front. The western end wall of this block has more stone-mullioned windows and an ancient doorway with a moulded oak frame. The later, seventeenth century, west section completes the picture, set slightly back and fronted by an attractive terrace. Over its pretty doorway is a sundial, once decorated with a ram's head joined by a swag or perhaps a fleece, but now only the swag and one ram's horn survives.

In the garden there is a stone removed from the parapet of the gable end of this block, which is carved with the initials N B and below them the date 1695, the two separated by a line of ropework

MAPPERCOMBE MANOR. A painting from the south in about 1870.

MAPPERCOMBE MANOR. The approach from the drive in early summer.

carving. There is also a weathervane with the initials N B and the date 1699, re-set on the gable of the small building to the west of the house, which bears a date of 1736. It can just be picked out on the roof of the main house in a painting of around 1870, before major alterations took place in the early twentieth century. The initials probably refer to Nicholas Browne, grandson of the Nicholas who bought the house in 1638.

The manor originally belonged to Cerne Abbey and was part of the tithing of Nettlecombe and these two manors seem usually to have been treated as one. In 1293 the Abbott of Cerne's land in Nettlecombe and Mappercombe was valued at £7.11s. 4d and in 1318 the Abbott had a 'grant of free warren', which was a royal licence to hunt small game on the manors, mainly rabbit, hare, and partridge. After the Dissolution the manors still seem to have been considered together, although they were separate manors in their own right, but eventually Mappercombe became the sole survivor.

In 1547 and 1554 the manors of Nettlecombe and Mappercombe and Milborne St Andrew were granted to Alexander and William Brett. The manors then descended together through various owners until, by 1582, they had become the property of Thomas, Viscount Howard of Bindon, and through him came to Thomas, Earl of Suffolk.

In 1622 the Earl sold them all to a Basil Dixwell of Kent, who gradually broke up the estate. In 1638 he sold Mappercombe to Nicholas Browne, who was already the lessee, for £1,367. His son, Henry, and his nephew, Hugh, inherited the estate and in 1675 it was divided, including the house, into two halves. H.S. Poole in his pamphlet, *Powerstock – A Short Social History,* suggests that this was because of a disagreement between the cousins.

Henry Browne's son Nicholas was the last male heir of the family. He had four daughters, of whom two had no children and one remained single. Therefore Henry's half of the estate was eventually inherited by the heirs of the third daughter, who had married Richard Churchill from Compton Abbas. Their daughter, Elizabeth, married Thomas Burt in 1705.

MAPPERCOMBE MANOR. The south front of the house with its lovely terrace to the left.

By the 1780s Mappercombe was owned by Captain Francis Roberts, who was born in Burton Bradstock. It is not clear whether he bought it or inherited it, but it is possible that his wife, Fanny, was a descendant of Elizabeth Churchill. They had no children. Francis was first Lieutenant on the frigate *Quebec* in 1779 during the American War of Independence and was the only surviving officer when it blew up during an engagement with the French ship *Surveillante*. He was captured but escaped and later commanded HMS *Helena*.

In 1781 the twelve year old Thomas Masterman Hardy (later captain of the *Victory* at Trafalgar) joined the *Helena*. A year later, in a letter written to his brother in Martinstown, young Thomas wrote, 'Captain Roberts has promised that when an opportunity offers, to send me home to go to school for some time to learn navigation and everything that is proper for a sailor'. Captain Roberts endorsed the letter saying, 'Am glad to inform you that Thomas is a very good boy, and I think will make a complete seaman one day or other'.

Roberts kept his word, and soon Thomas left the navy to attend school for three years. He then served with the merchant navy for some years before rejoining the Royal Navy in 1790. Sadly Captain Roberts did not live to see his protégé fulfil his early promise as he died of yellow fever in 1794 on board the *Success* in the West Indies. However, his nephew, Francis, also joined the Royal Navy and served under Hardy, although not at Trafalgar.

Hugh Browne's half of Mappercombe eventually came to the Burts of Cattistock (probably through marriage) and then to the Rev. George Burt of Askerswell. The census of 1841 shows that the estate was still two farms, with one part occupied by Thomas Burt and his wife Sarah. In 1865 it belonged jointly to James Burt of Ilminster, Giles Burt of Mapperton and Mrs. Sara Burt, widow of Thomas Burt the third son. Throughout the nineteenth century the house and farm remained divided and leased to tenants. *Kelly's Directory* of 1895 describes it as 'a fine old manor house called Mappercombe. Now a farmhouse divided into two portions.'

MAPPERCOMBE MANOR. The original main entrance with the eastern fifteenth century wing on the right.

In 1900 Captain Hugh Blomfield Nicholson bought the estate and set about modernising the house. He removed the old porch on the south front, replacing it with windows and built a new porch on the east end. He partly demolished the old north-east wing and built a much larger version. The old dovecote was pressed into service to house equipment to supply gas to the house. He also made considerable alterations to the interior. One of his innovations, in 1911, was to have piped water from Eggardon Hill supplied to the parish in cast iron pipes, which were still in use in the 1980s. Mappercombe's water still comes from the same spring.

Captain Nicholson's son had no wish to live in the house and in 1937, Admiral Sir Victor Crutchley, VC, KGB, DSC, bought the Manor. The Admiral had won his Victoria Cross in 1918 at the age of 24, for an action at Ostend, whilst serving aboard HMS *Vindictive*. He took command of the ship after the captain had been killed and, when it was sunk, he transferred his crew to a motor launch and brought them to safety under heavy fire: his citation is one of the few that commend seamanship as well as gallantry. He went on to serve in the Second World War, commanding the battleship *Warspite* and serving in the Norwegian campaign, destroying a German destroyer flotilla at Narvik Fjord. Following the outbreak of the Pacific war, he was seconded to the Australian Navy, taking command of a cruiser squadron and was second in command to the American Admiral, Richmond Turner, during the Guadalcanal campaign in 1942.

Admiral Crutchley's final command was Flag Officer Gibraltar. After his retirement from the Royal Navy in 1947, he lived at Mappercombe until his death in 1986. He was a well known figure in West Dorset, becoming involved with many local activities as well as running the Mappercombe Estate. After his death, the manor was inherited by his son, Lieutenant Commander William Crutchley RN, who continued to manage the estate.

The Crutchley family still live at Mappercombe and in 2005, to commemorate the 200th anniversary of the Battle of Trafalgar, they arranged the planting of a 16 acre wood on the Mappercombe Estate, to be called Africa Wood. The name commemorates HMS *Africa*, which took a leading part in the battle, commanded by Captain Henry Digby, one of the three Dorset men who commanded ships at Trafalgar and who is buried at Minterne. Lieutenant Commander Crutchley died early in 2007 and the farm is now managed by his son, Victor.

Mapperton House

MAPPERTON STANDS at the head of a deep valley not too far from Beaminster. It is an elegant house, with mullioned windows, balustrades, twisted chimneys and armorial finials. On the gate piers stand two stone eagles, as though poised for flight over the handsome stable blocks.

The Domesday Book divides the manor into two parts, Malpertone and Mapertone. The first recorded owner was Reynold de Moion, or Mohun, in 1235-6. It passed into the hands of Sir Robert Brett (or Bryte) in the reign of Edward I, and later, Maud, an heiress of the Bretts, married into the Morgan family, who came from Morganshay, Devon. In 1424, we come across an interesting story about Robert Morgan who received a patent from the King allowing him, when in the King's presence, 'to use and were his bonnet on his hed forasmoche as wee bee credibly enformed that our welbiloved Robert Morgan, esquire, for diverse infirmities which he hathe in his hedde, cannot, conveniently, without his grete daungier be discovered of the same.' Strangely enough, nearly one hundred years later, on November 6th 1522, another Robert Morgan received the same concession, plus an exemption from jury service, all issued under a

MAPPERTON HOUSE. What surely is the most decorative main façade of any manor house in Dorset, Mapperton's west front, built between 1540 and 1560.

Above MAPPERTON HOUSE. The Tudor wing built by Robert Morgan in about 1540.

Opposite page MAPPERTON HOUSE. The east front of the house from beyond the summer house and fishponds.

privy seal. This Robert Morgan, who died in 1528, was then living at Little Comberton in Worcestershire.

The third Robert Morgan succeeded to the manor in 1535. He had married Mary, daughter of John Wogan of Silvinch near Ilminster, and between 1540 and 1560 they rebuilt the house using Ham Hill stone. From the courtyard rise buttresses to twisted pedestals bearing armorial finials, which are such a feature of the exterior. Only the north range remains of the original house. The inner porch doorway is also from the time of the Morgans with a four-centred head where the griffin heads of the Morgans can be seen in the spandrels. In the drawing room a late Elizabethan plaster ceiling shows the fleur-de-lys arms of Morgans and the lions of Brett plus the name, possibly, of Hodges, in the panels. The room above still retains the original fireplace and overmantel with a cartouche of the Morgan arms and motto. The plaster frieze, with heads in roundels held by putti, is amazingly well preserved. The ceilings in both these rooms are perfect examples of the high quality workmanship of the sixteenth century.

MAPPERTON HOUSE. Tudor barley-twist chimneys and the four heraldic finials of the Morgan griffin on the gable of the north wing.

133 / MAPPERTON HOUSE

In the hall, which has seen a few changes through the centuries, Hutchins, in the eighteenth century, read the following inscription:

'Robert Morgan and Mary his wife, built this
house in their own lifetime and at
their own charge and cost.
What they spent, that they lent;
What they gave, that they have;'
What they left, that they lost.

Unfortunately the wording is no longer there.

Robert and Mary had four sons, John, Christopher, George and William, and four daughters, one of whom was Anne who had married Nicholas Turbervile of Winterborne Whitechurch, High Sheriff of Dorset in 1578/79. John Morgan was a hot-headed young man, not trusted by his father, Robert Morgan, who died in 1567. Later, his widow Mary married William Stourton of Worminster, near Wells.

One day, Nicholas Turbervile went to visit his mother-in-law in Wells. He went alone as his wife, Anne, was awaiting the arrival of her fifth child. Unfortunately, Anne's brother, John, was visiting his mother's house at the same time. The Turberviles, Morgans and Stourtons were all staunch Catholics, but Nicholas Turbervile had taken the Protestant Oath of Supremacy, as was required of him, in order to be High Sheriff of Dorset. John resented this bitterly and accused Nicholas of allowing his wife, Anne, to lapse in her Catholic worship. Arguments became heated, tempers flared and John stabbed Nicholas with a dagger. Nicholas died almost immediately, and John was arrested. At his trial, Anne Turbervile, having by then given birth to a son, testified against her brother. Her evidence turned the scales against John and he was hanged in March 1581. As a convicted criminal, John had to forfeit Mapperton to the Queen, but after his execution, his brother, Christopher, spent several years trying to recover the estate. He succeeded, but only lived to enjoy his triumph for three years.

In 1582, the plague swept through Mapperton, claiming eighty lives. It had been the custom to use Netherbury churchyard for burials because Mapperton church was built on rock.

MAPPERTON HOUSE. The late seventeenth century stables.

Understandably, during the plague, the people of Netherbury refused to honour this commitment, so many of the bodies were buried on Warren Hill. The story goes that mourners placed sweet herbs under what became known as the Posy Tree. A plaque identifies a tree on the same spot today, marking the beginning of the track to Netherbury.

In 1608 Christopher died, and his daughters, Mary, who had married Richard Brodrepp of Huntstile, near Bridgwater, and Elizabeth, wife of Sir Thomas Trenchard, inherited the estate, but it was not divided between them until 1618, when Mary and Richard Brodrepp took possession of Mapperton. The couple lived there for forty years and made various alterations to the house, but it was their grandson, also called Richard, who built the magnificent stables and coachhouse. The date 1670 is cut into the keystone of the eastern door on the southern side. He was also responsible for the main porch of the house, constructed in mellow stone and displaying the Brodrepp coat of arms above it. Inside the porch is the inscription R.B. 1661, which most likely indicates the year it was built. The splendid dovecote can be attributed to him as well, with his initials RB 1665 on the lintel of the north doorway. In 1693 he bought Melplash Court for his son Thomas, and in 1704 rebuilt the nave of the church.

His successor, also called Richard and who died in 1737, is commemorated by a monument in the church designed by Scheemakers, the sculptor of

MAPPERTON HOUSE. The Italianate gardens designed by Mrs. Ethel Labouchere in 1926 and enlarged by Victor Montagu MP in the 1960s.

Shakespeare's memorial in Westminster Abbey. Mapperton then passed to his nephew, the son of Thomas Brodrepp of Melplash Court, the fourth Richard, and a successful lawyer. In the 1750s he added the classical front to the house and a Georgian staircase in the north wing, the work of the Bastard brothers of Blandford. This Richard was the last of the line. He died in 1774 and his estate passed to his nephew, Bennet Combe, son of his sister Catherine. In 1788 it passed to Catherine Richards, another niece, wife of John Compton of Minstead in Hampshire. From that time the Comptons owned Mapperton until 1919. During the early part of the twentieth century, two large overmantels were removed from Melplash Court and relocated in Mapperton. Melplash Court had belonged to Mapperton for over two hundred years. The first one, now in the library, displays the arms of James I, and the second, which is in the Hall, is encrusted with the Paulet arms and motto: 'AMES LOYAULTE'.

In 1919 Mapperton was purchased by Mrs. Ethel Labouchere. During her time the interior was renovated with a Renaisance style ceiling in the hall and screens passages, but above all else she is remembered for creating the beautiful Italianate gardens. The Fountain Court and topiary garden were completed in 1926 in memory of her late husband. Following her death in 1955 the house was bought by Mr. Victor Montagu, M.P. for South Dorset. He rescued the then overgrown gardens and between 1966-68 built the Orangery at the north end. He added an arboretum and a spring garden rolling away down the valley. The display of flowering trees, wild flowers and daffodils each springtime continues to delight visitors to this lovely house and garden which is now owned by his son and daughter-in-law the Earl and Countess of Sandwich. Their family connection with Mapperton goes back to the 1760's, when Lady Mary Paulet, a descendant of Lord Paulet, Marquis of Winchester, who, in Elizabethan times had owned Melplash Court, married the 5th Earl of Sandwich and inherited the surrounding lands in nearby Hooke.

Never have the gardens looked as magnificent as they do today, complimented by the softly mellowed stone of this ancient house. There is a delightful summer house, complete with chimney, which looks down upon seventeenth century fishponds. From here the valley rolls away, and its path unfurls into the distance, the epitome of peace and tranquility, its sense of history being almost tangible.

Melbury Bubb Manor

JOHN BETJEMAN's poem *Dorset* opens:

> 'Rime Intrinsica, Fontmell Magna, Sturminster Newton and Melbury Bubb,
> Whist upon whist upon whist upon whist drive, in Institute, Legion and Social Club.
> Horny hands that hold the aces which this morning held the plough'

conjuring a vision of a countryside where the days and seasons of the farming year turn much as they have for centuries. Sadly, this is no longer true for much of the country. However, at Melbury Bubb Manor, beside the little church with long views of the Blackmore Vale to the east and protected to the west by the steep slope of Bubb Down with its crown of trees, the rolling uncluttered landscape evokes a time when life moved at a slower pace. It is the high ridge of Bubb Down, which gives the manor its peaceful isolation. There are two other Melburys within a couple of miles of Melbury Bubb but, close as they are geographically, to get to either of them, other than on foot over the hill, requires a good few miles of travel by road.

The Domesday Book does not differentiate

MELBURY BUBB MANOR. Although largely rebuilt by the Foye family from about 1602, the section to the left of the porch with the steeper roof is probably older.

MELBURY BUBB MANOR. May flower, manor house and church from the slopes of Bubb Down.

between the three Melburys but for the last nine hundred hundred years or so they have been distinguished by the addition of the name of a one-time owner. The first historical indication of the name Bubb occurs a hundred years after Domesday when Peter and Walter Bubb held two knights fees in Dorset, but Bubba is a Saxon name, so perhaps an even earlier owner is responsible.

The village is so small as to hardly warrant the name and the Manor House, quite literally at the end of the road, must surely have been its *raison d'être*. It is a delightful, small, stone manor house, largely rebuilt in the seventeenth century but incorporating part of an earlier house. The older part of the house is at a slightly lower level than the rest so there is a step down into it and the pitch of its roof is steeper. The floor of the main room here is made up of huge, irregularly shaped stone slabs, like giant crazy paving instead of the more usual large squared flagstones, which appear in other parts of the house. Everywhere there is lovely old oak panelling and ancient doorways and fireplaces, which with the beautiful mullion windows and low ceilings, make this a truly atmospheric old house. Even the little two storey stone porch, a twentieth century addition, with its re-set, ancient, nail-studded door, seems to have been absorbed into the general air of antiquity.

Evidence of the house's early history is sparse and we know no more than the names of some owners until the fourteenth century. Certainly the Bubbe family were here for at least a hundred years, because it was not until the late thirteenth century that Ralph de Bubbe passed it to Alan de Plukenet, and by 1329 it was in the hand of Thomas de Melberghe. In 1370, Elizabeth and Roger Folville brought a court case for the re-possession of their shares of the manors of Melbury Osmund and Melbury Sampford from Alan Cheyne, the widower of one of Elizabeth's sisters. Elizabeth was one of the three daughters who were the sole heirs of Sir John and Joan Matravers of Melbury Sampford. The case was found in Elizabeth's favour in 1375 and in 1383 an agreement was made with her surviving sister over the partition of their various shares in the two manors. Melbury Bubb seemed to be excluded, for when Roger died in 1383 he left his eighteen year old daughter Joan as his heir, and in 1384 her husband Philip Maubank was cited as the owner of Melbury Bubb.

Hutchins' *History of Dorset* then baldly states that in 1393 it belonged to Michael Fin and that 'after a long interval' it came to the Warres of Hestercombe, Somerset. It is certain that by 1500 it was owned by Joan Warre and in 1602 it was the Warres who sold it to the Foye family, who must have been responsible for building or rebuilding the later part of the house.

The church was rebuilt in the later 1460s during the ownership of the Warres and when Walter Bokeler was the rector. The tower is all that now remains of that church, apart from its bells and the font, which is of Saxon origin and is wonderfully carved with strange animals and dragons. On the outside of the tower, about eight feet from the top is a carved frieze, which includes leaves and shields and the initials W and WB. Considering these family references (a buckler is a small shield) and that the impressive tomb of Alexander Buckler, presumably of the same family as Walter, who died in 1568, lies just outside the church door, it seems reasonable to speculate that the Bucklers were of greater importance to Melbury Bubb than is apparent in the records. The family must still have been there under the ownership of the Foys because there is another, later tomb in the churchyard of Thomas Buckler who died in 1634.

For almost the next two hundred years the Foy family owned the manor and at least some of them were probably residents of the manor house, certainly at least two seventeenth century generations are buried in the churchyard. In 1713, Walter Foy of Bewley Wood, a descendant of a younger branch of the Foyes of Melbury Bubb, bought Duntish Court from John Churchill and in 1735 when John Foy of Melbury Bubb died unmarried, the manor came to the Foys of Duntish.

In 1784 Sidney Hollis Foy, the last male heir, died of tuberculosis, leaving two unmarried sisters. The younger sister, Harriet inherited Melbury Bubb. She married Samuel Shore from Derbyshire and the manor was sold as a tenanted farm.

In 1883 the manor was again sold, this time by auction. There is a framed plan in the house designating the area for sale, which shows that it was not part of the Ilchester Estates at this time, but adjoined them, so possibly the Strangways purchased the manor then.

In 1924 Commander and Mrs. Maurice Brind bought the manor from Ilchester Estates, by which time the house was in a poor state of repair and its thatch was replaced with tiles.

In 1935 the house again changed hands when Olive Brind sold it to Major Thomas Blain, MC and his wife Helen. The Blain family were originally grain merchants and Major Blain's grandfather was one of the founders of The Royal Insurance Company. Melbury Bubb then became a family home and the Blain's two sons grew up in this idyllic spot.

Melbury House

MELBURY HOUSE, which can just be seen amongst the trees to the west of the Dorchester to Yeovil road, seems more a stately home than a manor house. The imposing building is on high ground, an unusual choice of site before the seventeenth century, and surrounded by a glorious park, designed and laid out by Capability Brown. Immaculate lawns sweep down from the terrace to the ornamental lake below, with views of the rising slope of the park beyond. However it began life as an English country manor and its present appearance is the product of many alterations and additions to the medieval core carried out by the Strangways family, its owners for the last five hundred years. Viewed across the lake, against a backdrop of magnificent trees, the sixteenth and seventeenth century part of the house with its unique hexagonal tower is on the right, and on the left are the nineteenth century additions, dominated by a massive tower.

The first impression is of windows, chimneys and towers. There are three towers. To the west of the house, separate from it and standing on a little hillock, is a small octagonal tower complete with battlements and pinnacles, known as the Garden House. Its date and original purpose are uncertain, but in 1762 Horace Walpole referred to it as 'ancient' and added that its interior was 'newly adorned with shields'. At the western end of the house is an imposing neo-gothic tower, which is part of the nineteenth century alterations, and last,

MELBURY HOUSE. The entrance front, and the neighbouring fifteenth century church.

MELBURY HOUSE. The 'loftie' octagonal lantern tower built by Sir Giles Strangways in about 1530.

but certainly not least, is the lovely sixteenth century lantern tower at the centre. The lantern was designed as a belvedere for the owner and his guests to take the air and enjoy the view and must have been one of the earliest to be built in England.

Thomas Strangways made major alterations to the house in the late seventeenth and early eighteenth century and his daughter Susannah continued beautifying the house into the eighteenth century. The whole of the east front and the central portions of the north and south fronts between the gable ends were redesigned with Classic features and much of the interior redecorated. Thomas was also responsible for the two staircases, arranged back to back, which are behind the old entrance hall. The ceiling above the grand ascent, the southern one of the two, is painted by Lanscroon and represents the Council of the Gods. On the north wall alongside the staircase is a huge canvas depicting Thomas Strangways and all his family, painted by Thomas Hill. In the old entrance hall itself are two magnificent carved overmantels, one composed of musical instruments and the other of fish and game, almost certainly by Grinling Gibbons. The ground floor rooms leading from the old entrance are pure eighteenth century, either panelled or hung with silk damask, some of which was brought from Redlynch, the Fox home in Somerset, for which it was bought in 1735. The walls of one room are hung with Mortlake tapestries showing the Labours of the Months, which also came from Redlynch. Many of the possessions of Holland House were also absorbed into Melbury, most recently the pictures which, providentially, were removed from London to Melbury for safety in 1939, just a year before Holland House was destroyed in the Blitz.

There are three Melburys within easy walking distance of each other in this part of Dorset, each distinguished by the name of a past owner, Sampford, Osmund and Bubb. Melbury Sampford is no longer a village and has become just the great house with its satellite buildings and the church. For most of its history it has been joined with Melbury Osmund and also, at times, with Melbury Bubb. Its earliest name seems to have been Melbury Turberville, but by the thirteenth century it was owned by the Sampfords, who probably acquired it through marriage to a Turberville heiress. The name Sampford remained, even though it became the property of Sir John Mautravers, through marriage to Joan de Sampford in the early fourteenth century.

The Mautravers had three daughters, Alice, Joan and Elizabeth, who inherited various parts of the three manors. In 1370, Elizabeth, who owned Melbury Bubb, brought a court case against Alan Cheyne, Joan's second husband, to recover her share of the other two Melburys. The third sister, Alice, was also involved because she had leased half of the manors of Melbury Sampford and Melbury Osmund to Alan and Joan for their lifetime. Alan argued that Elizabeth had no rights in the manors because she was illegitimate but she proved her legitimacy and won the case and in 1373 Alan signed over her share of the manors.

MELBURY HOUSE. The Garden House.

In 1387 Alice and Elizabeth came to an agreement to reallocate their shares of Melbury Sampford and Melbury Osmund. This seems to have been a complicated legal procedure, which was not completed until 1412. Elizabeth then held her parts of the manors for life for a token annual rent of a red rose and was entitled to sixteen wagon or cart loads of oak and ash for fuel, 'each wagon load being as much as eight oxen can draw and each cart load as much as can be drawn by six horses at the most'. This was to be delivered to her by the bailiff of Melbury Sampford and if not delivered at her request, she had the right 'to fell and take away the said fuel on her own authority'.

Alice's second husband was John Bruning from Gloucestershire, who made arrangements for his elder son, William, to inherit his Gloucestershire estates, 'if he should die before he returns from beyond the seas in his passage to Acquitaine', and later for his younger son John to inherit his manors of Melbury Sampford and Melbury Osmund, also 'if he should go beyond the sea and die there'. In 1420 John died childless and the Dorset manors duly passed to William, whose eldest son William and his wife, Catherine, had no children, so in due course, their nephew, another William, inherited the whole estate. Catherine was left Melbury Sampford and Melbury Osmund for her lifetime but they were to revert to William after her death.

Catherine's second husband was Henry Strangways and in 1500 he bought the reversion of Melbury Sampford from William Bruning, with the provision that if William had children, he would regain the reversion and repay Henry in instalments. As the Strangways have owned the manor ever since, that contingency never arose. Quite remarkably, that is the only time in its history that the property has changed hands by sale and even then there was a family connection, if only by marriage.

The Strangways family originated in the north of England and their main house was Strangways Hall in Manchester. The first of the family to settle in Dorset was Thomas, who came south in the household of Thomas de Grey, Marquis of Dorset, and settled in Stinsford. He married Alianor Talboys, the granddaughter of Sir Humphrey Stafford of Hooke, and Henry was their son and heir.

Catherine Bruning was Henry's third wife and his heir was his son Giles by his first wife, Dorothy Arundel. He is frequently referred to as Sir Giles the elder, to distinguish him from his grandson, and was the first of the Strangways to own both Melbury Sampford and Melbury Osmund. Henry Strangways died about four years after buying Melbury and it was Giles who began rebuilding the ancient manor house and creating the park. His house was built around three sides of a square, with an open entrance to the east and a wing projecting centrally to the west. In the centre of the wing forming the back of the square Giles built his beautiful lantern tower.

Leland wrote in about 1540 that 'Mr. Strangeguayse hath now a late much buildid at Mylbyri quadrato, avauncing the inner part of the house with a loftie and fresch tower' and also said that he used three thousand loads of stone from the Hamden quarry nine miles away. A century later, Coker, in his *Survey of Dorset*, said that there was still 'much old building' remaining at Sir Giles 'faire and strong house', but it is now impossible to establish if anything from the pre- sixteenth century house had been incorporated into the new building.

Giles was appointed one of the commissioners for the Dissolution of the Monasteries in Dorset. The Abbey of Abbotsbury was surrendered in 1539 and two years later he leased the Abbey lands for twenty years. In 1543 he paid Henry VIII £1096.10s. for the site of the monastery, 'the manor and land there, the fishery of the Fleet, the manor of Elworth, and land in Bexington and Portesham', all part of the monastery's holdings, thus hugely increasing his wealth.

His son, Henry, pre-deceased his father, dying during the siege of Boulogne in 1544 and Giles's grandson, 'Giles the younger' who was then 20 years old, became the heir. He married Joan Wadham in 1547 and in so doing 'acquired a fair estate' as she was co-heiress of her father, John Wadham, of Merifield in Somerset. She bore Giles six children before his death in 1562, then married Sir John Young and bore him three more. In Bristol Cathedral, the tomb of Sir John Young and Dame Joan depicts two men in armour kneeling either side of a prone woman and eight kneeling children. Despite two marriages and bearing nine children, Joan survived to the grand age of 70 at a time when longevity was the exception, especially for women.

Giles's heir was his eldest son, John, whose wife was Dorothy Thynne of Longleat. She also bore nine children and died in 1592, a year before her husband. It was John who obtained a grant from

Elizabeth I of 'the water, soil and fishery called East Flete and the flight of wild swans called the game of swans' – the famous Abbotsbury Swannery, which is still the property of the Ilchester Estate. Their eldest son died childless and the estate was eventually inherited by the youngest, John, who was only nine years old when his father died. He married Grace, daughter of Sir George Trenchard and had seven children. Their heir was another Giles, born in 1615.

The Strangways family was deeply involved in the Civil War. Sir John at first supported Parliament in trying to curb the excesses of the King, but as the movement became more revolutionary, he became a staunch Royalist, raising a Regiment of Horse and Foot at the beginning of the war. Anthony Ashley Cooper described him as 'a wise, crafty experienced man, but extremely narrow in expenses, a great enemy of the Puritans'. He was, however, an honourable man and in 1643 prevented Prince Maurice's troops from burning Dorchester after they had ignored the terms of surrender accepted by the town, and began looting and destroying houses.

Sir John suffered heavy penalties for his loyalty to the Crown. He was fined, his property confiscated by Parliament. He was imprisoned in the Tower after being taken prisoner after the siege of Sherborne Castle in 1645, and had to pay a huge ransom for his release. His son Giles and son in law, Sir Lewis Dyve, were also taken prisoner at Sherborne and sent to the Tower. Although Sir John bought his freedom, Giles was still held, remaining a prisoner for two and a half years. After the Restoration he had a medal struck to commemorate his incarceration. All pleas to allow Sir John's pregnant daughter, Howarda, permission to visit her husband, Sir Lewis, in the Tower were refused and she died in childbirth whilst he was still in prison.

In 1651 when Charles II was in hiding at Trent after the Battle of Worcester, Francis Wyndham rode to Melbury, where Giles Strangways was under virtual house arrest, to ask him for help in finding a ship to get the king to France. Giles was unable to recommend anyone to provide a ship either in Weymouth, Poole or Lyme, but sent £100 in gold (the equivalent of about £10,000 today) to Charles.

Sir Giles Strangways. Royalist commander in the Civil War.

Grace Trenchard, John's wife, was a redoubtable lady. In April 1643, 250 Parliamentary troops marched on the Strangways house at Abbotsbury in search of arms and provisions. Her husband and all the men had gone to join the King at Oxford and Grace was there with only the female servants. The commander of the troop reported, 'all the neighbours and men servants were fled and the Lady and women servants said that there were noe armes', but 'after much seekinge' they found arms and ammunition but no money or plate. Grace's refusal to pay to 'ransome her stocke and household stuffe' enraged them so much that they did £200 worth of damage, demanded that she should pay £500 within ten days or the house would be sacked and said that 'her Ladyship deserved noe better usage for shee is of a most malignant spirit'. Sadly, Grace's courage did not save her house for long. The following year, whilst being defended by her son James, it was destroyed by an explosion and fire during a fierce battle with Parliamentary forces commanded by Sir Anthony Ashley-Cooper (*see* St Giles).

In 1645 Grace wrote to her brother Sir Thomas Trenchard, an ardent Parliamentarian, for his help in recovering part of her husband's confiscated estates to support herself and their children. The appeal was at least partly successful, because in 1646 she wrote to her sister-in-law asking her to thank Sir Thomas and other friends who had supported her plea, adding that 'they did allot my fifth part here unto me about the house, but I think not the full portion . . . they deal upon harder terms with me than anybody else'. Sadly, Grace did not live to see the Restoration but died in 1652, six years after her daughter.

In May 1660 Sir John Strangways read the declaration of the Restoration of Charles II at Sherborne, even though he was not able, 'by reason of his age, to utter it with so loud and distinct a voice as requisite'. In June of the same year a Thanksgiving for the King's Restoration was presented to Charles II at Whitehall and amongst those present were Sir John and Sir Giles Strangways.

Giles was married to Susanna Edwards and had nine children, three of whom died in childhood. The heir was Thomas, born in 1643, and later described as 'a complete gentleman, an excellent scholar and the ornament and delight of his county'. When he inherited in 1673, he embarked on major alterations and additions to Melbury. He redesigned the whole of the east front and the central parts of the north and south fronts with Classic features. The courtyard was enclosed and made smaller by the addition of a staircase hall on the east side and connecting corridors on the north and south side and much of the interior redecorated. At this time the entrance to the house was by the east front, approached by a bridge over a small lake, but in the next century, when the park was laid out to the plans of Capability Brown, the lake was moved from the east to the south side and the entrance changed to the north, as it is today.

Thomas was married to Susanna Ridout and their eldest son, Thomas junior, inherited from his father in 1713 and died childless in 1726. As four out of their five surviving offspring died childless, their daughter Susanna eventually inherited the estate.

Susanna was married to Thomas Horner of Mells and they took the name Strangways-Horner. Legend has it that his ancestor was the Little Jack Horner of the nursery rhyme. At the time of the Dissolution, Thomas Horner was steward to Richard Whiting the last Abbot of Glastonbury. The story is that Horner was sent to the King with a 'gift' of the deeds of twelve manors and that to guard against theft they were hidden in a pie, a favourite ruse at the time. En route, Horner extracted the deeds to Mells, the plum of the manors, for himself. The bribe was unsuccessful and Abbot Whiting was tried for treason. His ruthless erstwhile steward, Horner, was on the jury that convicted him and the abbot was hung, drawn and quartered on Glastonbury Tor. The family version states that Horner purchased the manor legitimately after the Dissolution.

Thomas Horner died in 1741 and Susanna 'spent the latter part of her life in acts of piety, charity and generosity'. Among her benefactions was £5 yearly for the maintenance of a schoolmaster at Melbury Osmund and Melbury Sampford to teach twenty poor children of the parishes to read, write and cast accounts. She also gave a house at Melbury Osmund for the residence of the master and gave £50 to the poor of the two parishes. She also built, repaired or ornamented several churches, including St Catherine's Chapel at Abbotsbury. In her will she endowed a foundation to provide a school in Abbotsbury. She died in 1758 and was buried at Mells with her husband.

Her only child, Elizabeth, married Stephen Fox, son of Sir Stephen Fox and elder brother of Henry Fox, Lord Holland, father of the brilliant Whig politician Charles James Fox. Sir Stephen, Elizabeth's father-in-law, had risen from fairly humble beginnings to become steward of Charles II's household in exile. He managed his impoverished master's finances so successfully that after the Restoration he was made Earl of Ranelagh and granted various profitable offices. He was the main instigator of the building of Chelsea Hospital and contributed more than £13,000 to it, saying, 'I could not bear to see the common soldiers, who had spent their strength in our service, beg at our doors.' He was widowed at the age of 69 after forty-five years of marriage and seven sons, six of whom died in childhood, and married again at the age of 73 to a wife fifty years his junior, fathering two more sons, Stephen and Henry. The only surviving son of his first marriage predeceased him so Stephen became his heir.

Elizabeth and Stephen had ten children, seven girls and three boys. He was elected MP for Shaftesbury in 1726 and served in two succeeding parliaments until he was created Lord Ilchester in 1741 and Earl in 1756. He was a member of the Privy Council and died in 1776. Elizabeth died in 1792, aged sixty-nine.

In 1764, their daughter Susan scandalised family, friends and London society by eloping with an actor. In 1759, sixteen year old Susan was sent to London to stay at Holland House with her uncle and aunt and be companion to her aunt's fourteen year old sister, Sarah Lennox, who was to be launched into society. The two girls cemented a friendship that was to last a lifetime. Until then they had both led a fairly sheltered life, Susan in Dorset and Sarah in Ireland, and moving in London social circles with its round of balls, parties and theatre was a heady mixture. Famously the nineteen year old Prince of Wales, later to become George III, became enamoured of Sarah, and Susan, always close by, was often used by the painfully shy George as an intermediary. One of the girls' favourite pastimes was the theatre, which they attended several times a week, and they produced their own 'theatricals' at home. Susan fell in love with William O'Brien, a protégé of Garrick. He was incredibly handsome, regularly played the romantic roles and was hero worshipped by half the young ladies of London. They began meeting regularly during the winter of 1763-64 and in the spring of 1764 Susan's parents discovered the affair. They were appalled, not only was he an actor and totally unsuitable, but he was also Irish, Catholic, and impecunious.

In April 1764, faced with her parents' implacable opposition, Susan and William eloped and were married. This put them beyond the pale of society, her parents disowned them and they were shunned by the family. O'Brien left the stage, which placated nobody, but after a few tense weeks, Susan's uncle,

Susan Fox-Strangways and William O'Brien.
In 1764 Susan scandalised society by eloping with William O'Brien, an actor, who, although handsome and the darling of the London theatre, was Irish, Catholic and impecunious. Despite predictions of disaster, their long and happy marriage lasted until William's death in 1815.

Henry Fox, offered to give them an annuity of £400 a year and buy them some land in New York for O'Brien to become a gentleman farmer, safely out of sight in the colonies. They were outcast and penniless and had little choice but to agree and they arrived in New York in September. They both disliked it and were not successful, always looking for ways and means to return to England. After a few years they did return, regained grudging acceptance by the family and occupied the Strangways property at Stinsford.

The heir, Henry Thomas, was married twice, firstly to Mary-Theresa O'Grady of Limerick, by whom he had five daughters and one son, Henry Stephen Fox-Strangways. Two of the daughters married into the Talbot family of South Wales. In 1794 Mary married Thomas Mansell Talbot, the heir, and her son Christopher later developed Port Talbot. In 1796 Elizabeth married another brother, William Davenport Talbot. Their son was Henry Fox Talbot, the pioneer of photography, born at Melbury in 1800. His father died when he was 11 months old and Henry spent much of his childhood at Melbury. In 1841 he patented the calotype, the first process for photographic negatives from which prints could be made, and there is a permanent exhibition devoted to his achievements at Lacock Abbey, his Wiltshire home.

Mary-Theresa died in 1790 and Henry's second wife was Maria Digby, by whom he had three more sons. Henry Stephen inherited the title, becoming the 3rd Earl of Ilchester, but as his two sons predeceased him, his half brother, William Thomas Horner Fox-Strangways, Maria's son, succeeded to the title as 4th Earl in 1858.

William Thomas was not only a distinguished diplomat – his appointments included Under Secretary for Foreign Affairs and Minister Plenipotentiary to the Germanic Federation – but also a botanist and horticulturalist of international repute. He was an authority on the flora of Europe and a considerable plant collector, introducing many new plants to this country. It was he who was mainly responsible for the development of the famous sub-tropical gardens at Abbotsbury, begun by the first Countess and her son.

Opposite page MELBURY HOUSE. The house from across the lake. The engraving shows it prior to the building of the large range to the west by the 5th Earl of Ilchester in 1884.

On William's death in 1865, his nephew, Henry Edward Fox Strangways became the 5th Earl. He was only nineteen when he succeeded to the title, the son of the Hon. John George Fox-Strangways and Amelia Marjoribanks. A few years earlier, the Holland line had died out and the Fox-Strangways became the heirs to the Holland estates. Henry greatly enlarged the house. In 1872 he married Mary Dawson, daughter of the 1st Earl of Dartney and in the same year embarked on building the magnificent library designed by Anthony Salvin to house the books from Holland House. In 1884-85 he added the large range to the west. He died in 1905 and his son, Giles Stephen, became the 6th Earl.

Giles married Lady Helen Vane-Tempest-Stewart and their son Edward, the future 7th Earl, was born the year his grandfather died. He married Helen Ward in 1931 and they had two sons and a daughter. Tragically, both their sons died young. Giles, the younger, aged thirteen, in a shooting accident and Charles, at the age of twenty, whilst on active service with the army in Cyprus in 1958, which left their only daughter, Theresa Jane. Edward inherited the title and Ilchester Estates in 1959 but in 1964, when he died with no surviving male heirs, the title – but not Melbury or the Ilchester Estates – devolved to Walter Angelo Fox-Strangways, great, great grandson of the Reverend Charles Redlynch, younger brother of the 2nd Earl, and was inherited in 2006 by his grandson, Robin Fox-Strangways, who is now the 10th Earl.

The Ilchester Estates were inherited by Lady Theresa Fox Strangways, who married Simon Monckton-Arundell, 9th Viscount Galway, in 1953 and had one daughter, Charlotte. After Lord Galway's death in 1971, Lady Theresa married Richard Mark Agnew. She died in 1989 and her daughter, the Hon. Charlotte Townshend, and her husband are now the owners of Melbury.

Melplash Court

IN THE SMALL VILLAGE of Melplash, between Bridport and Beaminster, there lies a secluded manor house, first seen as a tantalising glimpse of a tall sixteenth century house at the end of an avenue of chestnut trees. This gabled stone building belonged to the de Melplash family until the reign of Henry VIII, when the heiress of the family married Walter More of Marnhull, and the estate came to the Mores.

An unlikely legend has come down concerning Sir Thomas More of Melplash Court, who was Sheriff of Dorset and Somerset. One night in 1533, 22 prisoners broke out of Ilchester gaol. Although the majority were recaptured and some were sentenced to death, Sir Thomas, as Sheriff, was responsible for the security of the prison. He wrote to Thomas Cromwell, Henry VIII's Chancellor, to give assurance that he was not at fault. A year later he wrote a similar letter to the Lord Chief Justice begging that he might keep his goods and honour as he was 'so disquieted almost out of his wits'.

Time has embellished this story with a touch of humour, accusing Sir Thomas of opening the gates of Dorchester gaol when drunk on the local cider, for which the area around Melplash was famous, and allowing all the prisoners to escape. Later, realising what he had done, he begged Lord Paulet, (afterwards Marquis of Winchester) to solicit a pardon for him from the king. This Lord Paulet promised to do on condition that his second son,

MELPLASH COURT. 'First seen as a tantalising glimpse of a tall sixteenth century house at the end of an avenue of chestnut trees.'

MELPLASH COURT. The east front and garden.

Thomas, could marry Sir Thomas More's daughter and heiress. Although this tale is more fiction than fact, the Paulets did become the owners of Melplash Court late in the sixteenth century.

The house contained two magnificent overmantels which were removed in 1909 to Mapperton. One displayed the Paulet coat-of-arms, a hawk with extended wings and the motto 'Ames Loyaulte' dated 1604, whilst the other showed the royal coat of arms and monogram of James I.

The main hall at Melplash was used as a court of justice for the area for over two hundred years. Two small rooms on the east front of the house, one on the ground floor and one on the floor above, were used as temporary detention cells for prisoners. The house was rebuilt early in the seventeenth century and much of the panelling as well as the staircase dates from that time; though its greatest glory remains the massive Tudor screen in the hall.

Richard Brodrepp, the owner of Mapperton, bought Melplash Court for his son Thomas in 1693. From then on the house descended with Mapperton, finally passing to the niece of the last of the Brodrepps, who, in turn, married into the Compton family in 1788 when Melplash became a farm.

In the early nineteenth century H.C. Compton altered the west side of the house and his initials 'HCC 1808' can be seen over a porch. A succession of tenants lived in the house until 1920 when it was owned and occupied, briefly, by Charles A. Goddard. The next owner was Mrs. Gundry, of the Bridport rope and net-making family, and who, in 1922, made extensive alterations to the west end, demolishing the Tudor barn in order to provide materials for the new extension. Behind the house lies a small dwelling once used as a chapel and in which was found an octagonal stone said to have been the base of the pulpit. This stone has now been set in the floor of the house.

MELPLASH COURT. The dovecote of 1604.

Mr. and Mrs. Timothy Lewis bought the house in the early 1980s. The previous owner, Lady Diana Tiarks, had laid out the gardens most beautifully, and the new owners have continued in the same tradition, each year adding more interest and variety to the planting. Today the house is surrounded by magnificent gardens while the house has been transformed and returned to its former glory.

Moigne Court

MOIGNE COURT at Owermoigne has the distinction of being one of the oldest houses in Dorset, perhaps the oldest. Its name derives from the family who owned the land from soon after the Conquest, being variously spelled as de Moyne, le Moygne, le Moyne, and le Moigne.

The house was built between 1270 and 1280 and is a rare survival of a typical medieval dwelling with its main living area, or hall, built on the first floor over a ground floor 'basement'. In the late thirteenth century, defence was still an important consideration and the placing of the hall on the first floor raised it to a defensible height. The need for defence is born out by a grant given to William de Moyne in the reign of Henry III, 'That he may close and strengthen his house at Ogre, county Dorset, with a good dyke and stone wall'. The moat, which still partially surrounds the house, and a fragment of medieval wall remain visible today. Despite the rarity of this type of house, Woodsford Castle only a few miles away, is of similar design.

MOIGNE COURT. The house in the nineteenth century when it was used as a dairy house.

Over the centuries the house has, of course, seen many changes. Approaching it today, the eye is immediately attracted by the three elegantly arched medieval windows of the first floor hall. Internally, its floor was raised early in the twentieth century to allow for higher ceilings on the ground floor and a new ceiling was installed, which means that its original proportions are no longer visible. In the north east corner is a small doorway, which once led to a wing containing the solar. This wing, according to Hutchins, was probably demolished in the eighteenth century. There is still a north-east wing, but it is a modern addition. On the eastern side of the hall is a medieval doorway, now converted to a window, which provided access via an exterior staircase, probably contained within a small tower. Hutchins also mentions the discovery of the foundations of a square turret and that the traces of its junction with the wall were still visible. In the last decade of the nineteenth century, after a major fire in 1890, the southern end of the house was demolished and rebuilt.

By the time William le Moyne built the house in the late thirteenth century, the manor had already belonged to the le Moyne family for close on two hundred years. When he inherited Owermoigne from his father Ralph, around 1270, it was recorded that the le Moyne family held the manor of Oweres from the King, 'for serjeanty of the kitchen and that their ancestors had held it from the time of Henry I by gift of that King by the said service'. This meant that they had been responsible for ensuring that their local area supplied provisions for the monarch and his court, as required, since the time of Henry I.

In 1377 John le Moyne inherited Owermoigne. He

MOIGNE COURT. A view from the west, showing the three arched windows of the thirteenth century first floor hall.

and his wife had no sons and their elder daughter, Elizabeth, was their heiress. She married Sir William Stourton in 1398 and, through her, Owermoigne passed to the Stourtons. The name of le Moyne thus disappeared, but the family connection endured for another three hundred years.

In 1557, during the reign of Queen Mary, Lord William Stourton, then owner of Owermoigne, was sentenced to death for arranging the murders of a father and son named Hartgill, with whom he had a long-standing quarrel. He appealed for clemency from Mary because he was a Roman Catholic. Her response was that 'he should be hanged with a halter of silk in respect of his quality'. This event has often been described as happening at Owermoigne, whereas the murders actually took place in Stourton Castle in Wiltshire, where he invited the two men to dine with him and then arranged for them to be murdered by two of his servants and buried in the cellars.

In 1703 Sir Edward Stourton sold the manor to William Wake, who later became Archbishop of Canterbury. He, in turn, sold it in 1732 to Sir Theodore Janssen, who had lost much of his wealth in the South Seas Bubble scandal. It eventually descended to Sir Theodore's granddaughter, Williamza, wife of Lionel Damer, Earl of Dorchester.

After her death in 1825 the house was sold to Mr. John Cree. He had been born John McMahon, in Dublin, but had been required to change his name to Cree as a condition of inheritance from his uncle, who had also been born a McMahon, but who had adopted his mother's maiden name of Cree. He had two sons, John and Robert, and a daughter Georgiana, but both sons became clergymen and remained bachelors. John, who inherited Moigne Court in 1853, was Rector of Owermoigne, founded the village school there and bequeathed funds for the restoration of the church. On his death Georgiana's son, George Stone, was named as heir and was also required to change his name to Cree as a condition of his inheritance. Since that time the house has descended directly, through three generations, to the present owner, Mr. Martin Cree.

Muston Manor

MUSTON MANOR nestles quietly in the fertile Piddle Valley not far from Puddletown. From the road it gives no hint of its existence and the approach down an unprepossessing little track does not seem promising. Then, facing you around a bend in the lane, is a delightful little, brick built, seventeenth century manor house, looking out over a pretty walled garden of lawn and flowerbeds and with its matching brick granary on the right.

The design of the brickwork is similar to that at Anderson Manor, some ten miles away, being bonded with one row of headers to two of stretchers and it has a simple but elegant two storey porch in the centre of the south front. The south end of the west front is mainly constructed of banded flint and stone, outlining a gabled end smaller than the present house, which raises the question of whether this is a relic of an earlier building. The house was originally single storey with gabled dormers but in the nineteenth century the dormer windows were removed and a further storey was added. In the 1930s an extension was added at the eastern end of the house, the dormers re-instated in the roof and the interior much altered, but in spite of these changes, the whole is still harmonious and attractive.

The earliest historical mention of Muston is in the Domesday Book, where it is included in the tithing of Little Piddle, one of the holdings of Cerne Abbey. Legend has it that this small manor and its hamlet

MUSTON MANOR. Brick, stone and flint in the Piddle Valley.

were given to Cerne by Edgar, King of the Saxons. His reign was an interlude of peace and prosperity in the troubled tenth century, when many new monasteries and abbeys were founded and religion, learning and art flourished. Sadly, there seems to be no evidence for this claim and probably the benefactor was someone less exalted and the suggestion of royal patronage was intended to raise the Abbey's status. For the next six centuries Muston remained as one of the holdings of the Abbey of Cerne and the lives of its tenants were governed by the turning of the seasons. They cultivated their land and paid their dues and were perhaps not greatly affected by the affairs of the wider world.

Following the Dissolution of the Monasteries, Muston was sold in 1546 to John Bartlett, or Bartelot, of Piddlehinton, who had relatives with influence at Court and had been employed as an Investigator of Monasteries by Thomas Cromwell. He seems to have been an unscrupulous character, who ruthlessly used his position to extort money from the monasteries and to acquire church lands at knock-down prices.

In 1609 Nathaniel Bartlett sold Muston to John Churchill of Stinsford, who had already been leasing it and who probably built the present house. His father, William, had bought land in Piddlehinton in 1586 and his grandfather, John Churchill of Dorchester, was both wealthy and respected and owned much property in and around the county town. He was Bailiff of Dorchester in 1525 and 1540, and appears to have been the brother of Roger Churchill of Catherston, reputedly the ancestor of John, 1st Duke of Marlborough, and his illustrious descendant, Sir Winston Spencer Churchill.

The house was retained by the Churchill family for more than three centuries and many were baptized, married and buried in Piddlehinton. There was a brief interlude between 1906 and 1915, when it was owned by Mr. Clement Tory. He purchased the manor and its 980 acres of farmland from the trustees of William Churchill's estate. Mr. Tory did not live in the house but took an active interest in the running of the estate.

MUSTON MANOR. Despite their quality, these two paintings give a good idea of the ways in which even the most modest manor house can evolve over time. The watercolour at the top dates to about 1800 before the roof was raised, creating an extra floor. The lower painting by Margaret Churchill of the house in the 1920s shows it before the addition of the new wing on the right and new dormer windows.

In 1915 the house, with some five acres of land, was bought back into the Churchill family by Commander Kenneth Churchill, after his marriage. He and his wife Margaret lived there for the rest of their lives, taking an active part in local life and raising their two children. They added the kitchen extension at the eastern end of the house, mounting two plaques on the wall there to mark significant anniversaries in their life, and re-instated dormer

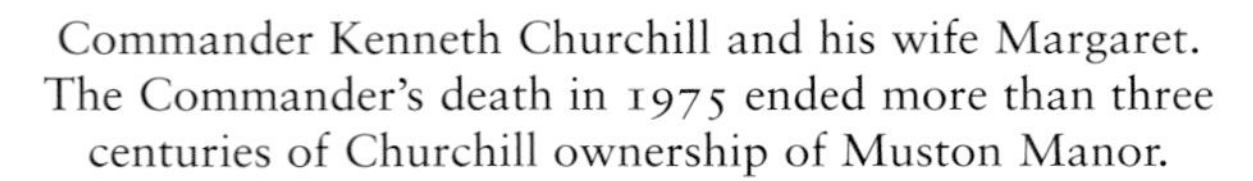

Commander Kenneth Churchill and his wife Margaret. The Commander's death in 1975 ended more than three centuries of Churchill ownership of Muston Manor.

windows in the attic floor. During the Second World War Commander Churchill was recalled to the Royal Navy whilst Margaret remained at Muston and served as a V.A.D. Evacuees were billeted at the house and the padre from the nearby army camp rented part of it. The staff of the house rapidly dwindled from a parlour maid, housemaid, cook and gardener to just the parlour maid until she also was called up.

In 1976, after Commander Churchill's death, his son John sold the manor to Mr. and Mrs. O.B. Paine who made it their family home.

Nash Court

NASH COURT is on the eastern edge of Marnhull with uninterrupted views over the lovely pastoral scenery of the Blackmore Vale. The Marnhull of a century or so past appears as 'Marlott' in Thomas Hardy's *Tess of the D'Urbervilles* and, although the village has expanded and altered greatly, the surrounding countryside would still be instantly recognisable to Hardy's characters. The house itself, whilst attractive, bears little witness to its venerable history, having undergone a massive nineteenth century makeover and in recent times being divided into two dwellings. However, the layout of the older house is still discernible and the part now known as Nash Court contains within it remains of ancient timbers and stonework which may date back to its medieval history.

In the middle ages there were two adjacent

NASH COURT. The east front with its central bell tower.

Giles Hussey (1709-1788). Renowned artist and owner of Nash Court until he gave it to his nephew in 1787.

manors in the parish of Marnhull, Burton Ashe, from which the name Nash Court derives, and Marnhull itself. Marnhull was owned by Glastonbury Abbey until the Dissolution and Burton Ashe was a separate entity under the overlordship of Glastonbury. In the seventeenth century both manors were purchased by George Hussey, who obtained permission to combine them into a single manor.

The earliest information about Burton Ashe appears in 1329, when it was owned by Walter de Tryll and ten years later in 1339, when it became the property of the Carent family. The Carents were substantial landowners and Burton Ashe was only a small part of their property. They owned it until at least 1517 when William Carent left it to trustees.

There is then a gap in its history of more than a hundred years until in 1641 Edward Henning, grandson of Richard Henning, conveyed it to John Churchill, who sold it the following year to Sir John Walcot of Sherborne. By this time it was called Nash Court and consisted of a manor house, farm and demesnes. In 1651, his grandson, Edward sold it to George Hussey, who had bought the manor of Marnhull in the same year. The Husseys were a wealthy family, whose estates in Cornwall, Wiltshire and Somerset had been acquired in spite of the financial and political disadvantages of being Catholic. They usually supported a 'gentleman', as Catholic priests were colloquially known, at Nash Court.

George's grandson, Giles, was born at Nash Court in 1709 and was destined to become a renowned artist. He was educated in France and, despite his father's misgivings, eventually became a pupil of Vincenzo Damini, a Venetian, who was considered one of the best painters of the time. While learning his trade Hussey was chiefly employed in painting less important areas of pictures, gradually progressing to helping finish those of his master, whom he also worked alongside, painting the ornaments of Lincoln Cathedral.

After four years he went to study in Italy, where he became well-known and highly regarded. On his return to England in 1737 he found it more difficult to be accepted. In 1742 he went to London where he worked as a very successful portrait painter. During his time in Italy, he had developed a complex theory about the principle of harmony in the musical scale, which he believed should also govern drawing. He was unable to persuade other artists to accept his ideas and he became depressed and exasperated by his surroundings.

In 1768 he retired to the country and in 1773, on the death of his brother, he inherited the Nash Court estate. He lived there until 1787, when, from religious motives, he gave all his worldly possessions to his nephew, John Rowe, the only descendant of the Husseys (who then adopted their name). Giles retired to Beaston, near Ashburton in Devon, where he died suddenly in 1788, and is buried. Much of his work is now in private collections and in museums and galleries around the world, including the Royal Collection and the British Museum.

In 1795 seventeen Benedictine Nuns came to Nash Court as refugees from the French Revolution. They had been imprisoned near Paris, and only escaped to England by selling their possessions. After being befriended by Lady Arundell, a relation of the Husseys, they found a home at Nash Court, which was untenanted at the time. They remained for about 12 years, and their rental of £12 18s 6d appears regularly in Squire John Hussey's account book, supplemented by Lady Arundell's contribution of ten guineas.

They seem to have been regarded with suspicion by the neighbourhood, and their library, brought in several chests by one of the priests who accompanied them, was suspected of concealing arms, or even people, and subjected to a strict search. On one occasion, the local magistrate even instituted a search for Napoleon Bonaparte, who was confidently expected to be concealed under their protection. When nothing was found, the Prioress informed him that they had already been searched, in their convent in France, for William Pitt, whom they were also suspected of harbouring!

The burial of one of the sisters in the garden, without a coroner's inquest, was another source of alarm to the neighbourhood. The site of her grave is not known, nor whether the legend that the nuns removed the body when they finally left the neighbourhood is founded on fact, but, within living memory, a superstitious dread of going up Love Lane under the garden wall remained, and children were recommended to hurry lest the nun should look over the wall at them. The somewhat gloomy path between the yews leading from the north gate to the walled garden entrance is commonly known as the 'Nun's Walk'.

John Rowe Hussey married his cousin and they had nine children. He died in 1811 at the age of 75 when his son John inherited the property. In 1836 John Hussey began remodelling the whole house. An east wing extending down to the lane, which is visible in a watercolour of the house in 1831, was pulled down and it is likely that the bell tower was added at this time. The old stone roof was still on the house in 1831, but about this date it slid off one night onto the drive and was replaced by the present slate roof. John remained at Nash Court until his death in 1884.

The Rev. R.B. Kennard, then the Rector, bought

NASH COURT. This rather odd little naive watercolour of the house and garden in 1831 first appeared in *The Marn'll Book* in 1952. The watercolour's whereabouts are now unknown but it does show an east wing that once extended down to the lane.

Nash Court for £2,600 and embarked on further alterations and renewals. He divided up the attics in the west wing, put in dormer windows and replaced the eighteenth century sash windows on the first and ground floors with stone mullioned windows. A new hall staircase was made from the timbers of an old merchant ship called the *Victory*. The porch was rebuilt and enlarged and the Kennard crest and motto placed over the door. For the first time in two hundred and fifty years Nash Court ceased to be a Catholic house and became a model of Victorian Anglican rectitude. It was later let to various tenants until, in 1921, his son, Stanley Kennard, sold it to Captain Brocklebank R.N.

Captain Brocklebank remained there until 1933 when he sold the property to the Misses Beausire, two sisters from Birkenhead. In 1969 it was bought by Mr. Morton Nance who remained there for the next ten years and then sold it to a builder, who renovated the house and divided it into the present two dwellings, calling the western half The Manor and retaining the name Nash Court for the eastern half. Mr. Jonathan Shackleton and his wife bought Nash Court in 1985.

Nethercerne Manor

NETHERCERNE IS A tiny parish lying on the banks of the River Cerne two miles or so below Cerne Abbas. From the Dorchester to Sherborne road, the lovely house and little church of All Saints can be seen below. At first glance they seem to stand entirely alone in the fields, but a second look reveals that there are a few small cottages behind them near the river. The settlement has probably never been much larger than the house, the church, and a handful of cottages, and is one of the smallest parishes in Dorset.

The house itself is built of stone, banded with flint rubble. The central, and oldest, part was built in the late seventeenth century and extended to the east soon afterwards. The west block was added in the late eighteenth century and there are some modern additions on the north side. The older part of the house is floored with magnificent, huge, stone flags, some of which are as large as seven feet by three. The house and church sit so closely together that only a couple of dozen steps separate them.

The churchyard now retains only one memorial in situ, the grave of Anthony Albert Slade, a previous owner and Lord of the Manor, who died in 1915 whilst serving with the Somerset Yeomanry. All the others have been moved to allow the grass to be mown, although, inside the church, there are still memorials to some past inhabitants of house and parish.

In Hutchins *History of Dorset* there is a rather strange description of some stone heads: 'In the walls of one of the outhouses are some very large stones carved into forms of human faces which Mr. Sherren said are so placed to command the gatehouse of the mansion – now taken down – and he supposes from the perforations of the eyes and mouth that they were intended for the discharge of wall pieces to protect the entrance from enemies'. One of these heads was discovered by Mr. and Mrs. Gallia, buried in the undergrowth in the garden and has been mounted in a corner of the garden wall. Its most likely source would probably be robbed stone from the destruction of the monastery at Cerne.

The Domesday Book seems to include Nethercerne in the survey of Cerne Abbey and it may have been part of Cerne's holdings since its foundation in the tenth century until, in 1536, Henry VIII granted the manor to John Bailly and his heirs.

It is probable that this family then held the property for at least 100 years. There was certainly a Bailly still in residence in 1623, because Coker, in his *Survey of Dorset*, tells us that it was 'the seat of William Bayley Gent' and that his neighbour, along the valley at Godmanstone, was Sir Robert Browne, cousin of John Browne of Frampton. It could just be coincidence that Nethercerne was bought by the Brownes of Frampton soon after the Restoration, but there was a much earlier connection between Nethercerne and the Brownes. In the late fifteenth century the church tower was erected and the church considerably repaired by Avice, wife of John Ferret (who was buried there) and who was the mother-in-law of John Browne of Frampton.

The manor was owned by the Brownes until, in 1833, Francis John Browne died without any direct heirs and left his estates to his brother-in-law, Sir Colquoun Grant KCB. He was a distinguished soldier who had seen service in Spain with Sir John Moore and commanded a brigade at the Battle of Waterloo, where he had no less than five horses

killed under him! He was seventy-one when he inherited and he died the following year, leaving the property to his daughter, Marcia Maria, who was married to R. B. Sheridan, grandson of the famous dramatist. Nethercerne remained the property of the Sheridans until at least 1898, when Algernon T. Brinsley Sheridan is listed as owner and Lord of the Manor.

By 1903 it was owned by Alfred Osmund Symes, whose family already had connections with Nethercerne, shown by memorials in the church to members of the Symes family dating back to 1808. In 1911, Kelly's *Directory* gives the owner as Anthony Albert Slade, whose executors sold the estate after his death in 1915 to Edward Claude Maby. The farm was then rented out until it was sold in 1966 to Mr. and Mrs. G. Gallia.

NETHERCERNE MANOR. Looking across the River Cerne to Nethercerne Manor and its little church.

NETHERCERNE MANOR. A much weathered carved stone head discovered in the garden, probably originating from Cerne Abbey.

Parnham House

THIS FINE Tudor house lies alongside the River Brit, just south of Beaminster. There has been a house on the site since 1400, the first built by John Gerard, with William Strode adding more buildings at the end of the fifteenth century. The Strodes were a local family based nearby at East Hewstock, their connections with Dorset going back to the eleventh century. They owned Parnham until 1764. In 1522 Robert Strode married Elizabeth, the granddaughter of Sir William Hody, Chief Baron of the Exchequer under Henry VII. It was probably on account of his wife's inheritance that he was able to rebuild his father's house around 1559. This date appears in the stained glass in the hall.

In early Tudor times the medieval plan of a Great Hall changed drastically when fireplaces and chimneys replaced the central hearth and open timber roof, so allowing rooms to be included on the upper floor. The porch became a more dominant feature, as seen here at Parnham, reaching up three storeys with a splendid two-tiered oriel window.

Robert Strode's Great Hall was entered from the porch through a screens passage with the kitchen wing to the north, but the wing to the right of the porch, altered around 1600, is almost certainly part of an earlier building. Around 1810 John Nash added copings and pinnacles to the gables, but for the most part the front exterior of this lovely Tudor house remains untouched.

In Hutchins' period there were more buildings in the grounds. He mentions 'the schoolhouse, the gatehouse, the wall about the inner court and the gardens', all of which he credits to Robert's son, John Strode (I), who died in 1581. He refers also to the 'base court set up by Robert Strode', and lists 'three orchards, out-gardens and ponds' comprising four acres. These facts appeared in a survey of the estate drawn up by Sir John Strode (II), a younger son of the Parnham family who bought Chantmarle in 1606. He succeeded his brother, Sir Robert (II), around 1628 and then moved into Parnham.

PARNHAM HOUSE. The three-storeyed porch on the entrance front, with a seventeenth century cartouche of the arms of the Strodes dividing the two oriel windows.

PARNHAM HOUSE. The house and garden from beyond the lake.

Sir Robert (II) had an only daughter, Catherine. He arranged her marriage to a relative, Sir Richard Strode of Newnham, in return for £2000, with which he acquired additional land, on the understanding that the property should go to their son. He bought eighty-four acres of freehold land adjoining the house from the Bishop of Salisbury, enclosing ten acres with dry stone-wall for a rabbit warren. He then annexed parcels of the prebendal manors of Beaminster, along with the deer park at nearby Horn Park. This he left to his wife Margaret for her to enjoy for the rest of her life. Richard and Catherine did not have a son, only three daughters, so Sir Robert went back on his word, altering the limitation and taking back this vast amount of land to himself for life. He chose his brother, Sir John (II), as his heir, providing he paid inheritance to Richard and Catherine's three daughters.

After a long suit in chancery and with the estates greatly diminished by the settlements, Sir John (II), a lawyer by profession, succeeded in his claim. He paid a reduced sum to the three daughters and moved into Parnham, dying in 1642, aged 81. His widow, Anne, however, suffered a violent death. At the time when Cromwell 'had totally routed the enemy in the West, one of his soldiers with his sword casually killed Sir John's wife Anne in the

PARNHAM HOUSE. The memorial to George Strode (died 1753), dressed in Roman robes, and his wife Catherine (died 1756) in St Mary's Church, Beaminster.

same place Parnaham which she so unlawfully kept', while her son Sir John (III) of Chantmarle, 'was taken prisoner for Parliament for his malignancy'. Eventually Lady Anne's son was released and his title restored, after paying for the release of his confiscated estate.

After the death of Sir John (III) in 1679, Parnham passed to his nephew George. It could be said that George 'modernised' the house by enlarging the rooms in the south wing, rebuilding the stables and garden walls though, at the same time, sweeping away the gatehouse and Elizabethan forecourt. Neither George nor his brother, Thomas, had any male heir, so in 1764, for the first time in three hundred years, Parnham passed through the female side of the family to Elizabeth Strode, daughter of Sir John Strode (III), and wife of Sir John Oglander of Nunwell, Isle of Wight.

From then on, the house remained empty for nearly fifty years, until their great-grandson, Sir William Oglander came to live at Parnham. In 1810 he married Lady Maria-Anne Fitzroy, daughter of the 4th Duke of Grafton, and between 1807 and 1811 he employed the services of John Nash who reconstructed the south wing, turning it into a library and drawing room. Nash also added a new dining room while furnishing the interior of the house with marble fireplaces and plaster cornices in the Regency Gothic style. On the south front, the parapets, gables and pinnacles are also of this time. Fortunately the beautiful Tudor armorial glass survived. Nash's only legacies left today are the ice-house, built in 1809, the walled garden and an exquisite, delicately curved

PARNHAM HOUSE. The south front.

staircase with a lantern above.

In 1896, after the death of Sir Henry Oglander, Parnham was sold for the first time. It was purchased by Mr. Vincent Robinson, who used the house for the display of his huge collection of European artwork and furniture. In the dining room he replaced Nash's windows with Jacobean stone mullion and transom windows from Lord North's estate at Wroxton Abbey. The hall door and carved oak chimneypiece he found in Taunton, and to his amazement, was informed they had come from Parnham during the time of Nash's renovations.

In 1910, Parnham was once again on the market. This time the buyer was Dr Hans Sauer from South Africa, a mining engineer and friend of Cecil Rhodes. Although he lived at Parnham for only three years, he completely changed the interior of the house. His designer, Colonel Harry Lindsay, stripped away the remainder of Nash's work, except for the Nash staircase. Dr Sauer searched the country for Elizabethan and Jacobean fixtures and gradually the house returned to its original period. He redesigned the south garden, with its now splendid pyramid yews, the terrace, formal gardens and the graceful pavilions, all in the style of Francis Inigo Thomas who, in the early part of the century, had landscaped Athelhampton and Montacute. At the same time, around 1912, came the creation of the lake and Dower House.

The next owner, in 1914, was Mr. Rhodes-Moorhouse, whose son, William Rhodes-Moorhouse VC, was the first airman to be awarded the Victoria Cross. He died of his wounds on 27th April 1915. His wish was to be buried at his family home and the small burial ground can be seen from the public footpath that runs from the back of Parnham House. Tragically, his son, Flight-Lieutenant William Henry Rhodes-Moorhouse DFC, was also shot down in the Second World War over Tunbridge Wells at the height of the Battle of Britain in 1940. One of the 'Few', his ashes share the same grave as his father.

In 1928 Parnham enjoyed a brief two-year period as a country club patronised by Conan Doyle and the Prince of Wales. In 1930, the owner, a Mr. Brown, sold it to Mr. Eric Bullivant, whose ownership lasted until 1955.

William Rhodes-Moorhouse VC died in 1915, the first airman to be awarded the VC.

During the Second World War it briefly saw service as a military hospital but in mid 1943 it became HQ of the 16th Infantry Regiment of the US Army under the command of Colonel George A.Taylor. The detailed planning for the Regiment's assault on Omaha Beach was carried out here. Units were billeted as far away as Lyme Regis, Abbotsbury and Litton Cheney as well as in huts and tents in the grounds. Vast amounts of armoured vehicles were assembled in local lanes prior to being moved to the coast. The oak room was converted into the officers' lounge. The Great Hall was the dining room with two long folding tables end to end. General Eisenhower visited the troops at Parnham during this crucial time. Afterwards the house was used briefly as a German prisoner-of-war camp. After the war Mr. Bullivant returned to Parnham and

PARNHAM HOUSE. The terrace and gardens on the west side.

replanted the North Avenue with lime trees. In 1953 his wife died and he moved to Anderson Manor where he lived until his death in 1972.

The National Association for Mental Health became the new owners in 1956, using the house as a home for elderly ladies, but it closed in 1973 due to non-compliance with fire regulations. It remained empty for three years and was then bought by Mr. and Mrs. John Makepeace and used as a School for Craftsmen in Wood. The student quarters were upstairs while the crafts were displayed in the main rooms. John and Jenny Makepeace began to restore the neglected gardens. With an English Heritage grant they repaired the ha-ha and the water rills which are such a delightful feature of the garden. The house and garden were then opened to the public.

In 2001 the house was once again for sale and received planning permission for conversion into flats with houses in the grounds. Fortunately this did not materialise, as in the same year it was rescued by Mr. and Mrs. Michael Treichl, who, with their architect, William Bertram of Bath, have sympathetically restored the house, turning it into an elegant family home. The park and gardens are being returned to their former glory and a new herd of deer have been introduced. The orchard has been replanted and once again the kitchen garden is well used. Mrs. Emma Treichl has recently founded The Parnham Press, with the aim of publishing books in aid of local and national charities. Her first book, *Eat Dorset*, which promotes Dorset produce, was published in 2005.

Pilsdon Manor

PILSDON MANOR, with its tiny church, sits in the Marshwood Vale, still a remote and unspoiled part of West Dorset. It is protected from the north by Pilsdon Pen, instantly recognisable by its flat topped, grassy outline, and by Lewesdon Hill beside it to the east, two metres higher, (at 277 metres, Dorset's highest point) steeper and densely wooded. Not far away is Racedown House, where William and Dorothy Wordsworth once lived and in this quiet valley you can still glimpse the little early wild daffodils braving the winds of March. To find the house you wind through steeply-banked narrow lanes, until it seems you may well be lost, when suddenly, there across a field, are the little church and the Manor House with a lane leading up to them.

The house was built on a rectangular plan at the beginning of the seventeenth century and extended to the north and north-east later in the same century. It is built of Ham stone and flint, and faces south down the valley towards Golden Cap and the sea. Although Newman and Pevsner describe it as having, 'an unusually fine manor house facade of the mid seventeenth century', its appearance seems austere and uncompromising. The grey slate roof, which slopes steeply down almost to the ground floor on the north side and has replaced the original stone tiles, does nothing to soften this impression. However, the south front has large and beautiful windows which overlook the garden and stretch the whole length of both ground and first floor,

PILSDON MANOR. The seventeenth century Ham stone south front looks out over the Marshwood Vale towards Golden Cap and the sea.

allowing light and sunshine to pour into the house.

Across the garden, through a little arch in the wall, is a small chapel, which, despite its Victorian restoration, predates the present house. Little is known of the history of the church. It may have been attached to an earlier manor house on the same site, or possibly was a chapel of ease for the see of Sherborne. Inside is a scroll listing names and dates of its rectors, the earliest being 1319, so its origins predate the present house by about three hundred years. Whatever its previous history, the chapel today has a simple beauty and an atmosphere of tranquillity and prayer.

Before the Conquest, Pilsdon was owned by a thane called Edric and then came to a family who called themselves 'de Pillesdon'. Many of the de Pillesdons went on Crusade, including Warresius de Pillesdon, who died on the way to Jerusalem in 1243-44, leaving a widow and young son. The family name of de Pillesdon survived until about 1337, when the manor was inherited by a daughter, Alice. She married John le Jewe and Pilsdon then belonged to the le Jewe family until, once again, it was inherited by a daughter, Elizabeth. She was the wife of Sir John Hody MP, Lord Chief Justice of England in 1440, whose main property was Stowell in Somerset. Stowell was inherited by his eldest son, whilst Pilsdon went to the second son, Sir William Hody, who became Attorney General and Lord Chief Baron of the Exchequer. The Hody family owned Pilsdon until about the 1620's when, with only daughters to inherit the estate, they sold it to Sir Hugh Wyndham. He built the present house, renaming it Pilsdon Court. In 1641 he was created a baronet and in 1651-52 served as Sheriff of Dorset.

Following the escape of Charles II after the Battle of Worcester, Pilsdon was considered as a possible refuge for the King, who was hoping to escape to France from the Dorset coast. Unfortunately, Parliamentary forces were searching the area and Pilsdon was judged too dangerous, so he returned to his previous hiding place at Trent, the home of Colonel Francis Wyndham, a trusted aide, who was Sir Hugh's nephew. Pilsdon was suspected of harbouring the fugitive and was searched by Cromwell's forces. An account of this event was included in a pamphlet telling the story of the King's escape, written by Mrs. Anne Wyndham of Trent, which was published in 1681. She writes,

> 'They took the old baronet, his lady, daughters and whole family and set a guard upon them in the hall whilst they examined every corner, not sparing either trunk or box. Then taking a particular view of their prisoners they seized a lovely young lady, saying she was the King disguised in woman's apparel. At length, being convinced of their gross and rude mistake, they desisted from offering any further violence to that family'.

Sir Hugh had no son, so the baronetcy died with him and Pilsdon passed to his nephew, Francis, who was created a baronet in 1673. The last Wyndham to inherit the property was another woman, Frances, sister of the 4th and last baronet. He died in 1719 at about the age of fourteen. The estate was sold to Sir Theodore Janssen in 1732.

The Janssens originated in Holland. Sir Theodore had suffered huge losses as a director of the South Seas Company and gone bankrupt. Because of this, Pilsdon was bought by one of his sons and conveyed to Sir Theodore a few months later. All the income from the estate was assigned to paying off his creditors. Pilsdon was now leased and was not to be occupied by its owners again until the twentieth century. The property was eventually inherited by Sir Theodore's granddaughter, Williamza, who was Mrs. Lionel Damer of Came, and later sold to the Rev. Gregory Raymond of Symondsbury in 1825. He subsequently left it to his niece, Mrs. H.T. Bower of Fontmell Parva.

In 1918 the estate was again sold, this time to Mr. Sherley H. Jenks, a farmer and horse breeder and in 1958 was bought by the Rev. Percy Smith and his wife Gaynor. They established a charitable foundation and set up a Christian Community 'to offer friendship and shelter to those defeated and broken and near the end of their tether'. The Community at Pilsdon still flourishes, upholding the aims of its founders.

Plumber Manor

THE APPROACH TO Plumber Manor is by way of an eighteenth century bridge over the Divelish Stream, a tributary of the River Stour. Situated one and a half miles from Sturminster Newton, the house was built in the late sixteenth or early seventeenth century. Though remodelled down the centuries, much original material has been reused. The large west range illustrated in Hutchins has gone. The walled inner garden shown in Hutchins still remains to the north of the house but all the other pavilions and walls have disappeared. The south range is a mixture of old and new, with the double chimneystack topped by an arch, shown in the engraving, still remaining. The interior of the house has been extensively and sympathetically altered.

Swain, one of the King's thanes held Plumbere at Domesday and in the reign of Edward III, the land was held by John de Plumber. Coker goes back even further, stating that the Plumbers were known here even from the time of Edward the Confessor. According to Leland, Roger de Plumber, in 1300, held land in exchange for service in the forest of Blackmore.

Between 1409 and 1430 the manor was held by the Monteacutes, and in the early sixteenth century passed into the hands of the Williams family of Dorchester and Herringstone. John Williams held it in 1550, followed by Robert Williams, a wealthy landowner who died in 1569. Robert's heir, Sir John Williams, was Sheriff of Dorset in 1582 and 1592, then MP for Dorchester in 1603. There is no record of a house at Plumber until after Sir John's death in 1617, when Coker describes a house there as 'a new house of the Lady Williams'. As Lady Williams was

PLUMBER MANOR. The house in the eighteenth century. The orangery on the left and garden walls no longer stand.

Sir John's widow this surely indicates that her husband built the house.

The estate was inherited by Sir John's third son, Major John Williams, a Royalist soldier in the Civil War. In August 1644, the Royalists attacked Wynford Eagle, home of the Sydenhams, who were Parliamentarians. During the attack Colonel Sydenham's mother, Mary, was killed by Major Williams. This tragic event led to more tragedy. In November, near Dorchester, Colonel Sydenham recognised Major Williams at the head of the Royalist troop. Crying, 'I will now avenge my innocent mother's blood, or die in this place', Sydenham charged and slew the major, so avenging his mother's death. Major Williams' son, John Williams, though married, had no children, so Plumber was sold. The new owner was Charles Brune.

The Brunes originated from Hampshire. Sir John Brune, in 1554, was living in part of Athelhampton House, the seat of the Martins. He married Jane, the widow of Henry Turbeville and daughter of John Bampfield. Their daughter, Jane, married John Williams of Tyneham in 1572 and their son, Henry, married Elizabeth, eldest of the four daughters of Nicholas Martin, who died in 1595. Henry inherited a substantial estate upon his marriage. This was further enhanced when Chidiock Tichborne was executed in 1586. He had married Nicholas Martin's second daughter, Jane, but became involved in the Babington Plot to assassinate Queen Elizabeth and replace her with the Roman Catholic Mary, Queen of Scots. Henry Brune was also arrested because of his family connection to the Tichbornes. He was imprisoned in the Tower of London but fortunately released after signing the Bond of Association for the safety of the Queen. It was a close shave.

Henry and Elizabeth had three sons, the eldest, Sir John, as his mother's heir, lived at Athelhampton but died childless in 1639. His younger brother, Charles had two sons, John, a colonel in the Parliamentary forces, who married Mary Hooper, and Charles, who married Jane Collier, and purchased Plumber. John died in 1645, aged twenty-three, leaving an only daughter Mary. In 1661 Mary married Ralph Bankes, who built Kingston Hall, better known now as Kingston Lacy. Mary's substantial inheritance of £1,200 a year certainly helped her husband with his costly project, even so, in 1670, he was obliged to sell her inheritance in order to meet his debts.

Charles Brune died in 1703 and his son Charles became Sheriff of Dorset in 1709. He had married Betty, daughter of Lorenzo Jeffrey of West Bagborough, Somerset. Their four sons all died without issue, including the eldest, Charles, who rebuilt and enlarged the house and garden at Plumber. This is the house illustrated in Hutchins. It was completed around 1750 and was certainly a building of distinction.

Charles died around 1770, therefore the estate passed to his sister, Betty. She was married to Neville Morton Pleydell of Shitterton. Their son, Charles Morton Pleydell added the name Brune to his own as requested in the will of his late uncle, Charles Brune. Charles Pleydell Brune died in 1785 and, as he had no heirs, the inheritance passed to his sister Jenny Pleydell who had married Humphrey Prideaux of Prideaux Place in Cornwall. In turn, their eldest son, the Reverend Charles Prideaux assumed the surname of Brune in addition to Prideaux and the name Prideaux-Brune has continued to the present day.

Unfortunately the house was badly damaged by fire. The exact date is not known, but it was around the time when occupied by Jenny and her husband Humphrey Prideaux, in the latter half of the eighteenth century. Sadly it was not rebuilt and the surviving part, which lies to the south, with the arch over the chimneys, was let as a farmhouse. The Prideaux family had property in Cornwall, which probably left Plumber Manor surplus to requirements. The family did not occupy the house again until after the Second World War.

In the 1930s the present owner's grandfather returned to Plumber and began to rebuild and renovate the house. The main part was extended northwards from the surviving wing. Reset in this part is a seventeenth century door-head, now

PLUMBER MANOR. The house was badly damaged by fire in the late eighteenth century and not rebuilt and renovated by the Prideaux-Brune family until after the Second World War. Today it is a distinguished country house hotel.

spanning a window. In the upper storey is a blocked stone window, again probably reset. There was a considerable reuse of seventeenth century material. The farm buildings were converted into staff quarters. The handsome eighteenth-century staircase from Cranborne was also installed at this time. The size of the staircase necessitated re-siting the front door. The wing projecting to the west from the main part of the house was originally built as a separate unit from the main house and designed as two cottages for servants' quarters. After the war it was joined to the main building. Alongside a doorway in this wing stands an old pump with a cast-lead head bearing the letter B, for Brune, and four rosettes serving as a constant reminder of the present owners' ancestors. After the war this wing was let to two ladies.

The rebuilding was not completed until 1939. With the outbreak of the Second World War the house was used to accommodate evacuees. Towards the end of 1946 or 47, the house was once again ready for occupation, but by this time Mr. Prideaux-Brune, suffering from arthritis, spent much of his time in Tucson, Arizona, where the climate was drier and where he had family connections on his mother's side. He died in 1952. His son and family then moved to Dorset from Cheshire and have remained here ever since. In 1973, the present owner, Richard Prideaux-Brune, along with his brother and sister, Brian and Alison, turned their home into a deservedly distinguished country house hotel and restaurant which continues to flourish today.

Portesham Manor

OVER THE CENTURIES Portesham Manor has gradually been engulfed by the village until it is now just a large house known as 5 Church Lane, with its front door opening directly on to the street. Look closer though and its venerable ancestry becomes apparent. It is a substantial stone-built house with five mullioned windows on the ground floor and three on the upper floor. A string-course runs along the front above the windows, which are quite low and the upper windows have hoodmoulds. Because the house has been heightened, the low string-course divides the house unevenly, giving it the rather curious appearance of being top heavy. The long, straight, early seventeenth century range is still the face it presents to the world but additions have been made to the back, and the interior has been rearranged but still contains some original panelling. The beautiful, ancient front door with its flanking niches, now sadly empty, and the mullioned windows bear witness to its different past.

Before 1066 Portesham was part of Canute's gift of land to Orc and was left by him to Abbotsbury Abbey. It appears as a holding of the Abbey in the Domesday Book and remained part of its possessions until the Dissolution of the Monasteries, when the manor, rectory, manor house and pasture for 750 sheep were granted to William Paulet, Lord St John, 1st Marquis of Winchester, whose principal house was Hooke Court.

The Paulet family remained in possession of the manor until the mid seventeenth century when it was bought by Andrew Riccard. His father, Walter, whose memorial stone is in the nave of Portesham Church, lived at the manor and presumably leased it from the Winchesters so it seems safe to assume that Andrew was born and grew up there. In 1627 he went to sea apprenticed to John Watkin, a member of the Turkey, East Indies and Muscovy Companies and made his fortune, probably either from privateering or trading with the East Indies, legitimately or otherwise. He became Sheriff of London in 1651, and was made President of the East India and Turkey Companies, and knighted in 1660. He bought his childhood home and sold most of the manor's subsidiary holdings to the tenants, who then became freeholders. He also bought the perpetual advowson of St Olave's Church, Hart Street, London, and left it in trusteeship for ever. When he died in 1672 he was buried under the communion table there and the Turkey Company erected a handsome marble memorial to him. His funeral escutcheon still hangs in the church at Portesham.

A contemporary recorded his attendance at the funeral in his diary, 'Sept. 5, 1672, died Sir Andrew Ricguard [sic] (once alderman and sheriff of London) very wealthy; leaving behind him one only daughter (Christian) married (first to Henry Lord Kensington, son to Henry late Earl of Holland, and then) to (Sir John Berkeley) Lord Berkeley (of Stratton). His funeral to St Olave Cruchet Friars, Sept. 17'.

His only surviving child, Christiana was actually married three times. Her first marriage was in 1655 to John Geare, whose father was Lord Mayor in 1647. She was widowed and in 1658 married Henry Rich, Lord Kensington, son of the Earl of Holland. This marriage was also short lived. They had no children and he died the following year. Within a year or so Christiana remarried again, this time to a man of over fifty, Lord John Berkeley, Baron

Stratton. He was the youngest son of Sir Maurice Berkeley of Bruton in Somerset and had a distinguished military career.

He became a Royalist general, Lord Lieutenant of Ireland and Ambassador Extraordinary. During the Civil War he operated mostly in the West Country, gaining a notable victory, amongst others, at Stratton in Cornwall over the Earl of Stamford in May 1643. He was knighted in 1639 by Charles I and raised to the peerage in 1658 by Charles II in exile. In 1647 he had assisted Charles I in his flight from Hampton Court to the Isle of Wight.

For a number of years from 1652 he also acted as the steward of the Duke of York's household, during which time, according to Samuel Pepys, he obtained some irregular benefit from the letting of the Duke's wine licences. (Pepys, 27 Sep.1668.)

He acquired Twickenham Park in 1668 and lived there until his death, at the age of 72, in 1678. Christiana died in 1698 and is buried with him in a vault beneath St Mary's Church. She obviously had a considerable fortune, being her father's only heir, which was considered worthy of note on her husband's epitaph as follows:

> 'His other felicityes were crowned
> By his happy marriage of Christina, daughter of Sr. ANDREW RICCARD
> A young lady of a large Dowry and yet larger Graces and Virtues.
> Who also Enriched him with a most hopefull progeny.'

Sadly the 'hopefull progeny' did not perpetuate the family line. Charles, who inherited the title in 1678 at the age of sixteen, became a sea captain but died of smallpox at sea aged twenty-one. His brother John then became the 3rd Baron. He was also a sailor and became Admiral of the Blue in 1693. He died in 1697 with no sons to inherit, so the title went to his youngest brother, William.

William's eldest son John became the 5th Baron Berkeley of Stratton in 1740. He had no children

PORTESHAM MANOR. Once among fields, now totally engulfed by the village.

and when he died in the same year the title became extinct. He left his considerable estate, which included Berkeley Square, Stratton Street and Bruton Street in London, to a distant cousin, Frederick Augustus, 5th Earl of Berkeley. By this time the manor was leased to a succession of tenants and continued to be so almost until the present day.

Towards the end of the nineteenth century or early in the twentieth, the manor and its estates came into the ownership of the Hardy family, of Admiral Sir Thomas Masterman Hardy fame, and remained their property until their estates were sold off in 1938. They already possessed a handsome house just down the road in Portesham so it is probable that they continued to lease out the manor house.

In 1947 Mrs. Violet Sutton of Greatham, near Winchester, bought the house and moved there with her mother. She then met and married Commander Jack Sutton and moved to Frampton House, once again leasing the manor house. Her husband died in 1985 and in 1987 she returned to live at the manor. Her great nephew, Mr. John Barker, who now owns the house, came to live with her and cared for her until her death in 2004.

Poxwell Manor

POXWELL MANOR lies about six miles north-east of Weymouth alongside the Wareham road, but a little aloof from the small cluster of cottages which make up the hamlet of Poxwell. Looking down from the hills above, the house is seen to nestle warmly into a fold in the downs, protected from the east winds off the sea and from the north by the Ridgeway. It was once easily visible, but is now hidden from passing traffic by a tall, dense, conifer hedge.

The house is of Portland stone, two storeys high with tiled roofs and stone slates at the eaves. It was built around 1600 and seems to have been planned as an H shape, with the cross wings at the north and south ends and a central porch on the east front, but the south wing was never built.

The main front faces east towards the road. Here the garden is surrounded by a brick wall with a pretty, two storey, hexagonal, gatehouse in the centre of the east wall with an external stair to the upper storey. The contrast between the stone house and the brick wall is unusual, but the wall and gatehouse were probably built a little later than the main house. There is a date of 1634 over the arch of the gatehouse, by which time brick was fashionable in Dorset. There was no longer any need for a defensive wall and gateway and Poxwell's seems to be a fashionable ornament to the house.

From about three feet on either side of the gatehouse the wall drops to about half its height for most of the length of the south and east wall. A son of the Dorset poet William Barnes, wrote in 1900 that the wall on each side of the gatehouse, which he refers to as the Porter's Lodge, had been lowered but that the characteristic coping had been replaced. He also noted that three ancient tiles 'found in

pulling down the wall will be seen built in over the doorway between this lawn and the garden'. If these are the three terracotta plaques over a gateway in the north wall, one with a crowned head of Anne Boleyn and the other two with her badge, this might raise questions as to the date the wall was built. When the house was built in 1600, they would have been a pretty compliment to Anne Boleyn's only daughter, Elizabeth I, but by 1634 such compliments would have been out of date. However, recycling is not a modern invention and the plaques may have been old materials re-used when the wall was built.

POXWELL MANOR. The manor house with its surrounding wall and two-storey brick gatehouse of 1634.

The upper room of the gatehouse is traditionally known as the Fool's Chamber as it was said that the family's jester was allowed a parting joke from the window as guests departed. Barnes also mentions the ghost of an old lady, who was said to sit knitting in the porter's lodge, which 'terrified the maids', but who had not been seen for some considerable time.

By the early twentieth century the house had been leased as a farmhouse for many years and was apparently in a sorry state. Thomas Hardy used Poxwell as his model for the decaying Oxwell Hall in *The Trumpet Major* and his description is said to be very close to the reality:

> 'Mustard and cress could have been raised on the inner plaster of the dewy walls at any height not exceeding three feet from the floor; and mushrooms of the most refined and thin-stemmed kinds grew up through the chinks in the larder paving.
>
> The iron stanchions inside the window-panes were eaten away to the size of wires at the bottom where they entered the stone, the condensed breathings of generations having settled there in pools and rusted them. The panes themselves had either lost their shine altogether or become iridescent as a peacock's' tail.
>
> The quadrangle of the ancient pile was a bed of mud and manure, inhabited by calves, geese, ducks and sow pigs surprisingly large, with young ones surprisingly small.'

In the early 1930's, when Arthur Oswald visited the house, he found it still in a sad state of repair. Much of the house had been abandoned and was used only for storing apples. The Great Hall retained some panelling, but its massive ancient refectory table was riddled with woodworm and rot. However, in 1934 thorough repairs were carried out and a member of the Lane family, descendants of the Hennings, who bought the house in 1575, once again occupied it.

In Domesday Book the manor appears as part of the holdings of the Abbey of Cerne under the name Poceswelle. Leofricus of Poceswelle gave it to the abbey and the grant was later confirmed by King Ethelred. The name Pokeswell first appears as a family name during the reign of Edward III and it seems that the family leased land here from Cerne Abbey. In 1430 Robert Pokeswell had a house and 90 acres here and his descendants leased the manor until the Dissolution.

In 1562 Elizabeth I granted 'the manor, farm house and advowson of the rectory, late belonging to the monastery of Cerne' to the infamous Thomas Howard of Bindon. (*see* Waterston) In 1575 he sold it to John Henning, a wealthy merchant from Poole, who also later bought Cruxton.

His son, also John, was Sheriff in 1609, but it was probably his grandson, Richard, who built the present house. In 1644 the Henning's estate at Pokeswell was sequestered and it seems probable that either Richard or his son Edmund died in Corfe Castle village in 1652. The family's fortunes were obviously restored after the Restoration, as from 1679 to 1694 Edmund's son, Henry, was MP for Weymouth and Melcombe Regis.

In 1699 when Henry Henning died, his heiress was a daughter, Elizabeth, who was married to Colonel Thomas Trenchard of Wolfeton. Thomas and Elizabeth had only one child, Mary, who married her second cousin, George, son of Sir John Trenchard of Bloxworth.

From this point until the mid twentieth century, when Bloxworth was sold, the ownership of both Poxwell and Bloxworth remained with descendants of the Trenchards, although at various times they were both leased to tenants. The house at Bloxworth, together with the manor at Lytchett Matravers, which was largely pulled down in 1849, became the main residences of the family and their history is therefore included in the description of Bloxworth.

Around 1840, after the death of his father, George Pickard, John Trenchard Trenchard, who had changed his surname from Pickard to Trenchard to comply with the terms of his great uncle's will, acquired the manor house. He was a barrister and Deputy Lieutenant of Dorset, whose home was Greenhill House in Weymouth. As well as repairing and renovating the house, he financed a free school in Poxwell and piped water from a spring on the hillside behind the house, building a conduit to

POXWELL MANOR. Lawns and lavender fill the formal garden in front of the main entrance of 1600.

replace the well, which until then had been the cottagers' only source of water.

In 1842 the old thirteenth century church, a few yards to the north of the house, was repaired, although not altogether successfully. In 1868 John had it demolished and a new church built some 70 yards further east. One hundred years later, in 1969, John Trenchard's church had deteriorated so badly that it was considered dangerous. The congregation had dwindled to one or two and the immense cost of repair was untenable so the church was demolished and not replaced. John and his wife Jane Tennant are buried in the little churchyard at Poxwell.

In 1934 Ernest Lane and his wife Jessie moved into the manor house, which had been neglected for many years. He was the eldest son of Mary Ellen Lane, only daughter of Jocelyn Pickard Cambridge, who had inherited a life interest in the Bloxworth/Poxwell estate from his eldest brother Henry. On Jocelyn's death the estate passed to Mary Ellen. Ernest Lane undertook major repairs and renovation, including a new roof. He installed a fireplace, taken from one of the upper rooms, into the north wall of the Great Hall and bought a fifteenth century refectory table and chairs to replace the ancient, rotted one mentioned by Barnes and Oswald. In 1941, his mother died and left Poxwell to him. Ernest died in 1958 but his wife continued to live there until 1972 when she became too infirm to remain and the house was again let. She and Ernest had no children and when she died in 1974 Poxwell was left to Ernest's nephew, Mr. Jocelyn (Jock) Lane.

In 1978 when the tenants left, the house was sold to Mr. Peter Bolton. In 1987 he sold it to Mr. Michael Cannon and his wife, who did considerable work in the house and garden, including deepening and enlarging the ornamental lake. They lived there until 1998 when they decided to sell and it was bought back by Mr. Bolton.

Poxwell had remained the property of the same family for almost exactly four centuries, descending from the Hennings, who bought it in 1575, to the Lanes, who still owned it until 1978. Although the Manor House no longer belongs to the Lane family, they still live at Poxwell, Mr. & Mrs. Jock Lane in Manor Cottage and their son and his family in Poxwell Manor Farm.

Puncknowle Manor

SIR FREDERICK TREVES, on seeing Puncknowle Manor nearly 100 years ago, described it as 'one of the daintiest and most beautiful of the manor houses in the country, a marvel of ancient dignity and peace.'

The manor house lies close to the church and was built by the Napiers in the sixteenth century. It was altered in the seventeenth century and the rear wing was rebuilt in modern times. The north, south and east fronts all retain their original windows. There is a broad porch in the centre of the east front, added around 1650. Inside the porch are two flanking staircases which merge for the final flight to the upper floor. On the first floor the rooms were lined with eighteenth century moulded panelling, with dado-rails and cornices. The overmantels were panelled and one of them had a seascape while another showed a landscape. The fireplaces were original. In the wall between the garden and the church is a stone door-head with a shield bearing the initials R. and A.N and a panel with a defaced date in the seventeenth century. The initials are probably of Robert and Anna Napier.

The original name of the manor was Pomacole, (still pronounced 'Punnell') the second part of the name referring to the 600 feet high hill south of the village still called the Knoll. In Domesday Book it was a small parish but in the fifteenth century it joined with Bexington and doubled in size. In the 1300s it was under the Whitefields, who were styled as lords of Puncknowle and in 1399 it passed to Elizabeth, daughter of Guy de Bryan, wife of Robert Lovel, whose heiress brought it to the Earls of Arundel. From them, around 1400, it passed into the hands of the Dukes of Clarence.

The Napiers, or Napper, as they were sometimes called, came 'out of Scotland' at the end of the fifteenth century, according to their monument in Swyre Church. James Napier lived at Swyre in the early 1500s but the site of his house is unknown. His son, another James, married Anne Russell of Berwick. She was the sister of James Russell whose son John became the 1st Earl of Bedford. Over the next century and a half, the Napiers acquired the manors of Puncknowle, Bexington and Baglake, building new houses in each manor.

James and Anne Napier had three sons. Their third son, Sir Robert, bought Middlemarsh. He became Lord Chief Baron of the Exchequer in Ireland in 1593 and High Sheriff of Dorset in 1606. Known for his generosity, in 1615 he endowed and paid for the building of an almshouse in South Street, Dorchester, which gave shelter to ten men. The building remains and is known as Napper's Mite.

Their second son, William, married Anne Shelton and they had five sons. Their fourth son Robert, who married Catherine Warham, was drawn into an adventure in the winter of 1629 involving Endymion Porter, gentleman of the bedchamber to Charles I. Porter was sent on an embassy to Madrid in 1628. Unfortunately on his return voyage, the Spanish ship on which he was sailing was caught in a storm and wrecked off Burton Bradstock. Porter, with 130 Spaniards and their captain, Don Antonio, managed to reach shore.

Sir Thomas Freke, the Sheriff, did what he could for the wrecked mariners and together with Endymion Porter supplied them with food and clothing for two months. Unfortunately the inhabitants of Burton Bradstock were not of such a charitable disposition. For them a wreck provided a

PUNCKNOWLE MANOR. 'A marvel of ancient dignity and peace.' The house built by the Napier family in the sixteenth century, with the church just over the garden wall.

chance for looting. This greatly upset Robert Napier and he and his Catholic neighbour, John Arundell of Symondsbury, met at Puncknowle to write an apology to Mr. Endymion Porter. Arundell's letter began:

> 'Your rustick friend presuming on your worth,
> dareth to salute you, not with a puritanical hart,
> as did the Burtonians or rather Brutonians, at your
> perilous arrival on our barbaro coast, but with a
> reall and Catholike hart, solely and wholely
> devoted ever to honour and serve you.'

Robert Napier also wrote a letter describing his vain attempts to meet Endymion Porter in London in order to apologise for the 'base abuses and beggarly insultings' he had endured at the hands of the people of Burton Bradstock. Eventually Porter and Sir Thomas Freke were able to reimburse themselves by selling salvage from the wreck. Robert Napier died in 1636. His family line ended and Puncknowle passed to a cousin, Robert Napier, son of Sir Nathaniel Napier who built Crichel House near Wimborne, which in time became the main seat of the Napiers.

During the Civil War, Robert Napier, second son of Sir Nathaniel, together with his elder brother Sir Gerard Napier, suffered great hardship for their loyalty to the King. Robert's farms at Puncknowle and Bexington were confiscated. Happily after the Restoration he was duly rewarded for his loyalty. In 1664 he was appointed Receiver of Dorset and Poole for the Hearth Tax and Master of the Hanaper Office, a department of Chancery, an appointment he held in the reigns of both Charles I and II. He died in 1686 and was buried at Puncknowle.

Robert, like his father before him, became Master of the Hanaper Office. He was appointed High Sheriff of Dorset, and created a baronet by Charles II. He also served in Parliament for the boroughs of Weymouth, Melcombe Regis and Dorchester. After his marriage he retired from court and public business and until his death in 1700, lived at Puncknowle.

Sir Charles Napier, Sir Robert's son, then sold the estate to William Clutterbuck. According to Hutchins, he was a naval officer who came from Devon in the reigns of William and Mary. He married Mary Chafin of Chettle. His son John died childless in 1746 but he had four sisters, one of whom, Arundel, married the Reverend George Frome, Rector of Puncknowle. Their grandson, the Reverend George Clutterbuck Frome, who died in 1844, inherited the estate on the death of his father Robert, Rector of Folke. He married Mary-Sophia, daughter of Edmund Morton Pleydell of Whatcombe House, by whom he had two daughters, Mary-Sophia, wife of Charles Kemeys Tynte, and Elizabeth-Arundell, who married Colonel Morton-Grove Mansel, the third son of Lieut. Colonel Mansel of Smedmore. Before his death in 1859, he purchased his sister-in-law's share of the manor and became the sole owner.

In the early half of the nineteenth century, the inventor Colonel Henry Shrapnel lived for a time at Puncknowle. His name lives on in the metal fragments thrown out of exploding shells. His shrapnel was first used in the Napoleonic Wars and was acclaimed by the Duke of Wellington. Those who have suffered the consequences of his invention would find less to applaud.

Around 1927, the then owners, Mr. and Mrs. R.H. Palmer, of the well known brewing family of Bridport, restored the house and in 1969 it was sold to Mr. J.R. Bridgeman of London. It now belongs to Mr. and Mrs. J. Wild.

Purse Caundle Manor

PURSE CAUNDLE is one of a group of villages in the Blackmore Vale, all named Caundle and all situated near the Caundle Brook, which joins the Lydden at Lydlinch and finally runs into the Stour. Caundle was originally spelt Candel, which refers to a small stream. The names of the other three, Marsh, Stourton and Bishop's, are self explanatory, but the origin of Purse is lost in the mists of time. The village is now, and probably always has been, an unremarkable little group of houses, which makes the beauty of its manor house all the more unexpected. It is only a short distance from the main Sherborne to Shaftesbury road, but set in such a peaceful, pastoral landscape that it seems remote both in space and time.

The lovely manor house with its stone slate roofs is on the northern edge of the village and its long south wing runs at right angles to the road, the end wall forming part of the boundary. In this gable wall is a beautiful fifteenth century oriel window projecting over the road. When the house was built in the fifteenth century, on the site of a predecessor, it was approximately L shaped. One wing, running north south, formed the stem of the L and contained two rooms, the Great Hall, and a further, smaller room, which provided a more private family space. The foot of the L formed a wing running east west and about half the length of the present south wing.

In the later sixteenth century the house was

PURSE CAUNDLE MANOR. The south front looking over the bowling green.

PURSE CAUNDLE MANOR. The mid fifteenth century oriel window in the Great Chamber looks out over the approach to Purse Caundle.

considerably extended, almost doubling its size. A large wing was added at the north west corner, the south wing was doubled in length and three small wings added to it, creating a fashionable E shape. In the four hundred years since then the house has remained almost unchanged.

The interior is just as attractive and interesting as the exterior. It is full of delightful surprises but pride of place must go to the oak panelled Great Hall with its magnificent roof and minstrels gallery. The tall, beautiful, five light, west window is a modern replacement. There is a small room here, behind the fireplace, which until the late nineteenth century, contained a stone newel stair and a well. The access to the well was apparently halfway up the staircase, which was demolished some time after 1873, when it was mentioned in the third edition of Hutchins's *History of Dorset*. The well still exists, although boarded over, and there is a strange tale about the removal of the staircase. Apparently the well was believed to be inhabited by a friendly sprite but the occupants of the house at the time were not happy with encountering this being when going upstairs to bed, so the staircase was demolished and the well covered over.

A close second to the Hall is the beautiful Great Chamber on the first floor, with its pretty oriel window and lovely barrel ceiling. In the 1920's, the then owner, Lady Victoria Herbert, chose the leafy Chinese-style William Morris wallpaper in this room, which, although anachronistic, works surprisingly well, enhancing rather than detracting from the atmosphere of the room. The oriel window is offset in the end wall, allowing a fireplace to its left, rather than being centrally situated under the arch of the barrel ceiling as one might expect.

The south front looks out over a beautiful lawn bounded by trees, part of which has been used as a bowling green by the village for many years. The garden is most attractive with lawns, borders, walled areas, a stream running through it and a delightful little courtyard between the north-west and south wings, overlooked by the magnificent tall window of the Great Hall.

There were originally two manors in Purse Caundle, one belonging to the nunnery at Shaftesbury and the other to the monastery of Athelney in Somerset. The Domesday Book only mentions Athelney by name, but says that there were two manors or parts of manors in Candel and that Alured held about 38 acres of land here. By the thirteenth century one John Aleyn appears as a landholder. He held land directly from the king 'for the service of caring for any sick or injured hounds at the king's expense when he hunts in Blackmore'. (Local legend has it that the hounds can sometimes be heard baying on the bowling green on Midsummers Eve and Christmas Eve.) His land also included some from Athelney (probably Alured's land) plus some from Shaftesbury.

In March 1292 an inquiry was held to establish the age of John's heir, his son Roger. The recollections of witnesses who had been at the

PURSE CAUNDLE MANOR. The east front and main entrance.

child's christening create a fascinating vignette of a family event in the thirteenth century. The witnesses were the rector, Roger Cosyn, who was also the child's uncle, Roger de Wyveleshulle, who was standing proxy for an absent godparent, and eleven parishioners who had been at the event. It was established that the child had been born and baptised on 9th December 1269 and that the rector had recorded it in his missal and the witnesses had all seen it. He also recorded that one of the witnesses at the christening had broken his leg and another her arm due to a fall from a horse because of the bad state of the roads, so perhaps that accounted for the absent godparent.

In 1349 Roger's son John died, possibly a victim of the Black Death, and left two small daughters, Elyanora and Johanna as his heirs. In about 1429 Richard Lang, or Long, bought Purse Caundle and 575 acres of land for 100 marks of silver from Alianor Peytevyn, a widow, who was probably John's granddaughter. In 1454 the name John Lange of Purse Caundel appears on a deed. John was almost certainly Richard Lang's heir and it was he and his son William who were mainly responsible for building the oldest part of the present house on the site of an earlier building. There is no record of the date of John's death but when William died in 1525, he owned a large estate. The impressive canopied tomb, which he built in the church testifies to his wealth and consequence. His heir was his only daughter, Elizabeth, who was four years old when he died and only outlived him by another five years. The property was then inherited by her aunt, William's sister, and three cousins, who were the children of his other sisters.

One cousin, Richard Hannam, the son of William's sister Margaret, who was married to William Hannam of Horsington, lived at Purse Caundle, his eldest son, William followed him and gradually all the parts of the estate were acquired by the Hannams. William died in 1576 and was buried

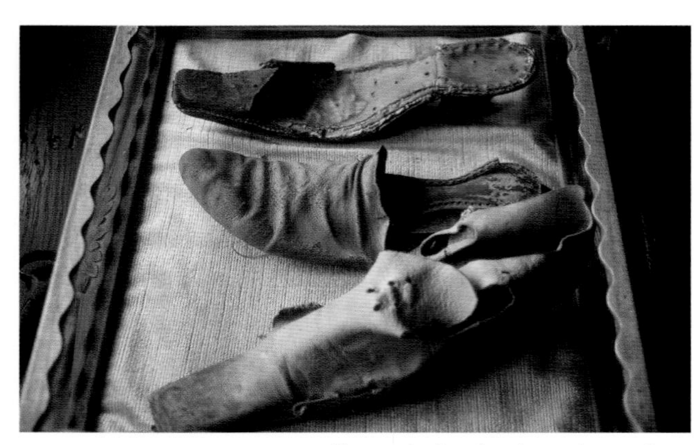

PURSE CAUNDLE MANOR. Shoes dating back to the early seventeenth century found during roof repairs.

at Purse Caundle. The Milborne register commemorates him as a good landlord, a friend of the poor and a benefactor of the parish. When his son James died in 1597 he was similarly praised and the register notes that he gave forty shillings worth of corn to the poor of Milborne Port 'in a time of dearth'.

James had married Mary Watkins, the wealthy heiress of Holwell, and their heir was also named James. Both father and son continued to add to the manor, bringing it more or less to its present form, which survived with only minor changes for the following 350 years. The Hannams were Catholics and Royalist supporters in the Civil War, which led them into severe financial difficulties. In 1640 James sold two manors near Weymouth to his cousin, Thomas Hannam of Wimborne, and granted him a twenty-one year lease of Holwell to pay his debts. At about this time he also sold him Purse Caundle. In 1645 the Hannam estates were confiscated by Cromwell's Commissioners and Purse Caundle was sold to John Hoskins of Beaminster.

John had no children and the property was left to his nephew, also John Hoskins, who was married to Mary Seymer of Hanford. John died in 1714 with no heirs and after his wife's death it was inherited by his nieces, daughters of his younger brother Peter. It was John who appropriated William Long's canopied tomb in the church. The original stone effigies were possibly destroyed during the Commonwealth and the tomb has been lowered to accommodate the Hoskins tomb, with its black marble slab and fulsome epitaph.

At the beginning of the nineteenth century, one of the descendants of the Hoskins family sold the property to a London merchant, who bequeathed it to a relative, Colonel Henry Huddlestone of the East India Company. He died at Purse Caundle in 1858 but the Huddleston family remained in possession until the beginning of the twentieth century, when it was sold to Mr. Merthyr Guest, of the Welsh steel-making family and brother of Lord Wimborne of Canford. In 1922 Lady Victoria Herbert bought the house from Lady Theodora Guest and lived there until her death in 1957.

Lady Victoria did a great deal of work on the house. She restored the entrance porch and added the small porch in the south-west corner of the little court. She was also responsible for restoring the minstrels' gallery, installing the seventeenth century panelling and replacing an existing window in the Hall with the present large five light window.

After Lady Victoria's death in 1957, The Honourable Mrs. Seymour Barnes, sister of Lord Methuen, bought the house and in 1959, a large part of the roof collapsed. This entailed major repairs, during the course of which three old shoes were found, including a slipper from the late sixteenth century and two high-heeled shoes probably dating from the time of Charles II. These are perhaps linked to an ancient tradition of concealing old shoes in the fabric of a house during building work to ward off evil or ensure good luck. These were traditionally concealed near openings into the house, doorways, windows or chimneys. There was also a wooden tool, unidentified, but thought to be connected with weaving. All these are still preserved at the house. After the repair work, which was partly funded by a government grant, the house was opened to the public.

From 1965 to 1967 the house was briefly owned by a Mr. Boxall, who then sold it to Mr. Ralph Winckelmann, who continued to open the house to the public but never lived there permanently himself. In 1984 he sold it to Mr. and Mrs. Michael de Pelet and it became their family home.

Quarleston Farm

QUARLESTON FARM lies in the Winterborne Valley almost midway between the tiny hamlet of Winterborne Clenston and the village of Winterborne Stickland. Quarleston was once a hamlet in its own right, but is now part of Winterborne Stickland. The house is one of the oldest in Dorset and was already well established by 1437, when a hall, bakehouse and kitchen were recorded as part of a dwelling there. The earliest part of the house now forms most of the western half of the north wing, although this was extended further to the west in the nineteenth century. In the sixteenth century the original rectangular building was extended eastwards, almost doubling its size and finally, in the next century, a further wing was added running north/south and creating the L shaped house that exists today. The beautiful timbered hall roof survives and is once again visible after the restoration of the house at the end of the 1980s. During the course of the work, two carved oak screens from the hall, parts of which dated back to the twelfth century, were temporarily removed for safety and, tragically, then stolen.

The house is built of banded flint and stone with tiled roofs with stone slate verges. The contrast between the superbly worked flint and the alternating bands of ashlar of the walls creates a lovely blend of texture and colour. Sadly, few of the

QUARLESTON FARM. The farm is now divided into two dwellings. The oldest part, which dates back to the early fifteenth century, is on the right.

original windows survive, although their replacements blend well. Internally few original features remain and during the restoration in the 1980s the house was made into two separate dwellings by closing off the north and east wings. This formalised an arrangement which had probably existed for much of the house's life. The first record of dual occupation appeared in the fifteenth century.

The name Quarleston seems to derive from the name of its owners in medieval times. In 1176 it was held by Osbert de Quarrel and was inherited by several generations of Quarrels, until in 1430 it passed to Alice, widow of Robert Quarrel, who had remarried a William Tybenham. In 1437 Christian Bedenhale, the daughter of Alice and Robert, and her husband were living there and made an agreement to lease out part of the manor, keeping the hall, bakehouse and kitchen for their own exclusive use. Christian was probably Robert's heiress, as there were no male heirs to carry on the Quarrel line. The inheritance seems to have continued in the female line, as the house became the property of the Chaldecotts. William Chaldecott of Kimmeridge, who died in 1483, had a son, George, in about 1476, who is referred to as 'of Quarleston'. William's wife is not named but she was possibly John and Christian's heiress, thus bringing Quarrelston to the Chaldecotts.

George married twice. Nothing is known about his first wife but his second was Edith of Bryanston, who had borne him a child before they were married. This child, William, was George's only child and must have been legitimized after his parents married, to become his father's heir. In 1543, George extended his property by buying East Whiteway and Swalland and after he died in 1558, left the estate to William who granted Swalland to his mother for life.

William married Margaret Rogers of Bryanston and they had three daughters. The eldest, Ann, married Robert Bingham of Bingham's Melcombe and inherited Quarleston. In 1587 it passed to their son, Richard, who died in 1656. There is a strange anomaly in the parish register regarding his death. It would seem that he died on the 9th August but was not buried until the 3rd of October. We can only hope that this was a clerical error! Their son, Colonel John Bingham, inherited the manor and when he died in 1675 it went to his daughter, Grace Skinner of Dewlish. The inheritance then passed through three more generations of daughters, all called Grace. The third Grace married Sir George Jackson, who sold the manor and farm to William Portman.

In 1849, the then Lord Portman exchanged Quarleston for some other land with the Earl of Portarlington and it became part of the Milton Abbas estate, which was later bought by Baron Hambro of the banking family. It remained a Hambro property until 1932 when the estate was broken up and sold as separate lots. Quarleston Farm, as it was then called, was bought by Mr. and Mrs. Fortescue.

In 1945 Mr. and Mrs. Upshall took the tenancy and lived there until 1976. Their daughter, Mrs. Steele, still lives in the village and remembers that when she was a child all the water for the house was pumped up from the well in the courtyard, which is still there, and was said to be the best water in the valley. Mr. Upshall remembered the house being used as two farm cottages in the 1920s. After her marriage Mrs. Steele and her husband lived in one half of the house, whilst the other was occupied by her parents. In 1974 Mr. Upshall was able to buy the farm from Mrs. Fortescue.

In 1976 he sold it to two American ladies, mother and daughter. Sadly they allowed the house to deteriorate, also removing many ancient fittings and shipping them to America for sale. They died quite close together and in 1986 the farm was sold for development.

The development included a small group of new houses to the rear of the manor house built around a courtyard. The house itself was sensitively restored under the supervision of English Heritage and was completed in 1991 as two dwellings. It is now the centrepiece of an attractive small development – a new lease of life for a lovely ancient house that had come very close to being lost to future generations.

Radipole Old Manor

THE OLD MANOR, with the church and a few houses and cottages, has managed to remain a little oasis of country on the edge of, and almost surrounded by, the Weymouth conurbation. It is situated on Radipole Lane, which runs from the Dorchester road through Radipole village to Chickerell. A map of 1839 shows the section of the lane leading from the manor to Dorchester Road as a footpath. The present road runs alongside the end wall of the house, but the lovely east front is largely hidden by shrubs and hedges. The little church of St Anne is behind the western side of the house and huddled so close to it that anyone standing between them could almost stretch out their arms and touch both. Behind the church the graveyard reaches right

RADIPOLE OLD MANOR. The front of the house remodelled by Richard Watkins in 1580.

RADIPOLE OLD MANOR. A line and wash drawing of the house in 1790 by Samuel Hieronymous Grimm.

up to the windows of the house. This is perhaps not surprising, because the manor originally belonged to Cerne Abbey and it is believed that the oldest part of the house may have started life as a priest's house or an abbey grange.

At the Radipole end of the lane, perhaps a couple of hundred yards from the manor and easily visible from it, is the northern end of The Backwater. This was a tidal reach behind Weymouth Harbour and until almost the beginning of the twentieth century small boats could sail to Radipole and dock at the jetty quite close to the manor. It is now a bird sanctuary, no longer tidal, and although now officially called Radipole Lake is still known locally as The Backwater.

The house is of two storeys plus attics, built of stone with slate roofs edged with two rows of stone tiles. The east front is L shaped with a porch the full height of the house in the angle of the L. Its three gables, two on the main front and a third on the porch, are crowned with baluster style finials. The main front is most attractive with its two sets of mullioned windows rising in diminishing widths of five, four and three lights and simple pedimented doorway in the porch bearing the initials R.W. for Richard Watkins, who was responsible for remodelling the house around 1580. The oldest part of the house ran east-west with a service wing to the north. On the eastern side this forms the projection of the L shape containing the porch and opposite, on the western side, is a projecting staircase turret, rising the full height of the house and containing a stone circular newel staircase. On the south side of the turret is a small doorway, which has been converted to form a window.

The name Radipole, recorded in the Domesday Book as Retpole, derives from the Saxon for a tidal or reedy pool, and reed beds still grow in The Backwater in abundance. From Domesday until the Dissolution, Radipole belonged to the powerful Benedictine monastery of Cerne. They held half of it in demesne, farming it directly, and leased out the rest.

In 1540 Henry VIII granted the manor, with a house and the advowson of the church, (which gave the tenant the right to nominate its incumbent) to Humphrey Watkins of Holwell for an annual rent of 21s.4d. In 1560 Elizabeth I granted him the property for life with the right to leave it to his heirs. His son Richard was responsible for altering and extending the original house and his initials

RADIPOLE OLD MANOR. The back of the manor house with the stair tower only a few paces from the church.

appear over the porch doorway. When Richard died in 1589, his daughter Mary inherited the estate. She was married to James Hannam of Purse Caundle, a member of the Hannam family who later owned Deans Court in Wimborne.

James and Mary had several children and the estate eventually became the property of their son James. During the Civil War James and his son Thomas were supporters of the king and their estates were confiscated in 1645. In his Hannam family tree Hutchins says, rather abruptly after Thomas, 'this branch soon after extinct'. It seems the estate went to the Wimborne branch of the family and was later sold. Certainly by 1663, it was the property of Sir Wadham Wyndham, who left it to his son John Wyndham of St James's, Middlesex.

The Wyndham family remained the owners until 1803 when it was sold to Edmund Henning of Poxwell. The Wyndhams had always let it as a tenant farm, a tenure that continued through subsequent owners until well into the twentieth century. In 1829 Edmund Henning sold the estate to his brother John and ten years later the house and part of the land was sold to William Eliot of Weymouth. He built himself a large new house further north than the old manor, which remained a farmhouse and continued gradually to deteriorate.

In 1929 the house was sold by Mr. E. B. Thresher 'on the retirement of his tenant, Mr. Powell, after many years occupation'. Ten years later, the house underwent careful restoration by the then owners, Captain and Mrs. Cemmington Leigh. The work was overseen by the well-known local architect, Mr. E. Walmsley Lewis. Mr. Lewis had a particular interest in historic houses and paid meticulous attention to authenticity in restoration work. A later project of his, in the 1960s, was the restoration of the Tudor House in Trinity Street near Weymouth Quay. Unfortunately the collection of his papers and plans held by the Record Office in Dorchester does not contain those relating to Radipole Old Manor.

The Cemmington Leighs remained at Radipole until some time in the late 1960s and since then the house has changed hands more than once. It still remains a private house.

Rempstone Hall

THE ROAD FROM Corfe to Studland, meandering through the Purbeck Hills, provides delightful glimpses of Poole Harbour and Bournemouth Bay. Along this road, Rempstone Hall sits well back in a sheltered, sunny position within a short distance of a Bronze Age stone circle and the remains of a Roman villa. The house is built of stone and brick with the oldest part at the western end. Though much altered, this was probably part of a small sixteenth or seventeenth century house whose two bay windows on the south front were added later.

According to Hutchins, on Treswell's detailed map of the Purbecks in 1586, a house, immediately under Kingswood, said to belong to George Uvedale of Sherborne, seems intended to be Rempstone. Hutchins mentions that the Rempstons were lords of the manor in the reign of Henry IV (1399-1413), though the source of this statement cannot be found. In the fifteenth century the Rempstons were recorded as living at Godlingston Manor. Subsequently the manor belonged to the Millers of Corfe Castle. In 1585 their heiress, Margery, married George Uvedale of Sherborne. It later came to the Trenchards of Wolveton and was then sold to the Framptons of Buckland, who lived there for several years after their own mansion was burnt down.

REMPSTONE HALL. The hall in the 1800s.

The seventeenth century part of the house is of stone, possibly taken from the ruins of Corfe Castle. Half of a Norman font is set into the south wall of the dining room with fragments of carved stone in the other walls. The looting of the ruined castle was considered fair game after the Civil War, so it is just feasible that the font also came from there. The house has undergone many structural changes, but probably the most elegant interior renovation was in the mid eighteenth century when Lady Caroline, wife of John Hales Calcraft, added a large drawing room with two bedrooms on the floor above.

In 1682, William Rose, rector of Swanage from 1667, bought Rempstone. He had already purchased Carents Court from Onesiphorus Bond in 1676 and the 'New House' from the marbler Anthony Serrell in 1681. He died in 1690 leaving Rempstone to his son William who, in order to cover his father's debts, passed it to his brother Thomas who took up residence there. Thomas died in 1709 and left Rempstone to his son William, who sold it to a John Gannet of Blandford. William had no legal right to sell the property and it was not until 1748 that his daughter and heiress recovered it, though nine years later, in 1757 she sold it to John Calcraft.

John Calcraft's family came from Grantham. It seems that he was the illegitimate son of his mother, Christian, and Henry Fox, 1st Lord Holland. Certainly Henry Fox played a strong part in furthering John's career. By the time of the Jacobite Rebellion in 1745 he was already Deputy-

Paymaster in the Duke of Cumberland's army, and saw service at the Battle of Culloden when Bonnie Prince Charlie was defeated. His next position was Clerk at the War Office when Henry Fox became Secretary at War.

During his twenties, John Calcraft began to amass a large fortune. He acted as agent to 57 regiments, with responsibility for their finances, as well as acting as a private banker for M.P.s and aristocrats, all under the guidance of Henry Fox. In 1760 he bought Ingress Abbey in Kent, which became his principal residence, and Leeds Abbey, adding them to his already considerable estates around the country. In 1763, Calcraft deserted Fox, linking up with William Pitt, Lord Chatham, consequently being dismissed from his lucrative position. By now he was very wealthy. Elected M.P. for Calne in 1766, he soon turned his sights upon the Purbecks, and Wareham in particular. The town was then what was known as a Rotten Borough, sending two members to Parliament, despite the small number of residents allowed to vote.

Calcraft regarded Wareham as a vehicle for achieving his main ambition – an English peerage. He was renowned for his ruthlessness, and his energy as well as for his egotism. Yet no one could deny his aptitude for business. In 1771 he bought the manor of Worth Matravers, including Winspit, with land stretching to three islands in Poole Harbour. By 1767, he had bought the manor of Wareham from Thomas Erle Drax as well as all the properties in the borough belonging to John Pitt of Encombe. He then granted freeholds to tenants who lived on his other estates in various parts of the country. At the General Elections these tenants travelled to Wareham at Mr. Calcraft's expense, as did the clay miners and quarrymen from the Purbecks. They were brought to Wareham by waggon to vote for Mr. Calcraft's chosen candidates, usually his son John and another friend or acquaintance eager to enter Parliament. In these times Rempstone was only used for occasional accommodation when John Calcraft was on business in the area. Its days of elegant living were yet to come.

Top The banker and politician John Calcraft, who bought Rempstone Hall in 1757.

Above Calcraft's mistresses included the actress Georgiana Bellamy.

John Calcraft died suddenly in 1772, leaving behind a number of children by two mistresses, both actresses, Elizabeth Bride and Georgiana Bellamy. He had no children by his long-suffering wife, Bridget.

John, the son of John Calcraft and Elizabeth Bride, became MP for Wareham from 1786 to 1790

John Calcraft the younger, MP for Wareham, worked hard to improve the working and living conditions of the poorer classes but died in 1831, one year before the Reform Bill became law.

and again from 1800 until 1831. He married Elizabeth Hales and made Rempstone his home. He dedicated his political life to improving the living standards of the poor, from prison reform, to abolition of the slave trade, to improving the lives of farm labourers. He also played a central part in the formation of the Corps of Yeoman Volunteers trained to defend the coastal regions against an invasion by Napoleon. He became Clerk of the Ordnance in 1806 and, by crossing the floor of the House and becoming a Tory, he was appointed Paymaster General in 1829. He and his wife, Elizabeth, restored Rempstone Hall and lived there for much of the time.

Living through a time of great poverty in Purbeck, Calcraft distinguished himself by his successful attempts to repeal the salt tax. The general unrest and uprising among labourers and the middle classes with the 'Captain Swing Riots' in 1830, led to the introduction of the Reform Bill of 1831, supported by John Calcraft. Under this Bill, a greater proportion of people would be allowed to vote and a fairer system of Parliamentary representation would bring to an end the status of the Rotten Boroughs. The Bill was passed in the Commons but defeated in the House of Lords. Calcraft was devastated. He suffered from depression and tragically committed suicide in September 1831. Only a year later the Bill became law and in due course Wareham lost one of its two seats in Parliament.

Following his father's tradition, John Hales Calcraft stood for Parliament for Wareham against John Erle Drax. From 1830 they fought in subsequent elections, winning and losing on each side until 1857, when Calcraft narrowly won by three votes, incurring the wrath of the unpopular and eccentric Mr. Drax.

John Hales Calcraft had married Lady Caroline Katherine Montagu, daughter of the Duke of Manchester. Rempstone Hall became the family home, with Lady Caroline adding a large, elegant drawing room to the house, and two bedrooms on the upper floor. Her husband rebuilt Wareham Town Hall in 1869 and was Sheriff in 1867.

Their son, Lieutenant John Hales Montague Calcraft, R.N. continued the struggle to oust Drax from the elections by arguing that Charborough Park, Drax's home, was outside the boundary of the constituency. He succeeded in having Drax struck off the list of candidates, but his was a short-lived victory as he died after winning the Wareham seat in November 1868, thus allowing Drax to be re-elected.

From the late eighteenth century onwards much of the Calcrafts wealth came from the clay-mining industry on Rempstone Heath. Purbeck stone from the local quarries at Worth Matravers had been carried across the heath from medieval times to ships in Poole Harbour, but during the eighteenth century the increased use of tobacco had led to a greater demand for the mining of pipe clay. The Hydes of Poole paid £30 a year for mining rights and had already made their fortune, but greater fortunes were around the corner. In 1759 Josiah Wedgwood set up his pottery near Stoke-on-Trent. His customers were looking for delicate china such as in Chinese porcelain. Wedgwood found the perfect clay in Dorset and Cornwall. By 1771

REMPSTONE HALL. A view of the front.

Thomas Hyde was negotiating with John Calcraft to dig 1,400 tons of clay each year for Josiah Wedgwood. The industry grew from strength to strength and the scars of clay mines appeared on the heath. Railways connected the pits to the Harbour, remains of whose tracks can still be seen on parts of the heath today. They ceased working in 1937 and were removed by the army two years later at the beginning of the Second World War. English China Clays (ECC) now manages the clay mines. In 1974 oil was discovered on the heath at Wytch Farm and Ower. Despite initial fears for the protection of the flora and fauna the area is now a Site of Special Scientific Interest. With the wild life protected, it gives endless pleasure to walkers and bird watchers.

The last Calcraft in the male line was William, who died a bachelor in 1901. Rempstone then passed to his eldest sister, Katherine, who married the Reverend C.D. Marston. Their son Guy died, unmarried, in 1927. The property then passed to Major Dudley Claud Douglas Ryder, known as Jack Ryder, grandson of William's second sister Georgiana-Emily Calcraft who had married Dudley Henry Ryder.

Major Ryder was well known in Dorset. He was Lord of the Manor of Wareham and Worth Matravers for fifty-eight years and presided over the Wareham Court Leet. He died in 1986 and now his twin sons, James and Ben, run the estate with James continuing the family tradition as Lord of the Manor.

Round Chimneys Farm

ROUND CHIMNEYS FARM, sometimes called Newland, Newton Montacute, or Blackmore Manor, lies one mile north of the church at Glanvilles Wootton. The turning off Stock Hill Lane to Round Chimneys was marked by two ancient oaks known as Gog and Magog, survivors, it is said, of the old Forest of Blackmore. Alas, only one now remains. The view of Round Chimneys is almost hidden by farm buildings, but the famous chimneys can still be seen outlined against the sky.

The first record of this manor comes in 1232, when a fair was granted to Blakemore. Thereafter Simon Monteacute and his descendants rented woods here from the king. In 1400 the Earl of Sarum held the land, as did his descendants, including the unfortunate Margaret, Countess of Salisbury, who in 1541, aged sixty-eight, was beheaded on account of her son, Cardinal Pole, challenging the right of Henry VIII to call himself head of the church in England.

During the reign of Henry VIII, Walter Holewale held the freehold of what was then known as Wotton Glanville, and it is reasonable to assume that he had a dwelling on the site of the present house. After his death the freehold was bought by John Clavell of Barnston in 1573. He built the present three-storey house or maybe rebuilt an existing house. The date 159- can be seen on one of the chimneys. On another chimney there is a clear mason's mark. The third storey had dormer windows with each gable supporting a chimneystack. The third floor was removed in the early nineteenth century and the chimneys were repositioned onto the stacks on the lower storey. The south front also underwent changes. The original doorway was moved to the left, the windows altered, though still transomed, and the north side was completely changed. The central chimney on the main wing is the original, but one was replaced in the 1800s and two others had to be replaced in the 1980s.

ROUND CHIMNEYS FARM. A drawing from the 1765 edition of John Hutchins *History of Dorset* showing the house before the roof was lowered.

Inside, the original layout is difficult to follow. A long thick wall divides the house into two equal parts with an equally thick cross wall defining the room in the south east corner. Hutchins' illustration shows two large mezzanine windows on the north-west side which probably lit a grand staircase. Only the wide decorated arches remain, giving us some idea of the size of the staircase. The service area on the north side appears older than the rest of the house and was, perhaps, part of an earlier house. Above, sections of the original attics are still visible. With so many alterations through the centuries it is amazing to find so much ancient fabric still in situ. The complexity of the design makes it difficult to

John Clavell, highwayman and poet, sold the house to John Churchill in 1630.

Sir Winston Churchill, father of the Ist Duke of Marlborough.

unravel, but it is certainly a remarkable house.

After the death of John Clavell in 1609, his son John and wife Frances lived at the house. They had six children, one of whom was John, born in 1601. He lived at home until he was eighteen and then moved to London to start his colourful career. He went to Brasenose College, Oxford in 1619, but was caught stealing the college plate and left university without a degree. Presumably he was imprisoned for the theft, but was pardoned in 1623 when his father died intestate and in debt. With no money at all, John went to London and from 1621 became involved with rogues and moneylenders. The goldsmith and moneylender, William Banks, had a hold over Clavell, though why this was so has never been established. Banks was well known in the city for his shady deals. Clavell, still penniless in 1624, took to the road as the leader of a band of highwaymen, calling himself 'A Knight of the Road'. In December 1625 he was arrested and sentenced to death, despite his pleas that he had never harmed his victims. In desperation he appealed to the King for mercy thus:

> 'I that have robb'd so oft am now bid stand,
> Death and the Law assault me, and demand
> My life, and meanes, I never us'd men so,
> But having ta'ne their money, let them goe;
> Yet must I dye? And is there no reliefe?
> The King of Kings took mercy on a thiefe,
> So may my gracious King in mercie save me,
> Although grim Death, and Law doe thus out-brave me.'

Though this poem may have helped his situation, by coincidence it came at the time of the coronation of Charles I, when a general amnesty was declared. Clavell, however, stayed in prison for a further two years, during which time he wrote *A Recantation of an Ill Led Life* which brought him fame, and in which he described the tricks of the highwayman's trade. The first edition soon sold out, and two more followed, giving him much needed financial security. Apparently Charles I and his queen were rather amused by his writings. There then followed

ROUND CHIMNEYS FARM. The farm was rebuilt by John Clavell of Barnston in the late 1500s.

a five act play, *The Sodder'd Citizen*.

Upon his release, Clavell found he had lost favour with his uncle, Sir William Clavell of Smedmore, whose heir he had hoped to be. Sir William arranged for him to go to Ireland to assist his lawyers in reclaiming some property in Munster. Once in Ireland, Clavell's life totally changed. He was soon a popular member of society, marrying the nine-year-old Isabel Markham in 1635. Her father, a rich Dublin vintner, was a friend of Loftus the Lord Chancellor, who approved of Clavell and of his marriage and made him a barrister, adding to his wealth.

For many years Clavell kept a *Notebook* into which he wrote poems and plays as well as details of his arguments with his uncle, who never totally trusted him. Not only was Clavell a lawyer, but he also practised medicine, though where he studied for this is not known. His marriage was, by all accounts, a happy one, though his wife was only seventeen years old when he died in 1643, just one year before the death of his uncle.

After his father's death in 1623, Clavell had made several desperate attempts to sell the family house, but not until 1630 was it finally sold to a lawyer called John Churchill. The date 1632 is written over the door, most likely signifying some alterations to the house. John Churchill is recorded as living here in 1641 but in the following year he leased Minterne from Winchester College and was known as John Churchill of Wootton Glanville and Minterne. In the Civil War he was a loyal supporter of the king, and his lands were seized by Parliament.

John's son, Winston Churchill, was born in London in 1620. A staunch Royalist like his father, he fought at the sieges of Taunton and Bristol. He was fined £4,446 by Parliament, which was a huge sum of money in those days, and in 1643, despite their different loyalties, he married Elizabeth Drake, a Devonian, whose family supported the Roundhead cause, and whose house at Ashe was almost destroyed by Royalist troops. Her mother later received some compensation for the attack, enabling her to repair the house well enough to accommodate Winston and his wife, and their son John was born there in 1650. One of twelve children, John was later to become the 1st Duke of Marlborough, the great military leader whose victory at the Battle of Blenheim in 1704 led to him being acknowledged as England's greatest general. His home was to be the magnificent Blenheim Palace at Woodstock, where, in 1874, was born perhaps the most famous of all Englishmen, Sir Winston Churchill. The Churchill links with Dorset span many centuries.

In 1661 Winston Churchill was elected MP for Weymouth and became a Fellow of the Royal Society. He was knighted in 1663 and in 1675 wrote *Divi Britannica*, or *Remarks on the Lives of all the Kings of this Isle*. He died in 1688 and was buried at St Martins-in-the-Fields. Before he died he sold Newton Montacute, as Round Chimneys was then called, to Dr. Simon Wellman of Poundisford, near Taunton. It remained in the Wellman family for 154 years, during which time the north front was taken down and the remainder renovated. The grounds were laid out into formal gardens with fishponds. Hutchins considered the house to have been one of the best planned and most comfortable of Elizabethan houses. It was known as Golden Grove until the early 1800s and consisted of 800 acres.

In 1839 the estate was sold to Mr. J.C. Dale and became a farmhouse. It remained in this family until 1906, when it was purchased by Mr. Thomas Holford of Castle Hill. The family of the present owner, Mr. B.E.J. Rich, have lived and farmed here for over forty years, and are caring custodians of a house which, although in need of constant repair, is filled with the atmosphere of past centuries and remains an unsung memorial to the Dorset origins of the Churchill family.

St Giles House

ST GILES HOUSE lies in Wimborne St Giles on the southern edge of Cranborne Chase. The River Allen rises nearby, and in old documents the village was known as Upwimborne, along with Upwimborne Malmayne and Up Plecy. The earliest record of a family dates to the thirteenth century, when a Malmayne daughter married Robert de Plecy, who died in 1301. His great grandson, Sir Nicholas de Plecy, died without a male heir and his daughter, Joan, married Sir John Hamely, who died in 1398. Sir John, by his second marriage, had a daughter, Egidia, who married Robert Ashley from Wiltshire and their descendants have continued to live at Wimborne St Giles to this day.

The memorial to Anthony Ashley Cooper, 1st Earl of Shaftesbury, in Wimborne St Giles. Beneath his bust are his three wives, Margaret (died 1649), daughter of Lord Coventry who he married when eighteen, Frances Cecil (died 1654), who bore his heir, and Margaret Spencer, daughter of the Earl of Southampton.

In the sixteenth century two of the Ashleys, father and son, were knighted. The second Sir Anthony, who was briefly Elizabeth I's Secretary for War, is worthy of a culinary footnote in that he is thought to have introduced the first cabbage into England from Holland. He also built the lovely range of brick almhouses adjoining Wimborne St Giles church. He died in 1628, and at the foot of his canopied tomb inside the church is the kneeling figure of his only daughter Anne, who married Sir John Cooper of Rockborne and was the mother of Sir Anthony Ashley-Cooper, later the first Earl of Shaftesbury.

Anthony Ashley-Cooper was born in 1621, and was only ten when his father died. Much of his inheritance was squandered due to the incompetence of his trustees, but the uncertainties of childhood shaped the man. 'Sagacious, bold and turbulent of wit,' he grew into one of the most influential statesmen of the late seventeenth century.

First signs of his strength of purpose became apparent in the Civil War. Initially a Royalist and Governor of Weymouth and Portland, in 1644 he changed sides, leading the Parliamentary attack on Wareham and the much more ferocious onslaught on Sir John Strangways house at Abbotsbury. Here he showed a crueller side of his character, later admitting that he not only intended to refuse quarter to the garrison but did his best to burn them alive. Perhaps understandably, Sturminster Newton and Shaftesbury offered no resistance to his forces. Ten years later he changed sides again, resigning from Cromwell's Council of State in protest against his dictatorial policies.

Four years later he played a key part in the Restoration of Charles II and was duly rewarded by being made Baron Ashley and appointed Chancellor

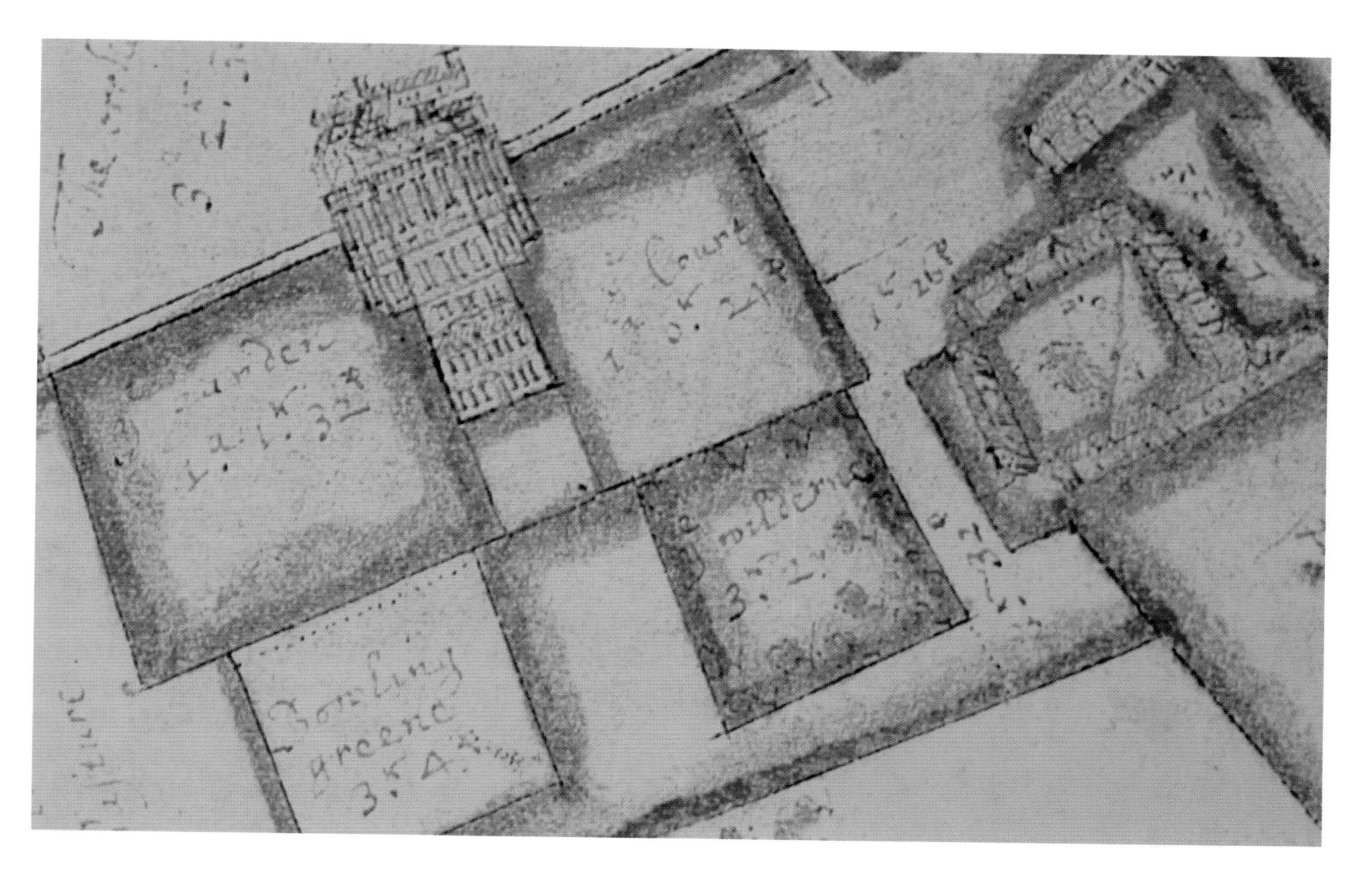

ST GILES HOUSE. A view of the house on an estate map of 1672. Note the 'Bowling greene' on the left. The range of buildings on the right includes the early seventeenth century Riding House.

of the Exchequer. In 1672 he became Lord Chancellor and was created Earl of Shaftesbury. Aligning himself with the Duke of Monmouth against the succession of the Catholic Duke of York, he fell from favour. He was twice imprisoned in the Tower. In 1681 he faced a charge of high treason. Although the charges were later dismissed, he fled to the Netherlands where he died two years later.

The bare facts do not do justice to his achievements, or his failings. He was unscrupulous, bore grudges, and made enemies more readily than friends. But as the founder of the Whig party and a brilliant parliamentary debater he was also perhaps the first truly modern politician. He was anti monopolies, pro immigration, in favour of religious toleration and the supremacy of parliament ('the power of the king does not extend further than the laws parliament determine'). He had the tastes of a country gentleman, dabbled in alchemy and horoscopes, and had three wives, two of whom predeceased him, and to all of whom he was devoted.

He also built the nucleus of St Giles House. In his diary of March 19th 1650, he wrote, 'I laid the first stone of my house at St Giles's.' He had been born in Wimborne St Giles, and it is quite probable that the previous house was incorporated into the new one. St Giles House is architecturally amongst the most complex of all Dorset's great houses. Successive generations of Ashley-Cooper have both added to it, and subtracted from it. Though a plan of the original house cannot as yet be clearly defined, thick walls of red brickwork can be seen in the lower storey of the present central range. In a cellar are the remains of a moulded sixteenth century stone doorway. Other relics include fragments of oak panelling, and a fifteenth century carved alabaster panel with a shield of arms

ST GILES HOUSE. The house in the eighteenth century, showing the battlements removed in Victorian times.

showing Ashley quartering Talbot: John Ashley married Edith Talbot in the reign of Richard II. There is also a roundel of stained glass showing the same arms with the inscription 'scutum Henrici Asheley,' as well as three square pillars of rusticated ashlar, probably early seventeenth century.

The earliest drawing of the first Earl's house is a small bird's-eye view from the north-east on an estate map dated 1659. A branch of the River Allen is shown flowing between two groups of buildings, and to the south can be seen a small structure, probably a mill. On a later map of 1672 the mill had disappeared.

Although the name of the architect employed by the earl is not known, the influence of Inigo Jones is obvious in the Renaissance north and east fronts with their Classical facades. The original plan was for a square courtyard to which was added two large ground floor rooms with rooms above. Battlements once edged the parapet of the complete house, but these were removed in the nineteenth century. The east front, with its seven bays, remains much the same today. In the drawing of 1659, the long range on the east bank of the stream extends north to south beyond the ends of the 1651 building, and the south part of this range still stands.

The 3rd Earl was born in 1671 in his grandfather's London house, and it was he who played a crucial role in his upbringing. His own father, the 2nd Earl, was, according to one report, 'of 'feeble constit-ution and understanding.' No two men could have been less alike in temperament than the 1st Earl and his grandson. The latter's education was entrusted to the philosopher John Locke, who as a young physician had successfully operated on the 1st Earl and ultimately became his advisor and closest friend. The 3rd Earl was quiet and studious, and though he sat in parliament as the Whig M.P. for Poole, ill-health and asthma brought on by London's smoke forced him to abandon politics for literature, and it as a philosopher that he is remembered.

Put simply, he believed that it was the role of philosophy to 'learn what is just in society and beautiful in Nature and the order of the world . . to have a sense of right and wrong.' 'Thus virtue is the good, and vice the ill of every one,' he once wrote. 'Taste,' he argued, 'should be expressed in human conduct no less than in architecture and painting.' He wrote widely, and his collected essays were published in 1711 as *Characteristicks of Men, Manners, Opinions, and Times.*

Although the 3rd Earl made no changes to St Giles House, his interest in the estate never flagged. His letters to his steward and housekeeper ask that they show hospitality to strangers, report all cases of need, and find out which children on the estate show signs of justifying further education at his expense. One architectural legacy that does endure is the two story brick gazebo, reputedly built as a place of contemplation, that stands set back from the B3078 beside the turn to Verwood.

The 3rd Earl was nearly forty when he married. An earlier courtship foundered when his prospective father-in-law rejected him as a suitor for his daughter on the grounds that he was not well enough to sire an heir. In due course, a group of friends arranged his marriage to a Miss Jane Ewer, who he did not meet until their wedding day and who to his surprise proved to be a great beauty. The Earl found himself 'as happy a man now as ever'. A son and heir duly followed. In due course ill-health forced the Earl and his bride abroad, first to Holland [whose tolerance and freedom he admired], then to Italy, where he died in Naples in 1713 'with perfect cheerfulness and the same sweetness of temper he always enjoyed when in the most perfect health.'

The 4th Earl was a devoted admirer of his father, whose *Life* he wrote, and whose principles of good taste he adapted to suit the more fashionable mid-eighteenth century when in due course he began modernizing St Giles House. The great state rooms have all the craftsmanship and brilliance of the period. The dining room is the work of Stephen Wright, a protégé of the Earl of Newcastle. The Tapestry Room owes its name to a set of Brussels tapestries depicting the Triumph of the Gods. Two new west wings were built, and in due course the house filled with fine furniture and paintings. The Earl's first wife was a crucial influence. She was an early admirer of Chippendale and a friend of Handel, a frequent visitor to the house.

The surrounding park also benefited, and was landscaped by the 4th Earl as a tribute to his father's belief in a 'natural' pattern. Richard Pococke, visiting in 1754, described it as follows:

'. . beautifully laid out, in a serpentine river, pieces of water, lawns, etc., and very gracefully adorned with wood. One first comes to an island on which there is a castle, then, near the water, is a gateway with a tower on each side, and passing between two waters there is a fine cascade from the one side to the other, a thatched house, a round pavilion on a mount, Shakespeare's house, in which is a small statue of him and his works in a glass case. There is a pavilion between the waters and both a Chinese and a stone bridge between them.'

ST GILES HOUSE. A two storey brick gazebo used for contemplation by the 3rd Earl of Shaftesbury.

There was also a two room grotto, designed by a Mr Castles of Marylebone, whose walls were lined with shells, fossils, coral and stone. Visitors could warm themselves before the fire in the inner room, or inspect the architectural fragments placed in small compartments round the walls.

After succeeding his brother, the 6th Earl employed Thomas Cundy between 1813-20 on further alterations, including roofing over the inner courtyard to form the Stone Hall and completely modernizing the library, transforming it into a long south-facing Regency room divided by bays of bookshelves. Further changes followed in 1853, when P.C. Hardwick was employed by the 7th Earl to rebuild the kitchens. A year later he added a pair of Italianate towers at the junction of the eighteenth century west wings with the original building.

The 7th Earl of Shaftesbury was born in 1801, his mother Anne was the daughter of the 3rd Duke of Marlborough. He entered parliament in 1826, succeeded to the earldom in 1851 and died in 1885. Tall, handsome, quietly spoken, troubled only by deafness and gout in old age, the 7th Earl was one of the great philanthropists of Victorian Britain.

Writing in his diary aged 25 the earl described himself as 'neither wise, nor good, nor useful.' The

Above and right ST GILES HOUSE. The Library and Large Drawing Room when still furnished and in use by the family. Both photographs are from an article in *Country Life* published in 1943.

impetus for his transformation from landowning earl to social reformer was an 1828 enquiry into mental asylums, whose cruelty and often inhuman conditions awoke his conscience. A visit to the industrial north brought him face to face with the appalling injuries suffered by those working long shifts in mills and factories and the plight of women and children working underground in collieries. To a stunned parliament, he told of how, in darkness and for up to eighteen hours a day, bridled children as young as five dragged trucks of coal through mine shafts on all fours. Thanks to his efforts, an act was passed excluding anyone under thirteen working underground, and in 1847 the first of the Factory Acts limited the working day to a maximum of ten hours. He next championed the Ragged School movement, whose Union he was chairman of for nearly 40 years, and thanks to which 300,000 of the great invisible army of vagabond street children were given a basic education.

The building of model housing in inner cities, the setting up of childrens' refuges, the ill-treatment of apprentice chimney-sweeps and 'shoeblack' boys, the work of the Church Missionary Society, hospital sanitation and the reforms advocated by Florence Nightingale,, the evils of the Chinese opium trade, the building of training ships – few causes escaped his attention.

The public rewards were many, and included the Freedom of the City of London, but the one that gave him most pleasure was the gift of a donkey from the city's costermongers, which saw out its days grazing contentedly in Dorset. The memorial to this great statesman is one of London's most loved icons, Alfred Gilbert's fountain of 'The Angel of Christian Charity' (better known as Eros), which stands at the end of Shaftesbury Avenue in the heart of Piccadilly Circus, and whose arrow points in the direction of Wimborne St Giles.

The 9th Earl inherited the title and estate aged sixteen in 1886. Unlike his father, a Naval captain and earl for less than a year, the 9th Earl was to

A rare photograph of the 7th Earl of Shaftesbury and his wife Minnie at St Giles House.

ST GILES HOUSE. The house from the south east. The two lines of windows on the east front appear on the estate map drawing of 1672.

occupy St Giles House until he was ninety-three, living there through its late-Victorian heyday, the years of plenty that preceded the First World War, and the gradual decline of both the fortunes of the family and those of the house. His grandfather's extravagance and father's death within six months of becoming 8th Earl meant a period of uncertainty, during which the house was occasionally let, and which only ended when he married Lady Constance Grosvenor in 1899.

Grosvenor wealth enabled the earl to embark on a much-needed programme of modernization. The house was reroofed, the plumbing improved, electricity installed. Paintings and tapestries were restored. Trees were planted, new gardens designed. Oddly, for it is his grandfather that history regards as the paternalistic Victorian landlord, the 9th earl did just as much to improve the lives of those who lived and worked on the estate. A village green was laid out. Learning, leisure and prayer were catered for by the building of a village school, a pub – the Bull, and the virtual rebuilding of the church by the architect Ninian Comper following a fire in 1908. Comper also helped the earl build a small chapel in the south-west wing, at least in part to placate Lady Shaftesbury's High Anglicanism.

For a while it seemed that nothing could mar their good fortune. When the Prince and Princess of Wales (later George V and Queen Mary) came to stay in 1907 1,200 partridge fell to the guns. In summer the estate cricket team took to the field once a week on the Green. In winter the Portman Hunt met outside St Giles's House and the Hunt Ball was regularly held in its state rooms. In due course the countess bore a son and heir, Lord Ashley, followed by three daughters and another son. One daughter later married a neighbour, Lord Alington at Crichel, whilst their youngest son, the modest John Ashley-Cooper, went on to become a famous salmon fisherman and author of a series of acclaimed books on angling.

On the outbreak of the First World War many of the estate labourers left the harvest to join their regiments. Part of the house became a hospital for the wounded. Although as a general officer nominally commanding a brigade, the earl was entitled to remain saddled, most of the 20 or so horses in the stables were commandeered. The period between the wars was one of marking time. From 1916 until 1952, an extraordinary 36 years, the earl was Lord-Lieutenant of Dorset. Despite his title and status, he chose to enlist as a humble private in the local Home Guard during the Second World War, junior to his head gamekeeper, Captain Carter. The platoon's sergeant was also his lordship's butler, Mr Curry, who twice a week put out his uniform for meetings in the village hall or on the Green. Occasionally the earl offered the terrace in front of St Giles House as a parade ground when a senior officer came on a tour of inspection. Once again the earl and countess moved into a flat within the house, which now echoed to the blue-blooded shrieks of the 60 or so girls of Miss Faunt's Academy, a Parent National Education School, evacuated to Wimborne St Giles from London. Along with the girls came their teachers and matrons, who in reality were their governesses and nannies (amongst the pupils were the daughters of Lord Mountbatten).

The immediate post-war years were difficult times for large country houses. In a little notebook kept by the 9th Earl, he wrote, 'Domestic servants are practically unobtainable. Girls nowadays will not have anything to say to domestic service and footmen no longer exist – with the result that these large houses are no longer a practical proposition to live in.'

Within two years tragedy struck. The 9th Earl's heir Lord Ashley had already shocked London society by marrying the chorus girl Sylvia Hawkes, who later went on to marry a second English peer before sailing across the Atlantic and marrying first Douglas Fairbanks Sr and finally Clark Gable. In 1947 Lord Ashley died suddenly, leaving his French-born second wife a widow and a young nine-year-old son, also called Anthony. Death duties forced the sale of the family's Irish estates and large parcels of the St Giles estate. The 15,500 acres in Dorset inherited by the earl were gradually whittled away, ultimately leaving the 5,500 acres that survive today.

In 1954 the earl and his countess moved out of St Giles's House, temporarily defeated by the struggle to keep it running. Following his wife's death in 1957, and despite being in his eighties, the widowed earl moved back into the house. He soldiered on bravely, staging occasional concerts and opening the house to the public during the summer. He died, aged ninety-three, in 1961, one of the last survivors of a generation that had been born within a few years of the Charge of Light Brigade, had endured two World Wars, seen the invention of the motorcar and aeroplane, and what in old age must have seemed like the complete collapse of the way of life that had sustained the rural aristocracy and allowed houses like St Giles to flourish.

The 9th Earl lived long enough to pass on the estate to his grandson, the 10th Earl, largely free of the burden of taxation. Following his marriage in 1966, the new earl began planning how best to make the house habitable in changed circumstances. In 1973 the south west wing and the kitchen wing were demolished, as was the Victorian tower, leaving the chapel isolated from the house it had once been part of. His intention was to try and return the house to its original design. But although timber and other materials were acquired, he finally had to admit defeat, making his home in a smaller house on the estate, and instead setting up a successful joinery business in the basement of St Giles's House as a way of retaining a toehold in the house.

The 10th Earl shared his grandfather's love of music, and was chairman of the London Philharmonic Orchestra for nearly 25 years. But it was as a conservationist that he made his mark. The St Giles Estate is renowned for its woodland, planted over the centuries. The 10th Earl planted over a million trees on the estate, restoring woodland and creating habitats for specific species of birds and insects. In 1992 he was joint-winner of the Royal Forestry Society's National Duke of Cornwall's Award for Forestry and Conservation. Butterflies were a particular passion, and he was vice-president of the British Butterfly Conservation Society, as well as president of the Hawk and Owl Trust.

In 1976 he married as his second wife the Swedish-born Christina Eva Montan, the daughter of a former ambassador, by whom he had two sons, Anthony and Nicholas. Although they divorced in 1999, Lady Shaftesbury continues to live on the estate and has played a crucial role as its custodian, maintaining it in readiness to pass it on to the next generation. In November 2004 the 10th Earl was murdered in the south of France, a crime for which his third wife, a Tunisian from whom he was estranged, and her brother have recently been found guilty and given lengthy prison sentences. Six weeks after the body of his father was found in April 2005, his heir, the 27-year-old Anthony, died of a heart attack whilst visiting his younger brother Nicholas in New York. Both father and son have now been laid to rest in the family vault in the church, and Nicholas has become the 12th Earl of Shaftesbury.

On the front page of his notebook, in an entry written at the end of the Second World War, the 9th Earl wrote, prophetically: 'What is to become of this old family home where successive generations have lived so long is impossible to foretell.' In recent years tragedy has made these words even more poignant. And yet despite the setbacks there is a now a sense of optimism and renewal. The new earl is young, unencumbered by the past. The gardens may be overgrown, the lake in need of dredging, but with time and energy could be restored. St Giles's House still stands, its rooms empty, but one comes away from it today with a sense that new life may yet be breathed into it.

Slape Manor

NETHERBURY is surely in one of the most beautiful areas of Dorset, with its rolling hills and narrow lanes between lush, verdant banks. From such a lane, the driveway to Slape Manor flows gently downhill to the welcoming front porch on the north side of the house. The property has undergone major alterations in the nineteenth and twentieth centuries, yet the remaining parts of the original seventeenth century house have been well preserved.

In the thirteenth century Netherbury and Beaminster were divided into five manors, each attached to a prebend of Salisbury Cathedral. The prebend was the lord of the manor. He leased his manorial rights to the gentry who farmed the land. For centuries the area was renowned for its orchards and flax.

In 1585 John Strode, a descendant of the Strodes of Parnham, married Christian, daughter of John Poxwell, who lived at Slape. So began the Strodes tenure of Slape lasting until the eighteenth century. The first mention of a dwelling appeared in a survey in 1649. Robert and Mary Strode lived here at the time and Robert was described as a 'fee farmer of Slape'. It stated that 'the demesnes consisted of a dwelling-house, barn and out-house, 16 acres of meadow, 80 acres of arable farmland and 60 acres of pasture, valued in total at £80 a year.'

In 1730, the lease passed to Churchill Rose, son of the surgeon Thomas Rose of Dorchester. He did not live at the house, preferring instead to work and live at Slape Mills, a nearby flax mill. The manor house was leased to tenant farmers and the Court Barons were held there. The next occupant was John Cook, followed by his son Thomas, who, in 1798, was known as Lord of Slape.

SLAPE MANOR. A view from the north. An early seventeenth century window and doorway survive at the east side of the house.

In the 1850s the five manors were transferred by Act of Parliament to the Ecclesiastical Commissioners for England and Wales who, in 1870, sold them individually. Slape was purchased by Edwin Slade who started upon major alterations, employing the architect G.R. Crickmay of Weymouth. Thomas Hardy worked for Crickmay at this time and it was he who designed the library in the west wing. The front porch was also of this era.

More refurbishment was undertaken in the 1930s by Major Basil Keep Ronald, who employed the architect Edward Prioleau Warren (*see* also Chantmarle). A housekeeper's wing was added and also an octagonal cupola from where breathtaking views of the countryside can still be appreciated.

Despite so many alterations the remnants of the early seventeenth century house are clearly visible at the east end where three-light windows with labels remain, plus a doorway with a four-centred head and label. Two seventeenth century, two-light mullion windows also survive, which allow light into the cellar on the south side. Inside the house is an elegant, early eighteenth century staircase.

Through the centuries the house has grown into a graceful country house. The present owners lavish care upon the house and gardens and are constantly seeking ways to improve and enhance the beautiful landscape surrounding their home.

SLAPE MANOR. The south front, showing the octagonal cupola added by Major Basil Keep Ronald in the 1930s.

SLAPE MANOR. The library in the west wing designed by the young Thomas Hardy when working for the Weymouth architect G.R. Crickmay in the early 1870s.

Smedmore House

THE NARROW ROAD to Kimmeridge opens out to a dramatic view of sea, cliffs and fields. Smedmore House lies to the east of the village surrounded by parkland, with its beautiful garden hidden on the south side. From the house the sea can be glimpsed through the trees which provide protection from the winter storms. The twin bows on the north-west front, which were added to the house in 1761, are in local white stone. In contrast, the south-west side was built in the more mellow Queen Anne period.

The Smedmore Estate was sold in 1391 and since that date it has been passed down solely through inheritance. At the time of the Domesday Book, Ricardus, a sub-tenant of William de Braiose, held the land on which Smedmore now stands. Ricardus was probably the founder of the de Smedmore family who owned it until the end of the fourteenth century. In 1391 Henry de Smedmore sold the land to one of his tenants, William Wyot, whose daughter, Johanna, brought it to her husband John Clavell in 1427.

Johanna had also inherited Barnston, a thirteenth century manor near Church Knowle, from her mother's family, the Estokes. At the time of the Domesday Book, Barnston belonged to a Norman tenant-in-chief called Walter de Claville who owned five manors in Dorset and thirty in Devon. There is no record of a house at Smedmore until much later, so the couple would probably have lived at Barnston (for more, *see* Barnston).

Kimmeridge, which lies adjacent to Smedmore, was held by Cerne Abbey. In 1554, after the Dissolution, it was purchased by John Clavell, the great, great grandson of Johanna and John Clavell. His sons, John and William, were well known for their dealings with pirates along the Purbeck coast. Buying and selling pirates' plunder was a lucrative business. Eventually the Clavell brothers were arrested, along with others, and sent to London for questioning. Some were sentenced to death but the Clavells were pardoned and John Clavell was even appointed M.P. for Corfe in 1586. He lived on until 1609, and a memorial to him and his family can be viewed in the church of St Peter the Apostle at Church Knowle.

SMEDMORE HOUSE. The house and grounds in the eighteenth century.

John's son, William, was another colourful character and knighted for his service in Ireland during Tyrone's rebellion. In 1620, after returning to Smedmore, he built 'the little newe house' mentioned by Coker, the remains of which, consisting of two and three light windows in two storeys, the lower ones with transoms, are situated at the back of the present house.

William's courage as a soldier and pleasure at returning to Dorset was not matched by a talent for

SMEDMORE HOUSE. Described by Coker as 'the little newe house', Smedmore was built in 1620 by Sir William Clavell.

business. His first venture was the extraction of alum from the cliffs at Kimmeridge but unfortunately a patent had already been issued to someone else! He then turned his not inconsiderable energy to extracting salt from the sea, and into the production of glass, using the bituminous shale as fuel. His workers suffered dreadfully from the appalling smell of burning shale. He built a large quay, part of which is still there today though the remainder was destroyed by a storm in 1745. Another obstacle, though, blocked Sir William's way. Sir Robert Mansel, Treasurer of the Navy, acquired the monopoly to make glass by using coal, instead of wood, and set up a glassworks in Newcastle. Anyone wishing to make glass would have to pay him a premium. Sir William, undaunted, went into partnership with a glassmaker, Abraham Bigo, and after agreeing to pay the necessary fees, was granted permission to make green glass to sell solely in the south-west of England.

Sir William had no intention of keeping to this agreement and sent his glass to London. He even had an interest in a glassworks in Scotland. For two and a half years he refused to pay his dues to the Admiral. Twice he was imprisoned in the Marshallsea. His losses totalled an amazing £20,000. Upon his release the glass works were closed and he was forced to sell Barnston and rent out Kimmeridge Farm, finally dying in 1644.

In the nineteenth century there were more attempts to regenerate the shale industry. The Duc de Malakoff who was the French Ambassor to London at the time, drew up a contract to use Kimmeridge shale to light Paris! But along with other companies they found it unprofitable due to transport costs and the strong, unpleasant bitumous smell from the shale.

Sir William's successor should have been his nephew John who had once been a highwayman. He had been arrested and sentenced to death, yet

William Clavell in the uniform of Colonel of the Volunteer Dorset Rangers.

reprieved after sending a touching appeal in verse to King Charles I (*see* Round Chimneys).

Sir William refused to leave the estate to John and it passed instead to a distant cousin, Roger Clavell of Winfrith who became Sheriff of Dorset in 1664 and Deputy Lieutenant in 1665. Being a prudent and cautious farmer, he gradually restored the family fortunes and his grandson, Edward, was able to repay Sir William's last remaining debt as well as adding the impressive façade to the south-west front of the house. An estimate of £1450.16s.7fi d. for the new north-west front, added in 1761 by his son George, is still on display in the house today.

George died childless and the estate passed successively to his two nephews, William and John Richards, sons of his sister, Margaretta, who had married into the Richards family of Warmwell. Both nephews changed their names to Clavell. There is a portrait of William in the uniform of Colonel of the Volunteer Dorset Rangers, formed in 1794 by Lord Milton, when an invasion by Napoleon seemed imminent. As William had no heirs, Smedmore passed to his brother, the Reverend John Clavell who built the Clavell Tower in 1831. He died a bachelor in 1833 and his heiress was his niece Louisa Pleydell, who had married Colonel John Mansel.

Three months later the Reverend Clavell's housekeeper produced a will, supposedly signed by him, leaving the entire estate to his farm manager, a Mr. Barnes, to whom the housekeeper's daughter was engaged! Louisa, however, had made a fortunate choice when she married John Mansel. He was a descendant of Sir William's old adversary, Admiral Mansel, and inherited the admiral's determination and tenacity. After a distinguished career in India he served on St Helena when Napoleon was exiled on the island. He worked tirelessly to overturn this will, and though there were many anxious moments during the court case,

The Clavell Tower, built by John Clavell in 1831. It now belongs to the Landmark Trust and is in the process of being moved slightly back from its eroding clifftop site overlooking Kimmeridge Bay.

SMEDMORE HOUSE. The north-west front with twin bows added in the 1760s.

he was eventually vindicated and the estate was saved from falling into the hands of a 'set of forgers', as Colonel Mansel called them.

His heirs were twin boys, George and John. George founded the Dorset Rifle Volunteers in 1859 and his brother John was a founder of the Dorset County Museum in Dorchester. The next owner was another Colonel John Mansel, a keen huntsman who lived at Wincanton and who was killed in a riding accident in 1915. From 1896-1924 the house was occupied by a tenant, Mr. Van de Weyer. Thereafter Major Rhys Mansel came to live at Smedmore with his family until the outbreak of the Second World War. He was then recalled to his regiment and the house was let to the Tolmers Park School for Girls from Potters Bar.

In 1940 the army requisitioned the house and used the surrounding land as an anti-tank range, setting up a target railway between Swalland Farmhouse and the sea. It was not until 1960/61 that the Ministry of Defence carried out a major clearance, which left the area safe to farm once again. During the 1950s the house was let to Sir Arthur Bryant, the historian, who worked diligently to restore the gardens to their pre-war glory. Major and Mrs. J.C. Mansel returned to Smedmore in 1958. Mrs. Mansel, being a keen gardener, continued to enhance the beautiful gardens, as well as establishing a small market garden. Now their son, Dr. Philip Mansel, an historian, as the fourth generation of Mansels, owns Smedmore. He takes a great interest in the estate and has added a significant number of trees to the surrounding landscape.

South Eggardon House

SOUTH EGGARDON HOUSE is just north of Askerswell below the impressive hillfort of Eggardon in a stunningly beautiful setting. The house is of lovely, mellow, golden stone and its views down the valley to the coast are nothing less than spectacular. It is surrounded by beautifully planned and planted gardens, overlooking a small lake in the valley below. The majestic yew tree at the end of the lawn opposite the house is about 2000 years old and its situation close to a spring suggests the existence of a pre Christian sacred site. In 1959, a large Bronze Age decorated shale disc, now on display in the County Museum, was discovered in a ploughed field just to the west of the house by Wing Commander Newall, the then owner. A Roman brooch, Roman settlement remains and evidence of post medieval settlement have also been discovered nearby. This beautiful place has an impressively long history of habitation and it is interesting that the present farm consists of around 280 acres, approximately the same as that recorded in the Domesday Book.

SOUTH EGGARDON HOUSE. Stuart and Georgian extensions combine with a more recent extension without losing the Tudor character of the original house.

There is evidence that the oldest parts of the present house date back to the sixteenth, or possibly even the fifteenth, century, but as with all houses which have survived the vicissitudes of centuries it has seen many changes, some beneficial, some not, and has become an amalgam of different periods. Disentangling its architectural history is well nigh impossible and assigning some parts of the structure to certain periods is about the best that can be achieved, none of which detracts from its charm, but adds to its fascination.

The main part of the Tudor house possibly incorporates part of an earlier building and was extended to the north in the seventeenth and eighteenth centuries. During alterations, the present owners discovered an ancient window inside the roof space, suggesting that the seventeenth century work may have been alterations and additions rather than new building.

The name Eggardon derives from a Saxon person's name, 'Eohhere', and 'Dun', meaning 'down' or 'hill' and the later owners of South Eggardon took their name from the place. In the Domesday Book it is described as a manor and hamlet. In 1312, the Abbot and Convent of Milton were receiving a yearly rent from a tenement belonging to Henry de Ekerdone, gifted to them by his ancestor, Robert de Ekerdone, 'from time immemorial', suggesting that the Ekerdones had been established here since well before the fourteenth century. John Hutchins says that the

SOUTH EGGARDON HOUSE. The manor house from the south with Eggardon Hill rising behind.

family name of Ekerdone had the reputation of being ancient, but 'we meet with little account of them, nor does their pedigree rise very high'. He then quotes the following rhyme, current among the villagers:

'When William the Conqueror went out for a roam
He always found John of Eggardon at home.'

Whether this was complimentary or derogatory is open to question.

In 1526 Thomas Eggardon owned the manor and manor house of South Eggardon and his son and heir was Richard, aged sixteen. The manor then continued to be inherited by successive generations of Thomases, Richards and Johns until the eighteenth century. By 1741 the family seem to have fallen on hard times and the house and the last of the land was sold after at least five centuries of Ekerdone ownership.

In 1790 it belonged to the heirs of the late Mrs. Sansome and by 1864 it was the property of a Mrs. Helyer of Combe Flory, near Taunton. In 1938 it was bought by Colonel and Mrs. Lumby. At that time the house was divided into two dwellings and the Lumbys converted it back to a single family home. Colonel Lumby was an Indian Army officer and their son, Michael, was born in Simla. He became one of the youngest submarine commanders during the Second World War and rose to be Vice Admiral Sir Michael Lumby, KCB, OBE, DSO, DSC. Colonel Lumby was killed in an air crash at the end of the war and in 1946 Mrs. Lumby sold the house to Wing Commander Bradbury, who farmed there until 1951 when he sold the house and land to Wing Commander and Mrs. Newall. After her husband's death Mrs. Newall sold the farm in 1984 to a Mr. Burbidge, who apparently made considerable changes to the interior of the house during his tenure.

Ten years later it was sold to Mr. and Mrs. John Sacher, who have carried out a great deal of sensitive restoration and refurbishment with some guidance from English Heritage. This includes adding a new wing to the western side of the house, creating a large kitchen and extra bedrooms with magnificent views down the valley, and re-planning and replanting the gardens. So South Eggardon's long history of continuity and change is perpetuated under the guardianship of new owners who have fallen under its spell.

Stafford House

UNTIL THE LATE 1800s West Stafford was known as Frome Billet, Frome Belet, or Frome House. It is all that now remains of a parish on the south side of the River Frome at West Stafford, just two miles east of Dorchester. In the 1400s a church lay near where the present house now stands. It disappeared along with its parishioners, the latter probable victims of the Black Death, as in so many other Dorset villages.

In Domesday Book the area was surveyed as two or even three manors. William Belet held the land here for the king. It was listed under 'Land of the King's Servants', valued at £6. Robert Belet, William's grandson, in 1199-1200 was Sheriff of Dorset and Somerset. He also owned Woodsford Castle. The last mention of the Belets was in 1230.

During the reign of Edward I, in 1278, a William Everard held the principal manor. It remained in the same family for around a hundred years and became known as Frome Everard. The family wealth came from land in Wiltshire, Berkshire and Somerset. Sir Edmund Everard and his wife Felicia, having no children, in 1371 left the estates to Sir Edmund's sisters, Elizabeth, wife of Robert Loundres, and Mary, widow of Thomas Remmesbury. It seems that one or maybe both of the sisters pre-deceased him, for before his death he

STAFFORD HOUSE. The east front is considered one of the best examples of seventeenth century architecture in Dorset. It incorporates an earlier sixteenth century house in the south wing.

STAFFORD HOUSE. The east front in the nineteenth century.

gave the manor and advowson of Stafford and Frome Belet to Milton Abbey.

John Bradley, the last abbot of Milton Abbey, leased 'the chyffe mansion' of Frome, in 1530, to William Long of Stafford. After the Dissolution, in 1539, the manors were granted to Sir Edward Nevile, with the Longs continuing as tenants of Frome Billet along with another estate in West Stafford. By 1560 the estates were held by the Longs in the gift of Sir Edward Nevile; Giles Long died in possession of the manor in 1592. His memorial can be seen in West Stafford church. In 1613 another member of the family sold both manors to John Gould of Dorchester.

John Gould, a merchant, owned houses in Dorchester and Fordington, as well as an estate at Upwey, purchased from the Framptons of Moreton in the early seventeenth century. His family came from Devon and after his death in 1630, aged 74, his son John, also a merchant, remodelled the old house. The date 1633 still remains over the porch. The Goulds owned the house until 1830.

The east front of Stafford House is one of the best examples of Jacobean architecture in Dorset. The uniformity of the round-headed windows on the eastern side is remarkable, with the exception of a ground floor pair in the south-east wing. Incorporated in the south wing is part of the earlier sixteenth century house. A stone newel staircase in the south projection is likely to have been part of the 'chyffe mansion' of William Long. John Gould (II) can be credited with an admirable design for the E shaped house while retaining much of the original structure, including the room at the north end which was originally the Great Hall. Placing chimneys on the gables was a fashionable feature of Dorset houses in the seventeenth century, despite the difficulties of construction. Other examples can be seen at Wraxall, Hanford and Upcerne. The seventeenth century woodwork in the entrance hall has gone but an unusual frieze from the early nineteenth century still remains.

John Gould (III) lived at Upwey. In 1676 he was Lt.-Colonel in the Dorset Militia. He died in 1681 and the estate passed through the families of three of his sons, John (IV), James and Hubert.

John Gould (IV), of Milborne St Andrew, (grandson of John Gould who built the house) inherited the estate but died childless in 1727, passing it to his nephew, Nicholas, youngest son of James Gould of Upwey. He too died childless in 1760. Frome Billet then passed to Thomas Gould of Milborne St Andrew, son of Hubert Gould. Thomas had six sons. His youngest, Nicholas, succeeded to Frome Billet in 1805 after the deaths of his five brothers. Nicholas consulted Humphrey Repton with a view to altering the landscape. The plans were printed in Repton's *Fragments on the Theory and Practice of Landscape Gardening* (1816) but his ideas did not bear fruit until much later. Nicholas, who inherited the house when he was 60 years old, died in 1823. In his will he directed his trustees to sell the estate and divide the proceeds between his five sons. His second son, the Reverend John Gould, rector of Beaconsfield, bought the house from his brothers, but in 1830, was obliged to sell it to John Floyer, son of the former rector of West Stafford

The house built by John Gould was only one room deep. John Floyer doubled the width between 1848-50, but the new work was totally in sympathy with the older part of the house. The windows at the west end of the south wing were altered yet still conform to those on the east front, for which they must have served as a model. The new west elevation followed the style of the east front with

STAFFORD HOUSE. An 1840s watercolour by the architect Benjamin Ferrey of the proposed west front.

gabled projections and chimneys rising from the tops of the gables. The central part has a ground floor arcade of four round arches. The two outer arches are blind with shell-headed niches. In the middle is the shield-of-arms of Floyer impaling Bankes. The interior has been much altered over the years but it is now a delightful house. The staircase, of 1848-50, has handsome arcaded balustrades between heavy square newels, once surmounted by heraldic beasts. The ceiling over the staircase is divided into nine panels with jewel-ornaments on the soffits and pendants at the intersections. Jacobean style oak bookcases grace the library.

Humphrey Repton's original proposals were reprinted in 1840. Nearly forty years had passed since the first drawings, but his two sons, John Adey and George Stanley Repton were alive and may well have worked on the plans. George Repton had married the eldest daughter of Lord Eldon of Encombe, the Lord Chancellor, for whom he designed the first church at Kingston (now converted into a house and superseded by Street's church for the 3rd Earl). The design of the new front at Stafford House followed the advice given by Humphrey Repton to Nicholas Gould. Detailed drawings still survive. None were signed, though one bears a seal of the architect Benjamin Ferrey.

In 1844, John Floyer married Georgina Charlotte Frances, daughter of the Right Hon. George Bankes M.P. who, in 1846-57 became Conservative M.P. for Dorset. He was again elected in 1864-85, when the county was divided into different constituencies and a few weeks before he died, in 1887, was appointed a member of the Privy Council. John was succeeded by his son, George William Floyer, a barrister and J.P. who died in 1927.

George William's successor was his cousin, Lt. General Arthur Nugent Floyer-Acland, who, under the will of George William Floyer, added Floyer to his name in 1928. He had a distinguished military career in the First World War when he was awarded the Military Cross, D.S.O. and Croix de Guerre. Knighted in 1940, he served as Military Secretary to the Secretary of State for War between 1940 and 1942. He was also High Sheriff for Dorset in 1953 and Deputy Lieutenant of Dorset in 1957.

During the Second World War the R.A.F. requisitioned the house. Conveniently situated close to R.A.F. Warmwell, Czech and Polish pilots were billeted here. Warmwell played a vital part in the first years of the war with Spitfires and Hurricanes

STAFFORD HOUSE. The west front added by John Floyer in the nineteenth century.

defending Portland Naval Base and the English Channel. In December 1942, Barnes Wallis stayed in the house whilst his revolutionary bouncing bomb underwent trials on the Fleet at Chesil Beach.

After the war, in 1947, Lt. General Floyer-Acland sold Stafford House to Lt. Colonel and Mrs. Richard St Barbe Emmott, whose daughter, Patricia Egidia, married Brigadier Stafford Nugent Floyer-Acland, son of the Lt. General who died in 1980 aged 94.

Lt. Colonel Emmott died in a hunting accident in 1949, and in 1954 the house was sold once again. This time it was bought by Sir Philip Grey-Egerton. Sir Philip had known and loved the house for many years. His mother was the daughter of Canon Reginald Southwell Smith who was rector here for nearly sixty years. After the death of his wife in 1952, Sir Philip was on board ship to Australia when he heard that Stafford House was for sale. He instructed his son to view and advise him by cable to Cape Town. The advice was – 'lovely house, but not suitable for you!' The reply came back 'buy it immediately!' The house was certainly in need of renovation. Drainage, sewage and water supply systems were installed, along with oil fired central heating. Bedrooms were converted and bathrooms improved. Afterwards, Sir Philip lived alone at the house with his housekeeper, gardener and the faithful butler who had served him since the war.

Sir Philip had succeeded to the title as fourteenth baronet in 1945. The family seat was Oulton Park in Cheshire, gutted by fire in 1926. Many of the family paintings were rescued and brought to Stafford House, along with Royalist memorabilia. Six months before he died, in 1962, he married Mrs. Dickson from Upwey.

A year later, Sir Philip's son, Sir John Grey-Egerton sold the house to Mr. and Mrs. Newgass who lived there for about twelve years. The next owners were Mr. and Mrs. Willis, followed, in the mid seventies, by Mr. and Mrs. Richard Pavitt who converted some of the rooms into flats and stayed there for around twenty years. After a brief time under the ownership of Mr. and Mrs. John Smith, Stafford House, in 2002, was once again for sale. The new owners are Mr. and Mrs. Julian Kitchener-Fellowes, who, while still retaining the historical features, have transformed this lovely house into a welcoming, comfortable home. Julian Fellowes is an author, actor, director and Oscar winning screen-writer of the film *Gosford Park*.

Stepleton House

STEPLETON HOUSE is close beside the road from Blandford to Shaftesbury, in fact the road takes a sharp semicircular detour around the edge of its park. It is situated in the valley of the little Iwerne stream, which gives its name to the villages of Iwerne Minster and Iwerne Courtney, the hamlet of Iwerne Stepleton having long ceased to exist. This is grazing country, sheltered to the west by the ancient hill forts of Hod Hill and Hambledon Hill and to the east by gentle downland.

The house, with its ashlar walls and roof of stone slates, faces south along the valley. A central, rectangular, two storey block with dormers in the roof, flanked on either side by smaller, two storey pavilions linked to the main house by single storey passages. The central block is the oldest part of the house and was built in the mid seventeenth century, originally with a small central courtyard.

The Fownes family, who owned the house from 1654 to 1745, moved the main entrance from the east front to the south and built the elegant, pedimented, central features on both these fronts. Its next owner, Julines Beckford, was responsible for adding the pavilion wings in 1758, having earlier covered the central courtyard to create a vestibule and insert a staircase. Set in its lovely parkland dotted with trees and with the gentle slope of the downland rising above it, the house seems only to lack a family on horseback with dogs and grooms to be the setting for an eighteenth century family portrait by Reynolds or Gainsborough.

The Domesday Book records Iwerne as held by 'Geoffrey', under the overlordship of the Mohuns, who owned enormous estates in Dorset, Devon and Somerset, including Dunster Castle. The name Stepleton appears in association with the manor in the thirteenth century. It was then held, first by a family called Iwerne and subsequently by Stepletons, both of whom appear to have taken the name of the place as their own. Early in the fifteenth century, it came to the Daccomb family by marriage with a Stepleton heiress, remaining theirs until Sir William Pitt bought it in 1623.

In 1654 George Pitt of Stratfield Saye sold Stepleton to Thomas Fownes, who pulled down the old house and rebuilt it in more or less the style we see today. A later Thomas was a keen huntsman and was responsible for building the magnificent classical-style stables to the west of the house for his hunters. He was a pioneer in the scientific breeding of hounds and his pack was one of the first to be kept exclusively for foxhunting. Not for the first time, however, a passion for field sports brought the family to the verge of bankruptcy and in 1745, to clear his and his father's debts, he sold his pack of hounds to a Yorkshireman and the manor to Julines Beckford. Stepleton's link with hunting was to continue however, as Juline's son, Peter, became an authority on hunting and breeding hounds and was the author of *Thoughts on Hunting*, affectionately known as 'the huntsman's bible'.

The Beckford family had amassed a huge fortune from slaves and sugar in Jamaica, which was inherited by two brothers, William and Julines, a third brother having died unmarried. In 1764 whilst on a business trip to Jamaica Julines fell ill and died suddenly leaving Peter, at the age of twenty-five, as his sole heir. Peter's keen interest in foxhunting was already in evidence but he was far from the stereotype of a 'hunting squire'. He was an accomplished scholar, fluent in Greek, Latin, Italian and French, with a deep love of music and it was

Peter Beckford. Enlightened scholar, lover of the arts and music but above all, devotee of fox hunting and breeding foxhounds.

Louisa Beckford, who Peter married in 1773 when she was seventeen. On the right is their daughter Harriet, the only one of three daughters to survive into adulthood.

said of him that 'Never had fox or hare the honour of being chased to death by so accomplished a hunter. He would bag a fox in Greek, find a hare in Latin, inspect his kennels in Italian and direct the economy of his stables in exquisite French.'

Once his affairs were settled he left Stepleton to travel on the Continent, where he lived for four years. In 1766, whilst in Rome, he heard a mass composed by Muzio Clementi, at that time aged 14, and was so impressed that he persuaded the boy's father to allow him to bring Clementi to England to further his education. After some years at Stepleton, living quietly and studying, Clementi was introduced to London society by Beckford and a brilliant career followed. In later life he often referred to the gratitude he felt towards his patron.

On his return to England, Peter stood for Parliament and in 1768 became the Member for Morpeth. In 1773 he married Louisa Pitt, who was young, vivacious, beautiful and the toast of London society. He was thirty-three, and the seventeen year old Louisa seems to have been swept off her feet by this well educated, much travelled, sophisticated, older man. Beckford resigned his seat in Parliament and brought his young wife to Stepleton. Their first child, a daughter, died in infancy and a second daughter, born in 1775 lived only until the age of six. In 1776 their first son was born, but only

Above STEPLETON HOUSE. A view from the north. The pavilion wings were added by Julines Beckford in 1758.

Left William Beckford, from the painting by George Romney. Known as 'England's richest son', and the builder of the incredible mock gothic Fonthill Abbey – and with whom Louisa Beckford carried on a long and passionate affair.

survived for a few months. In 1777, another son, William Horace was born, who survived to inherit Stepleton and in 1779 their daughter Harriet was born, who also survived into adulthood. During these years Louisa became increasingly unhappy and bored with country life, while Peter became ever more engrossed in his beloved hunting.

Not far away, at Fonthill in Wiltshire, lived Peter's young cousin, William, who must have seemed to embody all the glamour and excitement that was missing from Louisa's life. William's father had died when he was ten and he was brought up by an over-indulgent but autocratic mother. He saw himself as an aesthete, collected works of art, wrote poetry, entertained extravagantly and by the age of twenty was already thought of as an eccentric. Byron referred to him as 'England's richest son'. At Fonthill he built the extraordinary Fonthill Abbey, whose doomed tower soared over the Wiltshire countryside. Romney's portrait of him, painted in

STEPLETON HOUSE. Storm clouds gathering over the eastern slopes of Hambledon Hill form the backdrop to this view of the house. The lovely pedimented central doorways on the two fronts were built in the early eighteenth century.

about 1781 at the age of twenty-one, shows a handsome young man leaning against a piece of statuary in an elegantly languid pose.

He and Louisa fell madly in love and conducted a passionate affair over several years from about 1780. In her last letter to William in 1784, after the affair had ended, and when the Beckfords were living in Italy, ostensibly for Louisa's health, she told William that the time they had spent together had been the joy of her life. Louisa died in Florence in 1791 after a long illness and was buried at Leghorn. She was only thirty-four. Peter remained in Italy until 1799 when Napoleon's advance through Europe necessitated his return with his children to Stepleton. He died in 1811 and is buried in the little Norman church beside the house, which he had converted in 1809 to provide a family vault.

William Horace then inherited the estate, and in 1828 became Baron Pitt, taking the name of Pitt-Rivers on inheriting the title from his mother's brother, the second Baron Pitt, who had died childless. William married and fathered two sons but he was a drunkard and an inveterate gambler and brought Stepleton to the verge of ruin, signing away the income from the estate for years at a time to cover gambling debts. He died by drowning in 1831.

William was succeeded by his son, George Pitt-Rivers, who married Lady Susan Gower, the eldest daughter of Earl Granville. Repairs to the house were carried out in 1832 and the estate rented out, but there still seem to have been problems as the house was closed up for three years between 1834 and 1837. From 1839 until 1846 the family lived in the house, but after that it was again leased to tenants. This marriage was also dogged by tragedy. Of their thirteen children, all four sons died between the ages of fourteen and eighteen and a daughter, Alice, was struck by lightning and killed in 1865 whilst in the Bernese Alps on her honeymoon. George died in 1866 and was succeeded by his son Henry, who died the following year, aged eighteen. The estate was then inherited by Henry's uncle, Horace, who was the sixth and last Baron Rivers. He died in 1880 and was buried outside the church because, not inexplicably, the family vault was full. In the year before Horace's death, Thomas Hardy's sister Mary had attended a service in the little church and wrote to her brother describing it as: 'a very queer quire. It consists only of a shoemaker who plays a bass viol and his mother who sings the air'.

By 1896, the house was occupied by two maiden ladies, The Hon. Misses Pitt, who ran an orphanage for girls in one wing of the house. In 1917 Sir Randolph Baker of the neighbouring estate of Ranston bought Stepleton from the last surviving daughter of Lord Rivers, solely to acquire Everley Farm. He split the estate and sold the house and park to an American, Mrs. Cameron, who gave it to her daughter Martha and her husband, Sir Ronald Lindsay. Martha died young without children and Mrs. Cameron and her son-in-law shared the house until their deaths. Sir Ronald did not remarry and in 1949 left the estate to his nephew, the Earl of Crawford and Balcarres. It was then leased until 1972 when it was left to Patrick Lindsay, who again let it. In 1985 the house and park were purchased by Mr. and Mrs. Derek Coombs.

Stratton Manor

THE OLD MANOR HOUSE at Stratton, tucked away behind the church just two miles or so outside Dorchester, was bounded by open fields within living memory. Now it is part of the village, surrounded by houses and divided into two dwellings. From the outside it is still the attractive seventeenth century manor house, built of banded stone and flint with its stone mullioned windows and stone arched doorway. It has a long main range enhanced with climbing roses, with a smaller cross wing at the northern end. Sadly, internally almost nothing remains of the original house except a seventeenth century oak overmantel.

Stratton does not appear in the Domesday Book, but it was a prebend of Salisbury and was always owned leasehold from Sarum until modern times.

The earliest evidence of the ownership of the manor appears in December 1570, when John Colshell, Prebendary of Stratton, leased it to Robert Bond of Stalbridge, for 90 years at a yearly rent of £36. One of the conditions of the lease was that Robert Bond 'should build a convenient mansion house with necessary farm buildings at Wrackleford and also find sufficient lodging, man's-meat, horse-meat, and litter for the lessor or his successors, and his servants and horses once a year, provided they exceed not the number of six persons and remain not above three nights.'

STRATTON MANOR. Banded stone and flint divided by mullioned windows give the seventeenth century house its charm.

The manor was obviously sublet, as in 1626 Angel Smith died and was described in the Parish Register as 'having been Lord of Stratton fifty eight years and eight months'. Angel Smith originated from Montacute and owned land at Ilchester. He made an advantageous first marriage to Lettice, daughter and heiress of Robert Harys, lessee of Stratton Manor. Lettice died in 1575 and in the following May Angel married Catherine Prowte of Litton Cheney, also an heiress. The Parish Register for 1578 records that two sons of Angel Smith were buried in November, Angel on the 8th and James on the 10th. On the 7th his daughter Jane had been baptised and she was to be his only surviving child and sole heir. These dates recording a family tragedy also pose an intriguing puzzle, could this have been the birth of triplets, of which only Jane survived, or were the boys older children who died from an unknown cause?

In 1601 Jane married George Grey of Kingston Maurward. George died only a year later, but they did have a son, named Angel after his grandfather, who inherited both Stratton and Kingston Maurward.

In 1728 Stratton was inherited by Lora, Angel Grey's grand-daughter. She was married to George Pitt of Kingston Maurward and the manor was absorbed into the Pitt's huge estates. As a widow, Lora Pitt lived at Stratton Manor for some years. In about 1820, her grandson, William Morton Pitt, sold the leasehold to Robert Pattison. The Pattisons lived in Wrackleford House and the manor was leased. From at least the 1850s to the late 1930s the tenants of the Manor House and farm were the Chick family, well-known Dorset farmers.

The Pattison's only child married the Hon. Henry Ashley, a younger brother of the Earl of Shaftesbury and when she died in 1895 the manor reverted to the Ecclesiastical Commissioners for England, as representatives for the Prebendary of Stratton, who sold it to Alfred Pope of Eldridge Pope Breweries. He was President of the Dorset Natural History and Archaeological Society and a keen historian. The Pope family lived at Wrackleford House and the Manor House continued to be leased.

By 1939, the Chicks had moved on and the house was occupied briefly by James Douch, foreman to Major Ralph Pope. During the Second World War, Wrackleford House was taken over by the Women's Land Army and Stratton Manor became a store for furniture from the house. After the war the house was empty and local people remember it as becoming almost derelict.

In 1958 it was sold to a builder, Hayward of Maiden Newton, who did some restoration work and divided the house into two dwellings, now known as the Old Manor and Manor Cottage. In the 1960s Mr. and Mrs. Gill bought the Old Manor, which is the earliest part of the house, although the whole is seventeenth century, whilst the north cross-wing, which is now Manor Cottage, is owned by Mr. and Mrs. Boulton.

Toller Whelme Manor

IN THE PARISH OF Corscombe and north east of Beaminster lies the peaceful hamlet of Toller Whelme. The narrow lane off the road to Beaminster seemingly leads into a world little changed since 1150, when Henry II gave the land to the Cistercian monks of Forde Abbey. The walls of the seventeenth century manor house are of rubble with stone mullioned windows. The main part of the house is thatched. The Cistercians were a farming order, and the produce from the surrounding land would probably have ended up in the abbey's kitchen, ten miles to the west. Just east of the house rises the spring-head of a stream known as the Toller, which eventually flows into the Frome. The monks would have had a stew-pond here for fish and the clear, pure spring still supplies water to the house. The high walls surrounding the courtyard and gardens exude an aura of peace which must surely be a legacy from the time of the Cistercians.

Domesday Book states that Drogo (of Montacute) held Toller Whelme from the Count of Mortain and that Aelmer held it before 1066. In 1293 the land was valued at twelve pounds. The first building consisted of a refectory and dormer and could have been as early as 1390. Over the years the roof and floor of the dormer fell into decay leaving just the refectory intact. Now known as the Old Hall, it originally had two hearths, one at either end. Today the remaining hearth still supports a mantel of Ham stone nearly six feet in length. A doorway with an equilateral pointed arch and moulded stone jambs, which once led to the lavatorium, is now a window. There are still remains of original windows reset in other locations. The chapel was later converted into a stable, and the porch on the north wing of the house has been dated at 1470.

The Dissolution of the Monasteries forced the monks to leave and, from 1545 to 1630, the manor was owned by the family of William Paulet, Marquis of Winchester. In 1630 it was sold to the Pennes of East Coker, who were already leasing the manor. George Penne (I) built a south wing onto the original structure around 1644. Penne was a Roman Catholic and a staunch Royalist and incorporated a cupboard into the outer wall of his house concealing a shaft connected to the room above. Known as Penne's Hole, it was a hiding place for priests and Royalists and the remains of the cupboard can still be seen today. His lands were confiscated in 1645 but by then he had shrewdly leased the manor to his cousin Sir Robert Poyntz, whose family lived there for 31 years.

On Palm Sunday, 1644, Beaminster caught fire. The cause, some say, was Royalist soldiers firing muskets into the town's thatched roofs. There was no love lost between its inhabitants and the Royalist

TOLLER WHELME MANOR. A naive painting by an unknown artist showing the house during the time of William Pope in the early nineteenth century.

TOLLER WHELME MANOR. The home of the Pennes from 1630. Note how little the external character of the house has changed when compared to the painting on the previous page.

army under the command of Prince Maurice. His soldiers were quartered in private houses and helped themselves freely to provisions. No payment was ever offered, so resentment grew. While the fire was raging soldiers were seen plundering as the townfolk dragged their furniture outside to safety. In the wake of the fire Prince Maurice was petitioned for reimbursement, but to no avail.

The townsfolk then applied to Parliament and obtained an order to raise £2000 from the sequestered estates of George Penne. In 1646 timber worth £500 was handed over for the rebuilding of the town plus £300 in ready money. By 1651 the people of Beaminster were clamouring for the balance to be paid. Parliament ordered Sir Robert Poyntz's heir, Nicholas Poyntz, who still held the lease of Toller Whelme, to pay £100 per year until the remainder of the £2000 was paid. In this way George Penne and his family were forced to contribute substantially towards the rebuilding of Beaminster. As he was a Roman Catholic he had no access to litigation.

At the Restoration of Charles II in 1660, George Penne brought an unsuccessful petition against Beaminster to recover his money. He then appealed to the King but did not live long enough to receive any compensation. He died in 1673, eleven years before Charles II recompensed the Pennes by granting to George Penne's son, George (II), two fairs to be held annually on Toller Whelme Downs, one for five days at the end of August, the other for a week in May. These fairs took place until the accession of Queen Anne in 1702, who promptly declared them void. Ironically, in 1684, Beaminster once again burnt down.

The Duke of Monmouth's doomed Rebellion of 1685 brought the Pennes temporary respite from their financial woes. Hundreds of the unfortunate followers of Monmouth were taken prisoner and hauled before Judge Jeffreys in Dorchester, either to be hanged or deported to the West Indies. Of those to be deported, a hundred were allotted to George Penne, who in turn either sold them back to their families or friends, or on to plantation owners in the West Indies. Despite all this, George died a bankrupt in 1695.

George Penne (III) was a Brigadier-General in the army of James II who fought against William III at the Battle of the Boyne. Defeat for James plunged the Penne family even deeper into debt. William III put the estate into the hands of trustees who were ordered to sell it and raise £7000 to cover George Penne's debts. In 1708 it was finally bought by George Richards of Long Bredy who, from 1712, rented it to William Pope whose descendants lived there for over a century. In 1724 George Penne died, bringing to an end Toller Whelme's last link with a family whose loyalty to the Stuarts had brought about their financial ruin.

In 1786 tragedy struck. John and Thomas Pope and their sister Sarah were at home alone. The brothers decided to break open a trunk belonging to their father and took out of it fifty guineas. Sarah declared that she would tell her father what they had done. The boys panicked and strangled her. They dragged her into another room and cut her throat, later carrying her body out of the house and dropping it down a well. They then set out for Salisbury, dividing the money between them. John went to London and vanished without trace. Thomas took a ship from Poole to Newfoundland, but his guilty conscience eventually drove him to give himself up and he was deported to England on the sloop HMS *Echo* to face trial. Strangely enough there is no record of any trial taking place and he was never heard of again.

In 1802 the Reverend John Richards, grandson of George Richards, sold the estate to William Pope. In 1869 the third William Pope paid for the building of St John's Church near to the house. The population of the village was then nearly a hundred, and there was even a small school. William Pope's generosity cost him dear. The bills for building the church proved much higher than the estimates, and the estate had to be mortgaged.

Not until 1910 was the house lived in again. Then it was rented and eventually bought, along with 586 acres, by Benjamin Childs of Corscombe in 1919, for £8,075. Although he died in 1949, his daughter and son-in-law, Eleanor and Brinsley Walbridge, lived there until 1963. Once again the farms were sold and the manor left empty until 1966, during which time the house suffered vandalism. Colonel and Mrs. R.C. Hayward then acquired Middle Farm and restored the house. It was sold again in 1980, this time to Captain and Mrs. S. Maxwell-Hyslop. Finally, in 1989, it was purchased by Mr. and Mrs. Giles Marking. As a labour of love, they have spent many years carefully rebuilding the ancient outbuildings and sympathetically restoring this often neglected manor house into a dwelling of great beauty.

Tolpuddle Manor

Tolpuddle is a quiet village in the Piddle Valley between Puddletown and Bere Regis, which, for one day in the year, in mid July, plays host to a gathering of the great and the good of the Trades Union Movement. They and many ordinary working people come to commemorate the actions of six Dorset agricultural workers, who, in the 1830s, swore a secret oath to withhold their labour until their employers agreed to their modest demands for a living wage. The swearing of oaths was illegal and, when it was discovered, they were tried and sentenced to seven years transportation. This harsh sentence caused a great outcry in both country and Parliament and after three years the sentences of the Tolpuddle Martyrs were quashed and they were brought back to England. These events are seen as the roots of the modern Trade Union Movement. Once this day of celebration is over for another year, it again becomes a quiet little village not so very different from its Victorian predecessor.

The manor house is just behind the church. It faces south with an uninterrupted view across the Piddle Valley towards the tree covered ridge which, in Thomas Hardy's day, was part of Egdon Heath, the 'Great Heath' of his novels. It is a two-storied house with a variety of building materials incorporated in it. The south front is faced with ashlar, but other parts of the house are of brick or banded brick and flint and the roofs are of slate. There are some surviving original windows, but most have been replaced. The interior of the house has been much altered but it does include a delightful eighteenth century staircase. The front of the house is of five bays with a central, single story, gabled porch. This has a carving of the heraldic ape of the Martyn family, much worn, set above the arch. Over the doorway within the porch is a date stone inscribed 'I.B.N.A. 1656', which may indicate the date of rebuilding of the house, although at that time the lords of the manor were the Hull family. Today it is an unpretentious, attractive house set in lovely gardens, bordered on the south by the river, which is crossed by a picturesque brick footbridge.

Recorded history begins for Tolpuddle in 1024, when King Canute gave Orc, one of his retainers, substantial grants of land. These included several villages in Dorset and Orc's wife, Tola, bought Pidele. Tola and Orc had no children and they bequeathed their estates to the church. Tola gave Tolpuddle to the Abbey at Abbotsbury, whose property it remained until the Dissolution. The Domesday Book records that the abbot owned the manor of Pidela, which consisted of about 120 acres, that the Abbey farmed 50 or so of these and that the others were farmed by sixteen tenants who paid rent to the abbot. There was without doubt an important dwelling here from the time of Domesday.

There is a fourteenth century document dealing with an endowment of the church, which says that Thomas, the vicar, and his successors 'will have and keep for ever as his residence and dwelling, the principal house in the manor of Tolpuddle'. It goes on to describe the gardens, stable and other buildings and gives instructions to enclose the area with walls and to keep them in good repair. It also says that the vicar must have access and exit (to the church) through the graveyard from the house and land at all times. To this day there is a gate through the garden wall leading to the graveyard and the church from the manor house.

After the Dissolution the manor seems to have

TOLPUDDLE MANOR. A view from the mill stream.

changed hands several times in fairly short succession. In 1544 it was in the hands of William Riggs and Leonard Brown, who were given permission to pass it to Robert Martyn. Perhaps the worn carving of the heraldic ape of the Martyn family over the arch of the porch is a relic of his ownership. In 1560, the second year of Elizabeth's reign, it was granted to Richard Baker and Sir Richard Sackvill, who sold it the following year to Thomas and Margaret Argall. Its ownership then appears to become a little more settled and the Argall family remained there through at least three generations.

In 1625, Coker notes that it belongs to the Hull family, who had moved to Dorset from Larkbere in Devon. Once again the house remained in the family for several generations. Edmund Hull, grandson of George, the first Hull, was the owner in 1645. He was a Royalist supporter and had his rents here sequestered, paying a fine of £450 to regain his property. His son William became County Sheriff but died unmarried in 1709. The estate was left to his brother Francis and on his death, ten years later, was inherited by William's four sisters, or their children. By 1730 the estate was owned by George Pitt of Stratfield Saye. It was let as a tenanted farm and at the beginning of the nineteenth century his grandson, William Morton Pitt, sold it to a Bristol merchant, Samuel Fripp. In 1829 his trustees sold it to Rev. Edward St John of Oakley. His son Edward divided the estate in 1867 into two farms, Higher and Lower, which were let together to one tenant. When he died in 1887 it was left to his nephew, Captain StJohn Frederick, who sold it to James Crane.

James was a local farmer who seems to have prospered. In the 1851 census he is listed simply as a farmer but ten years later, in the next census, he had become a landowner employing seventeen men and sixteen boys. When he bought Tolpuddle Manor he was living nearby at Southover House, which he had built in 1862. In 1889 his son, also called James, married Mary Nash, who was the daughter of the vicar of Tolpuddle. Around 1904 they moved into the manor house and for the first time in at least two hundred years the house was occupied by its owners.

The Cranes continued to live in the manor house until the mid twentieth century. Edward Crane died in 1943 aged 80 and his wife in 1950. They are both buried in the churchyard at Tolpuddle. After Mrs. Crane's death the house was sold and over the next half century changed hands five times. Until, in 1991, it was bought by Colonel John Francis and his wife Jean as a permanent home at the end of a career spent serving and travelling with the Army.

Upcerne Manor House

SITUATED IN WHAT is arguably the most peaceful landscape in the county, Upcerne Manor House lies in a valley with its lake, while fields and hills rise all around, framing a distant view southwards towards Cerne Abbas.

In Domesday Book the manor was listed as belonging to Osmund, Bishop of Salisbury, as part of his Sherborne estates. The next mention is of the Percy family from Great Chaldfield in Wiltshire, whose family lived in Upcerne from the the death of Henry I (1189) until around 1347, when it was sold to the Haddons of Candel Haddon. Henry Haddon, who died in 1349, held the manor jointly with his wife Alianor. She died in 1362. Their daughter, Amicia, married Lord William Fitzwaryn, and the manor descended through three generations to her great grandson John Chidyok. At his death in 1450, his two daughters, who were co-heiresses, were Margaret, who was the wife of Sir William Stourton, and Katherine, wife of Sir John Arundel.

Upcerne came to the Stourton family. Their son Roger died childless and the manor passed to Roger's nephew, Charles, Lord Stourton who, in 1556, was hanged for the murder of William Hartgyll and his son, John Hartgyll. According to the custom of the times, his estate was then forfeited to the crown (*see* Moigne Court).

By 1572 the manor had been granted to John Marshe and Francis Greneham and the heirs of John Marshe. In 1592 the leases of Upcerne and Sherborne, along with Long Burton and Holnest, reverted to Queen Elizabeth I, who granted the lordship of these lands to Sir Walter Raleigh upon condition that he paid rent to the Bishop of Salisbury. Raleigh soon sold the lordship of Upcerne to John Mellor of Came, though he retained a small rent from the new owner, known as a fee-farm rent, or rent paid in livestock.

UPCERNE MANOR HOUSE. The house in the 1800s.

Where the Mellor family originated is not known, but during the reign of Elizabeth I they acquired a considerable number of abbey lands including Winterborne Came, Winterborne Faringdon, Uploders, Upcerne and others. John Mellor died in 1595, and his son Robert inherited Little Bredy, and Upcerne. After completing the house now known as Bridehead at Little Bredy, Sir Robert who was knighted in 1603, built, or probably rebuilt, the manor house in Upcerne, certainly before his death in 1624.

His son, Sir John, was heavily fined during the Civil War for recruiting and training troops for the Royalist cause, yet his grandson, John, who was also with the Royalist army, was excused. The Mellor family owned the manor until 1685 when Edward Mellor, who inherited the estates was forced to sell the land for payment of debts. He died childless in 1699 at Cheneys in Buckinghamshire.

The name of Sir Robert Mellor has been remembered and respected in Cerne Abbas and

Upcerne for over three hundred years. With his wife, Dame Margaret, Sir Robert founded a charitable trust in 1620, 'being desirous to dispose and impart some part of that which God hath mercifully and plenteously bestowed upon them'. A yearly sum of £40 was distributed around his estates for the poor and needy and aid was given to apprentices. Half of this sum was shared between Cerne Abbas and Upcerne and distributed quarterly at the feasts of the Nativity, the Annunciation, St John the Baptist and St Michael. As the years and centuries passed needs gradually changed, until the Second World War when cash was distributed to pensioners and 2s 6d per child allotted to parents with children of school age. This continued annually until 1964.

In 1943 Charles North, who for fifty-seven years was the vet in Cerne Abbas, left money for the needy of the parish. For several years it was used alongside Mellor's Charity and in 1996 the two funds were consolidated.

Since the eighteenth century, the house has endured many changes, especially to the interior. The exterior has fared better, and the porch on the west side of the house is probably the original entrance. The outer walls of the north wing, which was added in the late seventeenth century, show signs of a much earlier structure being incorporated into Sir Robert Mellor's house. The masonry in the main range contains unusual fragments of stone carvings, perhaps taken from Cerne Abbey. They include two capitals holding a man's head and two animal heads. Careful inspection of the walls of the house reveals lettering and scroll and floral decoration showing an interesting use of recycled material.

The west side of the house boasts a pair of two storey bow windows. The one at the south-west corner is from the seventeenth century, the other was added in the mid nineteenth century, to balance the original. Both provide splendid views over the surrounding landscape. The upper room, at the south-west corner, was known as the Great Parlour. A frieze of carved griffins once supported heraldic shields displaying the arms and intermarriages of the Mellors. There was a coved ceiling with oak wainscot and above the bow window, a stuccoed relief represented The Judgement of Solomon, while at the opposite end of the room a similar relief depicted Abraham's Offering of Isaac. All these

UPCERNE MANOR HOUSE. Sir Robert Mellor rebuilt the house around 1610-20 on land once belonging to Sir Walter Raleigh.

UPCERNE MANOR HOUSE. The house lies in a picturesque setting looking south towards Cerne Abbey.

decorations have now disappeared, probably removed around 1830 during the time of the early alterations. Similarly, the fireplaces mentioned in Hutchins have been despoiled or removed. In 1892 the house was re-roofed and a turret at the north end of the main block was added in 1909, but later demolished.

After the death of Edward Mellor, the next owner was Nicholas Cary, a goldsmith from London. He built a wing onto the east end for use as offices. Nicholas, his son, who became Sheriff of Dorset in 1715, married Catherine, daughter and co-heiress of Thomas March of Enfield, Middlesex, and also co-heiress of her uncle, Thomas Strode of Parnham. They had two children, Thomas Strode Cary and Catherine Cary, but neither had any children of their own, therefore, in 1784 the estate passed to their aunt Grace, Thomas March's other sister and co-heiress.

In 1764 Grace had married John White of Fairlee in the Isle of Wight and thereafter the manor passed to Grace's grand-daughter, Grace Eleanor, who, in 1841, married John Batten from Aldon near Yeovil. Their son, Colonel John Mount Batten restored and renovated the house and it remained in this family until 1946, when Winifred Eleanor Sarah Batten sold it to Mr. H.R. Ferdinando who remained the owner until 1963, when it was sold to Mr. R.M. Broadhead of Maidenhead

Mr. Broadhead certainly left his mark upon Upcerne. In 1964 he demolished most of the cottages as well as Tucking Mill Farm and Holly Bank, which had once been Glove Inn. Along with this came the dismissal of many workers on the estate. Mr. George Moore, the present estate manager, can still remember those days when the house and village were changed for ever. A few of the cottages were rebuilt, and the lanes resurfaced, but the interior of the house changed significantly as more of the original fixtures were removed, including fireplaces and carvings recorded as still in place in the 1950s. Garden walls, however, were rebuilt using stone from the demolished Yeovil Hospital. It was an unsettling time for this lovely manor.

Since Mr. Broadhead's departure in 1979, and under its present owner, the house slumbers in its beautiful grounds by the shimmering lake. A more tranquil setting would be hard to find in any part of Dorset.

Waddon House

WADDON HOUSE is close to Portesham on a little used country lane, which leads eventually to Upwey. It is built in the lee of a steep, south-facing hillside and has an uninterrupted view to the sea beyond the Chesil Beach. Unusually, the main part of the house runs out from the hill, not along it, and its tall, narrow frontage, with its lovely windows gazing towards the sea, is reminiscent of a ship. The house appears without warning, not hidden away down a private drive, but standing proudly, right alongside the lane with the hill behind and its garden beside it.

Although the first impression of the house is of the lovely classical façade of its west wing, it is actually a U shape building surrounding a courtyard, its north and east ranges being the older part of the house. These are single storey with attics, whilst the west wing is of two storeys with attics and a part basement. Waddon was originally a larger house built on an E shape plan, which can be seen in an old painting of the house from around 1700, but its west wing burnt down in 1704, soon after the tall surviving wing was built. Its traces can still be seen in the stonework on the western side of the existing wing.

The north and east ranges are part of the old house which was renovated and enlarged by Colonel Bullen Reymes. Around 1700 Harry Chafin, who had married the widow of Bullen Reymes' son, built the west range. After the fire of 1704 no attempt was made to rebuild and the house soon became just a farmhouse.

WADDON HOUSE. A painting soon after 1700 when the classical front was built. The west wing, just visible behind the trees was burnt down in 1704.

WADDON HOUSE. The white hounds, seen in the 1700 painting, restored to their rightful home after many years exile at Zeals House.

The main wing has flights of steps on either side, both surmounted with imposing stone pillars. The flight on the eastern side gives entry to the courtyard and its pillars are crowned with two delightful white hounds, which, although present in the eighteenth century painting, had long been missing. Some years ago they were rediscovered at the family's property at Zeals, painted black and unrecognised for what they were. Happily they were returned, both to their original home and their rightful colour. The pillars of the steps on the western side, leading to the garden, are crowned with their original ball finials.

The interior of the west range is a lovely example of late seventeenth, or early eighteenth century work, with elegant panelling and handsome doorways with moulded architraves and pediments. The 'White Parlour' at the south front is particularly beautiful with its large windows looking south to the sea and west over the garden. To the rear of the wing the dining room, which was originally the kitchen, is panelled in heavier style and has a large stone fireplace, appropriate to the kitchen it once was. In the angle of the room, above the doorway from the hall, is a strange triangular area, quite large and enclosed by an open wooden fence with a gate, which, in the past, presumably fulfilled some forgotten function in the kitchen. In the hall leading between the parlour and the kitchen is an imposing doorway with a handsome pediment, which originally led into the missing wing and now has a purely decorative roll, bearing mute witness to what once was there.

Waddon has a exceedingly long history of occupation. A Channel 4, Time Team excavation in the area in 1999 identified Iron Age occupation sites within the walled grounds of the manor and Roman artefacts and pottery have also been found. In the Domesday Book, Waddon is recorded as one of forty-seven manors held by the widow of Hugh Fitz Grip (also called Hugh de Wareham). Before the Conquest it was held by Alward. For most of its life Waddon has been known as West Waddon or Gerards Waddon. Documentary research by Robin Bush in advance of the Time Team dig has also thrown new light on the history of West Waddon.

It was previously thought that the manor had been the property of the church and that it was part of a grant made to Sir William Paulet by Henry VIII after the Dissolution and that Thomas Gerard acquired it from him. However the earliest documentary reference to West Waddon after Domesday is in 1212 and records that it was in the hands of the powerful de Mortimer family. By 1303 the Martyns of Athelhampton were lessees under the Mortimers and remained so until the end of the fifteenth century. In 1485 Roger Neuburgh, grandson of Cicely of York, conveyed it to John Gerard of Trent and it remained part of the Gerard family estate until Elizabeth Gerard inherited it from her grandmother in 1651, when the estate was divided between her and her sister Anne.

Elizabeth's husband was Bullen Reymes. A loyal soldier in the Royalist cause, Bullen Reymes remained a loving family man and showed great compassion to those less fortunate than himself. He was born in Devon but had strong connections with Dorset through his mother, who owned property at West Chelborough and whose sister had been married to Robert Coker of Mappowder. As a child and young man he frequently visited his cousins and step-cousins at Mappowder and had great affection for his 'deare Aunt Eme', Robert's second wife and Elizabeth's grandmother.

Bullen Reymes' family were not wealthy but he

would become a highly respected and important figure in the seventeenth century. At the age of fifteen, in 1628, he was part of the Duchess of Buckingham's household, where his father was 'gentleman usher'. His father considered that Bullen had a good chance of obtaining the post of 'chief attendant' to the 2nd Duke of Buckingham, at that time a boy of three, and decided that he should travel abroad and study to fit himself for this future appointment.

So in May 1631 Bullen Reymes set out for France to serve the English ambassador, Sir Isaac Wake. There followed six years of life abroad, travelling around Europe, living in Paris, Florence and Venice. He also visited Rome and sailed to Crete, Turkey and Greece, all the time learning the accomplishments of a gentleman and a courtier – from swordplay to dancing and playing the lute, which he loved and for which he had great talent. His diaries chronicle visits to the theatre, listening to music, buying books and pictures and meeting people from all walks of life. By the time he returned to England, he was an accomplished 'gentleman', but England was on the verge of war with Scotland and there was no place in the impoverished court of Charles I for a young courtier with little money.

In 1640 he marched north with Charles' army – and to its ignominious defeat by the Scots. Once safely back in Dorset, he married Elizabeth Gerard of Mappowder, the granddaughter of his 'deare Aunt Eme Coker'. Elizabeth and her sister were co-heiresses to Trent, Waddon, Broadway and Nottington, but for the first eight years of their marriage Bullen and Elizabeth lived at Mappowder with Elizabeth's grandmother.

During this time Bullen was away a great deal. In 1641 he was appointed Gentleman of the Privy Chamber at the King's court in exile in Oxford, where he served until the spring of 1643. He then fought with distinction in the West Country, under the command of Prince Maurice, rising to the rank of Colonel, until the surrender of Exeter to Fairfax in April 1646. The Royalist cause was by then effectively lost and he returned to his wife at Mappowder.

Colonel Bullen Reymes, owner of Waddon House in the mid-seventeenth century and one of the great personalities of the period.

In 1648, Elizabeth's grandmother died and Bullen and his family moved to the manor house at Trent to stay with Elizabeth's sister Anne, who was married to Francis Wyndham. They were there until 1651 when the final settlement of the estate was signed, with the Reymes inheriting the estate of Waddon and the Wyndham's that of Trent. Bullen went to Waddon in September of 1651 to supervise repairs and refurbishment of the manor house but Elizabeth remained at Trent with the children until the New Year.

She would thus have been there with her sister when the fugitive Charles II arrived with Francis Wyndham in September and when they later returned after the abortive attempt to get the king away by ship from Charmouth. Bullen Reymes was probably not actively involved in Charles' escape attempt. However, as he had previously organised the escape of his friend, Sir John Berkeley, by ship from Lyme Regis with the help of Captain William Ellesdon, it seems likely that he at least gave

Ellesdon's name to Francis Wyndham as a useful contact in finding a ship.

In January 1652 Bullen brought Elizabeth and their four children to Waddon. It cannot have been a happy start to life in their own home. In that year their two youngest children died, William, two, and baby Robert, just a year old, leaving Tabitha aged six and five year old Bullen. Their second daughter, Mary, probably born later in the year, suffered a physical disability of some kind. However, Bullen undertook the management of his new estate with his usual enthusiasm and efficiency and Waddon began to flourish. This allowed him to repay the money he had borrowed to pay his sequestration fine and to undertake extensive improvements to the house and grounds.

After the Restoration Bullen once again became involved in political life. In 1660 he became MP for Weymouth and Melcombe Regis and in 1661 he was appointed Vice-Admiral of Dorset. In the same year Elizabeth died and was buried in the church at Portesham. In 1660 he had formed a partnership with two friends in Weymouth, Captain George Cley and his wife Constance, for the sale of hemp, cordage and sailcloth to the Navy. The business prospered, but Reymes insisted that the lion's share of its success was due to Constance, saying that but for his 'woman partner' he would 'have been aground long since'.

In 1664 Bullen was again appointed Gentleman of the Privy Chamber and sent by Charles II to Tangier to investigate mismanagement. His report brought great praise from Samuel Pepys and gratitude from the king. In the same year he was appointed one of the four Commissioners for Sick and Wounded Seamen and Soldiers of the Second Dutch War. His district included Dorset and Hampshire, but his headquarters were in Portsmouth. He visited Dorset as often as he could, but the problems encountered in Portsmouth took up much of his time. He was a compassionate man and in the face of a lack of government money for the sick and wounded he repeatedly dug into his own pockets.

By 1667 the war was over and Reymes was back in London. Although busy, he managed to find time for friends, good talk, music and the theatre – of which he was particularly fond. Samuel Pepys once said of him, 'Colonel Reames understands and loves a play as well as I, and I love him for it'.

Reymes continued visiting Dorset when he could. Since his wife's death Waddon was empty, except for a caretaker, so it was to Melcombe Regis that he returned, where he had another house and where his daughter now lived with her husband, George Pley, son of his old friends, and her sister Mary. In the summer of 1672 he became ill but continued to carry out his duties in London until October when he returned to Dorset, where he died a week before Christmas and was buried beside his wife in the aisle of the church at Portesham.

Shortly before his death he commissioned the construction of a sundial bearing this inscription, 'The Gift of the Honble Coll Bullen Reymes, Vice Admiral of the County of Dorset to ye Ingenious Artists Navigators & Seamen of Weymouth and Melcomb Regis, Calculated by his order purposely for the meridian by a Person of Learning Ano Dom, 1672.' Sadly it seems never to have been set up as Reymes intended but at least it is now at his old home at Waddon.

His son Bullen succeeded him at the age of twenty-five and showed little interest in Waddon. Unlike his father, he seems to have been something of a wastrel and lived in London drinking, gambling and building up debts. In 1691, aged forty-three, he married his cousin, Anne Coker of Mappowder. By this time he was heavily in debt and no doubt Anne's fortune was a considerable attraction. The marriage was short-lived, as in 1695 he was found lying wounded in a street in Weymouth after a brawl. He was brought home to Waddon where he died after one of his wounds became gangrenous. Anne inherited Waddon and subsequently married Harry Chafin of Zeals in Somerset. Around 1700 Harry built a new central wing at Waddon in elegant classical style and shortly afterwards the picture, which still survives at Waddon, was painted. In 1704 a disastrous fire destroyed the west wing but mercifully left the new building and the east and north ranges intact. The lost part of the

WADDON HOUSE. The south front of Waddon House. The older parts of the house are on the right.

house was never rebuilt and the remainder was soon let as a farmhouse.

Anne Coker died childless in 1701 and Harry remarried. His second wife was Mary Cley, granddaughter of Bullen Reymes, daughter of Tabitha and George Cley, the son of his old friends and business partners.

In 1721, Mary also died childless and when Harry Chafin died in 1726 he left Waddon to his sister Mary who was married to John Grove. It was inherited by their son, Rev. William Grove of Manston. He had no children and bequeathed it to his nephew, William Chafin Grove, MP for Weymouth and Shaftesbury. In 1793 it again descended to a nephew, William Chafin Grove, who served in the Peninsula War in the 20th Foot. He died in 1859 and his nineteen year old son, William, an Ensign in the Coldstream Guards was his heir.

Six years later twenty-five year old William died in India and Julia Chafin Grove, his only surviving sister, inherited Waddon. She was also the heiress of the Chafin family of Zeals in Wiltshire. Julia remained a spinster and left her property to a cousin, George Troyte Bullock. Thereafter the ownership of Waddon descended through the Troyte Bullocke family to the present owner, Mr. Charles Chaffyn-Grove who, at the age of twenty-one, at his mother's suggestion, changed his name by deed poll from Troyte Bullocke to Chaffyn-Grove, deliberately altering the spelling slightly in the process.

In 1928, Mr. and Mrs. B. Corbett took on the tenancy of the house, which had deteriorated sadly in its years as a farmhouse, and proceeded to carry out admirable restoration work. Mr. Corbett owned the Winterborne Steepleton estate, which he farmed until he was eighty-six. In his younger days he was a keen sportsman. He played football for England in 1901, cricket and hockey for Derbyshire and ice-hockey for Oxford. He enjoyed hunting and served on the Cattistock Hunt Committee until 1940. He died, aged 90 in 1965.

After Mr. Corbett's death, when Mr. and Mrs. Charles Chaffyn-Grove and their family came to live there, for the first time in over 250 years Waddon House was occupied by the family that owned it.

Warmwell House

Warmwell lies within fair proximity of the sea, the hills between giving shelter from the strong winds along the coast at Ringstead. This handsome house, built around 1618 by John Trenchard, is often referred to as the earliest form of a sun-trap, with windows carefully angled to catch maximum light.

According to Hutchins, names beginning with 'Werm' or 'Warm' could have come from the Saxon name Weremund who may have owned a well here. In Domesday Book (1086) 'Weremund' or 'Warmemoile' was surveyed in three parcels owned by the De Tynhams, the De Warmwells (the latter owning the principal manor), and William of Earl Hugh, who also owned Little Mayne, later owned by the Sherards. By 1204 a number of charters are mentioned in Hutchins, of land leased or granted to different people.

In 1382 a charter gives the rights of Warmwell to John Faulconer and his wife Matilda, daughter of John D'Warmwell. The Faulconers were succeeded in 1431, by their daughter Alice and her husband Nicholas Coker, and again in the same year by their granddaughter, Wilhelmina, and her husband Henry North. In 1445 Henry Potter, who claimed to be the heir to Warmwell and the estate, brought a suit against the widowed Alice but, as with other claimants, he was unsuccessful.

In 1448 Alice, for reasons not explained, was awarded £32 from John Newburgh for the Warmwell estate. Part of the sale agreement was that Robert Morgan, whose wife had been the sister and heir of Henry Sherard, should have his chamber at the east end reserved for him for life with a stable for his horses and two loads of fuel for the fire every year and that he could occupy the chamber when he pleased. Whether this referred to a separate dwelling, or to a previous dwelling on the Warmwell site belonging to the Sherards is unknown.

At one time Warmwell was certainly held as two manors, one of which belonged to the D'Warmwells and the other to the Sherards. In 1450 one of these manors had come to John Newburgh and soon afterwards he acquired the other, as in October 1454 he held his first 'court' of the whole manor. In 1483 John Newburgh died and left the manor to his

WARMWELL HOUSE. This view of the house from the west, with the church visible beyond, gives some idea of the complexity of its design, of which the earliest part dates to the first quarter of the seventeenth century.

WARMWELL HOUSE. The delightful garden east of the house.

third son Thomas, ancestor of the Warmwell and Berkeley line.

In 1527 Thomas Kyrton Berkeley sold the manor to Sir Thomas Trenchard of Wolfeton. In 1617 or 1618, it passed to Sir George Trenchard's third son, John Trenchard, and probably at this time the rebuilding of the house was begun. After John Trenchard's death, his youngest daughter Jane inherited the house, bringing it to her husband John Sadler.

John Sadler came from an ancient Shropshire family. Born in 1615, he was educated at Emanuel College, Cambridge, went on to Lincoln's Inn and was appointed one of the Masters of Chancery in 1644. In 1649 he was chosen Town Clerk of London and in 1650 Master of Magdalen College, Cambridge. Fluent in Hebrew and several oriental languages, he was a friend of Cromwell. He is famed for his prophecy of 1661, when he predicted a plague in London, a great fire and the destruction of St Paul's. He spoke of sea fights with the Dutch and three little ships landing in the West Country causing uproar (the Monmouth Rebellion). Thanks to his influence, the Jewish community in London was granted permission to build a synagogue.

At the Restoration he lost all his appointments as well as the Crown property he had purchased in Bedfordshire and Vauxhall. In 1665 his fine house in Salisbury Court was burnt in the Fire of London. Soon after he lost his home in Shropshire. These misfortunes, combined with having fourteen children to provide for, obliged him to retire to Warmwell, where he lived privately till his death in 1674, aged 59, 'having been much disordered in his senses long before.'

William Smith, the husband of John Sadler's daughter Mary, 'purchased the estate from Sadler's widow and family, having previously advanced money upon it'. He sold it in 1687 to John Richards, a London merchant of The House of Richards, who dealt mainly with Spain but also with Holland, France, Italy and Russia. He rebuilt much of the house in 1689 and his crest can be seen above the front porch. He is said to have given £4,500 for the property and it remained in his family until 1806. He and his wife Alice Holmes had four children, Mary, William, John and Thomas. William married Susanna Savage and their son, William (1724-1803) married Margaret Clavell of Smedmore who was her brothers' heiress and who died in 1817 age 90. William and Margaret had five children, four of whom left no heirs. The fifth, Elizabeth-Margaretta married Edmund Morton-Pleydell of Whatcombe and their descendants became the heirs to Smedmore.

John Richards kept a diary rather like that of Samuel Pepys, dated 1697-1701, and a Day Book from 1713-18. The Diary gives a fascinating insight into the daily life of this family. At the time it was written, John Richards had owned Warmwell for ten years. Being retired from business, he led the life of a country squire, farming his land, breeding fighting cocks, coursing hares and gardening. He attended church and spent generously on the repair of the church. He was a friendly man who enjoyed dining with his friends and neighbours, and they with him.

He had married Alice Holmes and referred to her in the Diary as Alce, unless he was annoyed with her, when he spelt her name backwards, as Ecla. Alice was definitely a strong-minded woman. Her allowance from her husband was just £10 per year, so it seems fair to say that she must have had money of her own, as her husband on one occasion borrowed from her 15 guineas and a fortnight later, another 10 guineas. He noted down, or maybe Alice did, the date he borrowed money from her, and the date he repaid it.

In the autumn of 1699 the entries in the Diary record a stormy relationship between the pair which continued down the years. It involved a lady known at the outset only by her initials, M.L. On September 12th, Alice accused her husband of loving M.L. more than her. Indeed, Alice stated that due to the ill treatment she received in her home, she had often thought of killing herself. From then on 'domestic storms' in the household were frequently noted in the Diary:

October 15th 1699, 'This morning A. was mad to the greatest degree, telling me that I was got into such an ill-humour that nobody would serve me in a little while, and many other intolerable insolent discourses, which shall cost her dear.'

February 23rd 1700, after suffering a great scolding from Alice, 'losing all patience, I burnt my will before her eyes.'

July 21st, 'This night I slept in cellar chamber to be at rest from that Ecla'

The Diary continued in this vein until the following year:

May 19th 1701, 'Today A. became mad again, to the greatest degree, and treated me like a slave for nothing.'

The mysterious lady with the initials M.L., then appears in the diary:

May 26th 1701. 'Mary Lillington came hither'

More mischief ensued:

May 29th 1701, 'I kissed M.L. the first time'.

Perhaps the first of many?

Away from his wife, life was pleasant and calm. Cock fighting being a favourite pastime, it seems that some of his cocks were of a mixed strain, as Mr. John Williams' servant fetched a 'redish grey cock' and a 'black pullet with russet' which had been bred at Mr. Frampton's, along with 'two cock chicken of ye shak bag strain'.

As to medicines, Richards usually treated himself. For toothache he used 10 drops of 'juice of rue' to be mixed with garlic and brandy and dropped in the right ear! He applied leeches for his gout and anointed his feet with 'neat's foot oil' as well as sometimes dosing himself with 'spirit of buckthorne' and 'purging spirit scurvy grass'.

When surgery was required, Parson Read of Moreton was summoned, as when he 'cut a new issue in my left arm'. Yet when his wife needed attention he acted himself, 'I cut ye flesh from A's gum with my penknife'. There was no mention of anaesthetic!

Richards did indeed enjoy his garden, recording that his gardeners, 'Thos. Voss and Jno. Jasper rowled all the walks and squares in my garden, also the gravel'. Also, 'Ad. Cryde brot hither ye Mulberry from Mr. Plowman, and set it in my garden near the barberry tree'. The latter did well for he was able to send Pymer, his servant, over to Herringston with 'two baskets of barberry'. On another occasion, Mr. Williams of Lewell dined and after dinner set three 'graffs' of 'my Court Apple tree in pond on a stock in ye other garden'. He covered up his 'sparagrass' and artichokes in October and was able to send eight bundles of the former to Captain More on one occasion.

Alice also helped in the garden and we hear how she set a peck of beans in a ridge of the new 'broken ground' next to the old pond hedge, and also she 'gathered my wall pears, in all 33 besides yt which Mrs. Traheren had'.

Servants were usually engaged for a year. Richard Sansom, a 'working bayley' was paid £18 a year, while Richard Carly, in the same line of work was paid £16, 'he to diet and wash himself, came hither with his bedding, etc'. A dairy-maid received £3 and the under-dairymaid £2, while a ploughman earned four shillings and sixpence a week, due possibly to his work being temporary.

John Richards died in 1721 and Alice in 1723. His son William inherited the property and his descendants remained there until 1806 when Warmwell House and the estates were sold to Thomas Billett. He died intestate so they then passed to his only daughter, who, in 1823, married Captain Augustus Foster, formerly a captain in the 14th Light Dragoons, with whom Billet had served in the Peninsular War of 1808-1814. Captain and Mrs. Foster, around 1850, replaced the stone mullions and added the bay window in the morning room and they and their descendants were to own the house for the next 120 years.

They were succeeded by their son, Augustus Billett Foster, who died in 1892. His brother Lieut. Richard Bayntun Foster R.N. died in 1909. One of their daughters, Mary-Matilda-Willoughby married Mr. Thomas Pryor of High Elms, Hertfordshire. The Pryors often rented Warmwell House for the summer.

Major and Mrs. Foster, who lived there in 1928, had four pretty daughters and spent time (and more money than they could sensibly afford) at their London house presenting them as debutantes on the social scene. The rest of the time they lived at Warmwell, as Major Foster owned the local gravel pits. In due course they ran into financial difficulties and in 1936 Warmwell was sold to Lord Ellenborough, who spent the next three years restoring and refurbishing the house, living there through the Second World War until his death in 1945.

Mrs. Joan Crawley Ross Skinner was a cousin of Thomas Pryor and mother of Mr. H.J.C. Ross Skinner. Born in 1900, she had visited her cousins here in 1910. In 1945 she heard the house was for sale. She travelled down from Aberdeen, and sitting on the front stairs of the empty house at midnight, decided it was a happy house and bought it. All the present generation of Ross Skinners were born in this house.

The complex design of the house, built by John Trenchard in about 1618, suggests that it was built around an earlier house. Scarcely a room has four right angles. The south east front has an open recessed porch entered by an arcade of two round and partly moulded arches springing from a Tuscan central column. Above the porch sits a tablet representing a lamb, the crest of the Richards family. Projecting from the roof on either side of the porch are four original lead spouts They have serrated edges held on scrolled wrought iron brackets and give a dramatic effect to the front of the house. The wall is carried up into three gables with parapets of quadrants and semicircles, the latter flanked by circular, decorative chimneys. There have been many alterations to the windows, some replaced, as in 1850, and others, as in the dining room, blocked up.

Adjoining the morning room a stone spiral staircase leads to the first floor. Unaccountably it descends 4 or 5 steps into the ground though there are no cellars below. The main stone staircase in the house is splendid. It rises up over the lower passageway holding the upper floor on thin Tuscan newel posts. The sturdy balusters taper downwards

WARMWELL HOUSE. John Richards built the unusual porch with his crest above.

which is unusual. A little way up the stairs is an exterior door leading out onto two deep steps perhaps once used a mounting block.

Between the entrance hall and the main stair hall stands a reset seventeenth century archway decorated with rosettes. It was discovered blocked up in the north wall of the dining room. The jambs are moulded with three rolls and are probably medieval. The dining room could possibly have been part of the Great Hall of the original house. The fireplace with a late sixteenth century restored surround is said to have come from the Old Rooms, Weymouth, the town's first Assembly Rooms. The oak room, to the north, is lined with reset seventeenth century panelling. Here a splendid fireplace with a stone head has a decorated mantelshelf. The overmantel is divided into two bays containing mirrors. The windows of this room, which probably came from the church, as they are dated between 1377-1483, consist of a pair of two-light windows which seem to have been reset inside out.

The drawing room, on the first floor, was remodelled early in the nineteenth century. There was at one time a plaster barrel vault ceiling here, the remains of which can be found in the roof. The Long Gallery, across from the drawing room, retains the aura of the Trenchards. It is lined with seventeenth century panelling and the doors have original moulded oak frames. A small room leading off the gallery was Mr. Sadler's chamber. Here he dictated his prophecy, referring frequently to an unseen person in the corner of the room, unseen, that is, by his servant, Thomas Gray, and his minister, The Rev. Cuthbert Bownd, rector of Warmwell Church. The original document of the prophecy is now in the British Museum

In 1937 an airfield was built at the northern end of the parish. Hurricanes and Spitfires flew from R.A.F. Warmwell to defend Portland and played a leading part in the Battle of Britain. The house was undamaged during the war though Mr. Westmacott, the farmer, was killed by a bomb on the drive near Howe's Garden. Both the Allied and German dead were buried in Warmwell churchyard near the house, though the remains of the German dead have now been returned to Germany.

Jutting out from the back of the house is a walled courtyard in an oblong shape reminiscent of a Real Tennis Court. The windows looking down onto the court would have afforded an excellent view of the game. The extensive gardens of Warmwell and the views of the open landscape are pure delight.

Waterston Manor

WATERSTON MANOR is one of several manor houses following the river along the Piddle Valley. Its nearest neighbour, a few miles downstream, is the more imposing Athelhampton House, with which it once had close links, and, just upstream, delightful little Muston Manor. Despite many vicissitudes, including being almost destroyed by a disastrous fire in the nineteenth century, the house is still beautiful and is set in an elegant garden.

The oldest part of the house dates from the later sixteenth or early seventeenth century, when Thomas Howard, later 3rd Viscount Howard of Bindon, became the owner and began to enlarge and remodel the existing house. His classic frontispiece over the entrance to the east front is in the latest architectural fashion that Elizabethan builders were learning from the Dutch. The arched doorway is flanked by empty shell headed niches and fluted Doric columns, above which are two figures in their own niches, flanked this time by Ionic columns, with a three light window between and slightly above them. One figure with palm branch and staff represents Contempt of the World and the other is unidentified. Above the window is a third niche, flanked by Corinthian columns, containing a figure representing Justice with her scales. The whole topped by a handsome pediment reaching up to the gable, including a bull's-eye window and the date 1586.

His successor, Thomas Howard, 1st Earl of Suffolk, was probably the author of the more romantic, seventeenth century south front, with its two storey, bow fronted porch above a square entrance, completed by a pretty balustraded balcony at the third storey. The lower storey of this front is of red brick with a diamond patterning of black, the upper storeys have been rendered but in places it is still possible to discern the brickwork beneath. Its three gables are joined by little scalloped arches to let the rain off the roof, an attractive and unusual arrangement.

Just before the First World War the house was sold and the new owner carried out some further alterations and extension under the guidance of the architect Morley Horder, who also re-planned the gardens, the design of which remains substantially the same today. Until then the manor had been leased as a farm continuously since the mid seventeenth century and it is in this guise that Thomas Hardy used it as the model for Bathsheba Everdene's home in *Far from the Madding Crowd*. He describes it as 'a hoary building, of the early stage of Classic Renaissance' where 'Soft brown mosses, like faded velveteen, formed cushions upon the stone tiling, and tufts of the houseleek or sengreen sprouted from the eaves of low surrounding buildings.'

The name Waterston has had a variety of versions. In the Domesday Book it is Pidere, by 1212 it was Pidela Walteri and in fourteenth century records Vill Pudele Walterstone. Later it went through various renderings of Walterston or Waterston, all of which add up to 'Walter's farm on the Piddle', although Walter's identity is lost in the mists of time.

Henry de Pidele appears in 1280 as the earliest recorded owner and he also held Athelhampton. His heirs were his daughters, Alice, aged 18, and Joan, aged 14. In 1291 after Henry's death there was an enquiry when, in order to claim their inheritance, Alice and Joan had to establish that they were not minors and various friends and

WATERSTON MANOR. The south front which inspired Thomas Hardy's description of Bathsheba's bower in *Far From The Madding Crowd.*

neighbours were called to testify that they could remember the girls' births.

Alice married Nicholas Martyn, but it is not clear whether the Martyns were already at Athelhampton. It seems unlikely, as Alice was heir to both Athelhampton and Waterston. Alice and Nicholas, who is referred to as 'of Waterston' probably married between her father's death in 1280 and the enquiry held in 1291. Nicholas seems to have been the grandson of Nicholas Fitz Martyn of Poleynston. Thereafter different branches of the Martyn family lived both at Athelhampton and Waterston.

Alice and Nicholas' only son, Robert, died childless in 1377 and his sister Johanna became the heir. She was married to John Govis and their son Walter eventually inherited. History then repeated itself and in the absence of any direct heirs the estate descended to his sister Christiana. Her husband was Sir William de Newburgh who died in 1481. The house again passed down through the female line and eventually became the property of Thomas, 1st Viscount Howard of Bindon who had married Elizabeth Marney, Christiana's great granddaughter.

Waterston was settled on their second son, Thomas, probably as the younger son's portion, but in 1590 his elder brother Henry died and he succeeded to the title, becoming 3rd Viscount Howard of Bindon. Rachel Lloyd, in her book *Dorset Elizabethans,* describes him as being 'very spiteful and a cauldron of misdirected energy' and he was suspected, at least by Sir Walter Raleigh, of having poisoned his wife, Grace Duffield. When his brother died, Thomas inherited only the title, excluding the land, which came to Henry's granddaughter, Ambrosia. Thomas contested her

WATERSTON MANOR. The east front.

claim on the grounds that her mother, Douglas Howard, had been too delicate to bear a live child and that Ambrosia was a changeling. A long and bitter court case ensued, full of sensational accusations and 'evidence' about her mother's supposedly physical incapability to bear a child. When Ambrosia's father re-married, she was made a ward of the Queen. In 1592 Thomas was imprisoned for spreading slander about the Queen's ward, but eventually gained his release by giving assurances that he would hold his peace. He did finally gain Ambrosia's estates, but not until after her death in 1600.

Before inheriting his title, Thomas began to enlarge and 'modernise' the house but perhaps did not progress far with his plans because, when he inherited the title in 1590, he went on to build Lulworth Castle as his seat and fifteen years later sold Waterston to his relative, Thomas Howard, 1st Earl of Suffolk, who completed the building work.

In 1641 Thomas Howard's grandson, James, sold it to Sir John Strangways. Like the Earls of Suffolk, the Strangways never lived at Waterston but leased it as a tenant farm, which it remained for some 250 years. In 1863 a large part of the house was destroyed by fire and was rebuilt in 1864. Of the seventeenth century house, only the south front and part of the east front remain and little evidence is left of the original plan.

In 1911 Waterston found a saviour in Captain G. V. Carter, who engaged the architect Morley Horder to restore and enlarge the house and to lay out its gardens. After being used as a farm for many years the house had become down at heel and the old garden had totally disappeared.

The main entrance to the farm, on the south side under the circular bay, was converted into a garden entry leading into a small paved rose garden and a gatehouse was made through two old cottages which formed one side of the stable yard. Some old Jacobean stone arcades from the original house were used in the wing walls running out from the south front on either side. Similar arches were

WATERSTON MANOR.
The porch and gabled bay on the east front, dated 1586 and probably built by Thomas Howard. Then the height of fashion, all three Classical orders are incorporated into the design: Doric columns either side of the entrance, Ionic on the second stage and as mullions to the window, and Corinthian columns at the top.
The left hand lower figure is holding a palm branch and staff, the figure to the right is unknown, whilst below the gable and the pair of rampant lions either side of the circular window stands the figure of Justice with her scales.

inserted into the end of the farm buildings to form a garden house overlooking the rose garden, although the buildings have now lost their arches and the rose garden its roses in favour of a more easily maintained lawn.

A north-east wing was added to the east gable front and a newly formed hall was panelled in old oak. Thomas Hardy described the staircase in Bathsheba's house as 'of hard oak, the balusters, heavy as bed-posts, being turned and moulded, the handrail as stout as a parapet top, and the stairs themselves continually twisting round like a person trying to look over his shoulder.' This delightful description was used as a basis for its replacement, which was hand made locally in heavy oak.

In 1936 Capt. Carter sold the house to Col. H. W. Woodall and after the Second World War it changed ownership several times. In 1975 Mr. Adam Tindall bought it and has lavished love and care on it in his turn.

West Hall

WEST HALL is close to Longburton on the main Dorchester to Sherborne Road but it can only be reached from the village by a footpath to West Hall Farm. The approach by road is via a long country lane, running roughly parallel to the main road. It is impossible to see the house until, turning off a farm road, you enter a courtyard surrounded by a tall hedge. Even then little of the house is visible until you walk through an opening in the hedge, when a lovely gabled house is revealed, surrounded by lawns on different levels with steps, borders and mellow brick walls. The house, which is roofed with beautiful stone slates, is built of a stone called 'forest marble', from an old quarry on West Hall land. This has now disappeared under an area of housing called King's Close, named after the King family who once owned West Hall.

The oldest part of the house is the north-east wing. This has a fifteenth century roof and contains some plank and muntin panelling and seventeenth century doors. Apart from some modern additions, the house is mainly seventeenth century, with the possible exception of the drawing room on the south-east side and the rooms above. There are two staircases in the house, one is elegant eighteenth century and the other is magnificent seventeenth century oak with turned balusters, moulded rails and square newels to support the flights above.

The main front door of the house and the external door from the ante-room to the garden are

WEST HALL. The south east front of the house, showing the 'new' drawing room of the late seventeenth century with its tall sash windows.

seventeenth century and still retain their heavy timber locking bars which slide into recesses in the stone on each side of the doorway. Mr. Fielding, who bought the house in 1979, says that at that time the four inch thick oak locking bars were still the only means of securing those doors. The solid oak timbers sliding into deep stone sockets would doubtless be as secure as modern locks – if less convenient. Hutchins mentions 'chops' in this front door, which tradition says were made in the course of an assault by Parliamentary forces during the Civil War. They are still visible as three deep cuts which appear to have been made by an axe, the largest of them being about four inches long by about three quarters of an inch deep, substantial, but insufficient to cause any real damage to this immensely thick door.

The earliest record of West Hall seems to be in 1363 when John de Cerne settled land here on his wife Phillippa. The first mention of a house comes 68 years later, when Richard de Cerne bequeathed a house and land in Westhalle to a relative called John Herring, who in turn, left it his to his grandson, John Russell, in 1456. By 1462 it belonged to the Hymerford family of Folke, though whether this was through inheritance or purchase is not clear. In that year Robert Hymerford died leaving his estate to his two sisters, Avice, who was a widow, and Elizabeth, wife of Thomas Moleyns. Thomas and Elizabeth obviously took West Hall because it remained in the Moleyns family until the mid eighteenth century when, for lack of direct heirs, the estate was sold to the Reverend John King.

Allowing for a late sixteenth or early seventeenth century date for the present house, the most likely builder is Thomas Moleyns, son of Thomas and Elizabeth. He was married to Ann Thornhill, daughter of William Thornhill of Stalbridge, and in 1578 was Sheriff of Dorset. He may well have considered that his status warranted the extension and improvement of the old, medieval, single range house.

In 1663, Edward Moleyns, who was Thomas's great-great-grandson, died leaving his property to his daughter, Susanna, who was married to Thomas Chafe. In accordance with the law at the time, a detailed inventory was taken of all Thomas's property for probate. Mr. Robert Machin discovered this document some years ago, whilst carrying out some research in the Wiltshire County Records Office. He gave the present owners a copy of the inventory, which lists every room with its contents and their value, and gives a wonderful snapshot of the house as it was on 25th May 1668. The house was well furnished. For example, it contained three down beds, six feather ones and two flock ones, along with twenty three pairs of sheets, various blankets, rugs and quilts plus twenty tablecloths and ten dozen napkins, to name just some of the household linen.

Mr. Machin was able to establish the location of nearly all the rooms mentioned in the inventory with the exception of 'the little parlour', of which he could find no trace. Judging by the inventory it could not have been all that small, as it contained one small table, one leather couch, three leather chairs, six leather stools, one form, seven frame chairs, some old cushions and one old carpet, plus andirons, firepan, tongs and bellows. This would seem to have been the room used by the family as their main living room. It is certainly more comfortably furnished than the grander 'Great Parlour' which held 'two tableboards, one livery cupboard, one forme, three frame chairs, ten frame stools and one little chair, three carpets and one pair of brass andirons'. It seems likely that the present drawing room, on the south-east side of the house, replaced the earlier 'Little Parlour'.

It was probably Susanna and Thomas who built the drawing room sometime between inheriting the house in 1663 and Thomas's death in 1701. We know that they carried out some improvements of the north-east wing, which are commemorated by their plaster coat of arms dated 1671 in one of the rooms on the first floor. The drawing room is lined with large moulded panelling with a cornice and dado rail and has tall sash windows. In one corner, concealed in the moulding above the cornice and inaccessible at about fifteen feet above the floor, is scratched the name H. BALL and the date 1696. If

WEST HALL. The south west front.

this graffiti is genuine, it securely dates the building of the room to the end of the seventeenth century rather than the early eighteenth. The style of the room fits well with that date as sash windows began to appear during the second half of the seventeenth century and the use of large panelling from about 1675.

When Thomas died in 1701 his eldest daughter, Susanna, who had married Charles Kent the previous year, inherited West Hall. She died in 1718 two years after her husband. They had no children and her two surviving sisters were her heirs. They were both middle-aged married ladies and it seems likely that the house was leased out from that time until, in 1741, it was sold to the Reverend John King.

According to Hutchins, Reverend King, 'repaired the mansion house there' and for almost the next two centuries it remained the property of the King family. Many of their sons were ordained into the church and several of their daughters married clergymen. An exception to this tradition was Colonel Henry King, who commanded a battalion of the Buffs in the mid nineteenth century and was a keen sportsman. He devoted his life and possibly much of his fortune to hunting in the Blackmore Vale and from this time on the fortunes of the King family declined and they began selling off parcels of land. By the early twentieth century their money problems were acute and the house was once again let, but there was little or no money available for repairs and maintenance so it became gradually more dilapidated.

In 1923 the last member of the King family was able to break the entail and sell the property and 500 acres of land to Major Tom Eccles and his wife. Major Eccles was a keen hunting man, whose wealth derived from cotton and who was able to bring the house back to life once again. The Major died in 1939 but his wife survived him until the early 1950's. During the Second World War the house was requisitioned and used as an Officer's Mess for the Royal Army Medical Corps but it was partitioned to enable Mrs. Eccles to continue living in part of it. After the war she was joined in the house by her husband's nephew, Colonel Ireland-Smith and his wife, who lived with her until her death. The Ireland-Smiths inherited the property and remained there until they sold it in 1979 to Mr. and Mrs. R.W. Fielding.

Whitecliff Manor Farm

Taking its name from the white chalk cliffs at the foot of Ballard Down, this ancient house looks out over Swanage Bay, occupying possibly the most perfect location in the Purbecks. The area has been inhabited since the Bronze Age. The Domesday Book records that Aluuard, a Saxon nobleman, held the land here before 1066, being replaced by the Norman knight Serlo de Burci after the Conquest. Domesday also records that the manor consisted of 360 acres, double the area it covers today.

The house has been added to many times and is now of an unusual shape. The front of the house faces south. The oldest part on the western side dates from the early seventeenth century and could have been an addition to an even earlier dwelling, later replaced by the main range. This tallies with the date 1683 carved on a stone in a barn. On the north side of the main range an original small window with a rounded head is still in position, while the other windows have been modernised. At

WHITECLIFF MANOR FARM. The south front is probably a rebuilding of a previous dwelling.

WHITECLIFF MANOR FARM. A nineteenth century engraving.

the east end of the main range there is another wing running south. This too was possibly a rebuilding of a former structure. It is noticeable that the land falls away steeply from the east wing, as though there was once a stream or even a moat running alongside the house.

To the west of the house an ancient wall runs southwards towards a tower. On the inside a stone staircase leads to an upper floor from which there is a superb view over Swanage Bay. The area beneath the staircase might have been used for storage or even as a sentry post. Another possibility is that the tower could have been used for defence, similar to the tower at neighbouring Godlingston Manor.

In 1251 the land was owned by Albreda, wife of Ralph de Sumeri, and Anastasia, wife of Ralph Fitzgilbert. In 1333 Whitecliff became the property of Henry de Whiteclyve, whose family owned it for the next century.

Ralph Tresswell's *Survey of the Isle of Purbeck* of 1586 names the Laurences of Winterborne Stepleton as owners of Whitecliff. Richard Laurence died in 1597, passing the property to his son Richard and thence to his grandson George Laurence, the land being valued at £73 4s. During this time the main range was rebuilt and the family continued to own Whitecliff until the early eighteenth century. Then it was sold to Thomas Cockram, son of Brune Cockram, who was a rector of Swanage, and who preferred to live at Whitecliff rather than at the rectory. In 1829 the last of this family, John Cockram, sold the property to William Morton Pitt, owner of Encombe House, who, ten years later, sold it to the first Earl of Eldon along with Encombe House. It remained with the Encombe Estate until 1976 when the land was purchased by the National Trust and the house sold to Mr. and Mrs. N. Viney.

In 1926, Josiah Dorset White in his book *Reminiscences of English Country Life* conjured up a remarkable description of Whitecliff at the turn of the nineteenth century. His father was born there in 1816 and his ancestors had been leaseholders of the farm for many generations. He himself was taken to Whitecliff when about six years old. Josiah describes vividly his first recollections of the house. There was a courtyard at the front enclosed by a high stone wall which reached to the sills of the second floor windows. The gateway into the courtyard was guarded by a portcullis, with the keystone on the arch above displaying a rotund *J* in twelfth century script. Outside the gate was a bridge under which was a deep depression, suggesting evidence of a moat or stream at one time. Sited in one corner near the house was a well and at the opposite corner was the watchtower. The walled garden was laid out geometrically with rows of fruit trees and an abundance of vegetables. Seaweed was brought up from the beach below on donkeys and used as fertiliser. Perhaps seduced by its romantic position, Josiah believed the house to have been a hunting lodge for King John, with the watchtower serving as a lookout.

Inside the house he mentions the beautifully carved staircase, said to be Elizabethan. A few steps up to the left of the entrance hall was the parlour, whose fireplace could take four feet long logs. Above the mantel hung a picture of Abraham offering up Isaac. It was in poor condition, probably due to the smoke, but measured around four foot by six. To the right, or at the end of the entrance hall, was the huge dining room boasting a table which could seat twenty. This room was dominated by an immense chimney, the opening being six feet high by eight feet wide. Andirons

WHITECLIFF MANOR FARM. The north front features a small seventeenth century window to the right of the porch. Apart from the absence of the dormer window, externally the house is very similar to that shown in the engraving on the opposite page.

stood in the centre of the hearth and pots and pans were hung on hooks from the spit. The pair of settles at either side of the fire were fully occupied on cold winter nights. From the mantel hung copper kettles and pans while pewter plates and candlesticks sat on the mantelpiece. A copper bedwarmer hung from one side of the fireplace. This would be filled with hot coals on frosty nights and placed between the sheets to warm up the beds in the cold bedrooms.

Beyond the dining room came the milk room with its rows of lead vats for cooling the milk. The kitchen was here too as well as the bake-oven in which twenty loaves of bread were baked at one time. Nearby was the laundry with its massive steaming copper boiler.

From the hallway steps led down to the spacious cellar which was around sixteen feet high and usually contained two big hogsheads of ale or beer. The ale was brewed in the spring or summer to quench the thirst of the workers in the fields at harvest time. According to Josiah his father was a fair employer who looked after the welfare of his labourers.

To the east of the house there once stood a great stone barn with a doorway on either side large enough to allow the wagons to enter. On each gable end was a small opening for owls, a lovely example of the age old relationship between man and Dorset's wildlife, as the owls were essential for keeping vermin under control. By the turn of the twentieth century, the barn had disappeared.

The massive front door of the house with cleats across the inside, immense hinges, and a lock holding a huge key had been replaced by his father, and changed yet again by subsequent occupants, but the windows, which his father also replaced, still remain on the south side. Josiah emigrated to Canada in 1870, and the house underwent extensive changes during the next century, but its story still intrigues and fascinates. The house itself now patiently awaits further excavation and research, which will one day reveal its full history.

Winterborne Clenston Manor

Winterborne CLENSTON is about four miles south of Blandford in the northern Winterborne valley. It takes the first part of its name from the little chalk stream, which tends to dry up in the summer, and the second from the name of one of its earliest owners, a family called Clench. Approaching Clenston along the valley from Whitchurch, the road runs beside Whatcombe Park for about a mile, until a little Victorian church, isolated in a field, can be seen on the right. A little further on, the magnificent Tudor barn of Clenston appears, close to the road with the manor house set back from it just beyond the stream. The settlement is tiny, consisting of little more than the manor house, the rectory, and a farm, hardly sufficient to warrant the status of a village.

There were originally three hamlets here, Winterborne Nicholaston, Philipston and Clenston but by 1428, Clenston and Nicholaston each had less than ten inhabitants. By the 1460s Nicholaston and Philipston had effectively ceased to function as separate parishes. This depopulation was probably due to the ongoing effects of the Black Death and the increasing importance of sheep farming, which used great tracts of land but employed fewer workers than arable and dairy farms.

WINTERBORNE CLENSTON MANOR. The manor house in the nineteenth century.

The main part of the house is almost certainly late fifteenth or early sixteenth century, built of alternating bands of stone and flint and roofed with stone slates. It faces south-west towards the stream and has a central wing extending to the north-east. The original building was extended to the north around 1600. At the front of the house is an octagonal staircase turret, which has an unusual and rather top-heavy appearance because it is corbelled out above the first floor to give headroom for the stone newel staircase serving the first floor rooms and the attic. The first floor windows in the original section of the house have four light windows with arched heads, whilst those on the ground floor have been replaced by windows with larger lights and flat heads, probably around 1530.

The ground floor of the original part of the house was arranged as two rooms with a through passage. This part, now divided into three rooms, still retains the original pre-Elizabethan ribbed ceilings. The newel staircase leads to the first floor, which has two rooms separated by a passage formed of plank and muntin panelling. In a recess in the wall at the end of this passage is a rare survival of a stone socket for a cresset, with a drain for waste wax. In the sixteenth century this floor was probably a single great chamber, similar to the first floor chamber at Wolfeton, and was open to the roof, the

WINTERBORNE CLENSTON MANOR. A view from the south west with its gabled staircase tower.

present flat ceilings being inserted in about 1600. The original, high quality, decorative timberwork in the attic was obviously intended to be seen and there are also remains of some lovely sixteenth century plasterwork. The patterns of this plasterwork occur in two bedrooms at Mapperton, which can be dated to about 1545-55, and Oswald considers that there can be no doubt that the same plasterer, using the same moulds, worked at both Clenston and Mapperton. The decorative bosses of the ground floor ceiling also appear to have been made from moulds used at Mapperton.

The earliest historical records directly related to Winterborne Clenston appear in the early thirteenth century. In 1220 Walter de Winterburn held land here and in 1232 there was a dispute over the boundaries of the common pasture involving Robert Clench and Roger de Winterburn. By the 1230s, William de Winterburn was prosperous enough to give all his land at Thorncombe, a farm between Clenston and Blandford, to the monks of Forde Abbey. A century or so later, in 1371, another William de Winterburn was Sheriff of Dorset. He had no sons to inherit his land and his daughter's child, John Syward, became his heir. In 1402 John died childless and John Heryng, the grandson of William de Winterburn's sister, inherited the estate. This was the family who gave their name to Winterborne Herringston and Chaldon Herring. Once again there was a lack of sons and John Herring made his daughter Isolda and her husband John de la Lynde heirs to the de Winterborne estates. He outlived both his daughter and her husband and in 1455 his grandson, John inherited. John held Clenston for at least twenty years and

WINTERBORNE CLENSTON MANOR. The great stone and flint Tudor barn.

was followed by three more generations of de la Lyndes.

In 1483 his son, Thomas, was involved in the Duke of Buckingham's abortive rebellion against Richard III. He was attainted for treason, his estates were confiscated and he fled the country, probably to Flanders or Brittany, to join other supporters of Henry Tudor. When Henry finally won the throne in 1485, Thomas's estates were restored to him and he was knighted. It was probably Thomas, his star rising, who built himself a new house at Clenston.

The family continued to prosper and the next Sir Thomas de la Lynde was Sheriff of Dorset in 1516. In 1520 he was appointed, together with his brother-in-law Thomas Trenchard, to be one of the knights attending Queen Catherine at the Field of the Cloth of Gold. However, in 1556 when his son Sir George died, the heir was just eight years old and only survived his father by a few months, so the estates were divided between George's three sisters, Agnes, Warburga and Anne.

Clenston and several other properties came to Warburga, whose husband was Thomas Morton of Milborne St Andrew. He was the great nephew of Cardinal Morton, who, like the first Thomas de La Lynde, had supported the Buckingham rebellion and escaped to Flanders after being arrested by Richard III. Warburga and Thomas left Milborne to live at Clenston. Their son George and grandson, another George, inherited Clenston in their turn and continued to live there.

In 1611, their great grandson, the third George, inherited. He was created a baronet in 1618 and built himself a new, much grander house at Milborne and returned there to live. Milborne then became the family seat and Clenston was let to tenant farmers and was not occupied by its owners again until well into the twentieth century. The male line of the Mortons ended in 1698 with the death of Sir John, the 2nd Baronet and his heir was his daughter Ann and her husband Edmund Pleydell. Hutchins says that their son Edmund Morton Pleydell repaired and improved Milborne, but in 1750-53 he built a new house at Whatcombe, just across the valley from Clenston.

In 1835 his grandson Edmund Morton Pleydell died leaving four surviving daughters. The third daughter, Louisa, was married to Colonel John Mansell of Smedmore. Their second son, John Clavell Mansell, inherited the estate in 1871 from his mother's sister, Margaretta, who had no children. John added Pleydell to his surname and was succeeded in the 1930s by his grandaughter, Mrs. Pleydell-Railston, whose two brothers had been killed in the First World War.

In the mid 1950s, when Mrs. Pleydell-Railston's daughter, Mrs. Carlyle-Clarke and her husband came to live there, the house was occupied for the first time in three centuries by the family who owned it. At this time extensive repairs and renovation were undertaken. The house has been leased again intermittently since that time.

From the thirteenth century to the present day Clenston has never changed hands by sale and the thread of inheritance can be traced back to William de Winterburn in 1230, an incredible seven centuries!

Winterborne Tomson Manor

THE MANOR HOUSE at Tomson is a most attractive, early seventeenth century house of warm, reddish sandstone with some brickwork on the upper parts. It stands alone in its garden facing south across fields, with a beautiful, historic little church just a few yards outside its gates. It was not always so isolated, being once the centre of a little hamlet, and the remains of house platforms can still be seen in the field to the south of the house. In the mid nineteenth century it was referred to as being 'reduced to a farmhouse and some cottages'.

Its appearance from the front is pleasingly balanced but the rear elevation seems rather off centre. Some foundations discovered to the west of the house were suggested by Hutchins to be evidence that the house was originally longer and symmetrical, centred on the rectangular stair tower, but the Royal Commission on Historic Monuments is dubious about this interpretation. The drawing room at the west end of the house has its Tudor fireplace rather oddly situated in the western corner of the room, which suggests that the room should in fact be longer.

It is probable that the main entrance was originally at what is now the rear of the house, as was the case at Anderson Manor half a mile away. At the back of the house there is some evidence for this in a substantial doorway beside the stair tower, where there are still heavy brackets for hinges and a cavity for a locking bar. This is now an internal doorway inside a Victorian overshot, but would have provided clear access to the foot of the newel stair.

In the early 1970s, Mr. Desmond Hooper, the present owner's father, began a programme of much needed repairs and renovation to the house, which took some years to complete. This was not the first time in its history that the house had undergone major restoration, with the result that its internal features are now fairly difficult to unravel. The entrance hall is lined with magnificent oak plank and muntin panelling.

The third edition of Hutchins's *History of Dorset* mentions the 'large and well preserved remains of two plaster ceilings', the designs included one which was either a crown or a modification of an archbishop's mitre, perhaps a reference to the ownership of Archbishop Wake. By the 1970s just enough of these ceilings survived on the first floor to allow them to be part restored, part copied for Mr. Hooper. The main bedroom has a draught porch, partly made of carved and painted timber as well as plain oak panelling.

WINTERBORNE TOMSON MANOR. The little church of St Andrew at Tomson. Built in the early twelfth century, it was refitted in the eighteenth century and once again rescued and restored in 1929, with funds raised by the sale of Thomas Hardy manuscripts.

WINTERBORNE TOMSON MANOR. The original entrance was probably a doorway in the left hand side of the tower but is now part of the interior.

Tomson has an ancient history, the earliest documentary evidence seems to be that in 1316 Roger Chaumpayn was Lord of Thomaston and that at least another three generations of Chaumpaynes succeeded him. In 1347 Roger Champaigne is recorded as owner, succeeding Peter Champaign. By 1377 it had passed to the Hussey family and it remained in their hands until De La Lynde Hussey sold it to the father of Archbishop William Wake. This must have been after 1645 because in that year Thomas Hussey had his estate at Tomson confiscated by Parliament for supporting Charles I during the Civil War.

William Wake was born in Blandford in 1657 and became Bishop of Lincoln in 1705 and Archbishop of Canterbury in 1716. The lovely little church was completely refitted at his expense and the box pews, the pulpit, the screen, communion rails and matching table, together with the font cover and studded west door, date from his time. He died in 1737 and his daughters inherited the estate. In 1750 they and their heirs sold it to the Hon. John Spencer, later Viscount Althorp and Earl Spencer.

In 1773 Henry Bankes of Kingston Lacy bought the manor and estates of Shapwick Champayne from Earl Spencer, thus acquiring the manor and farm of Tomson. The existing tenant was Roger Pinchard, but at Michaelmas 1773 the lease was

Above WINTERBORNE TOMSON MANOR. The south front showing the buttresses either side of the porch and the courses of Purbeck stone slates on the lower part of the roof.

Right WINTERBORNE TOMSON MANOR. The back of the house with its stair tower.

taken over by Robert and Thomas Lillington. The rent was substantially increased, from £290 to £340 a year, but the farm must have been in a poor state because for two years the Lillingtons were allowed to deduct at least £150 from their rent for building repairs. The chapel was also in a bad state; ultimately housing an assortment of livestock until it was finally rescued and restored in 1929.

The manor remained the property of the Bankes Estate until it was sold in about 1910 to the sitting tenant, Mr. Ernest Genge. He remained there until 1922 when he sold it to Mr. Maurice Hooper, who continued to work the 600 acre farm. In 1972 it was his son, Mr. Desmond Hooper who was responsible for restoring the house to its present attractive state, a project which lasted for many years. The house is now let by his son, Mr. James Hooper, who still works some of the land in conjunction with his own farm.

Wolfeton House

THOMAS HARDY, in his intriguing story, *A Group of Noble Dames,* describes Wolfeton as an 'ivied manor house, flanked by battlemented towers, more than usually distinguished by the size of its mullioned windows'. The ivy has since been removed, revealing the full beauty of the stonework. This great house lies close to Dorchester, near where the River Cerne meets the Frome in the parish of Charminster, well hidden from the Yeovil road. The rough driveway gives little indication of the magnificence that awaits. The huge gatehouse and towers have guarded it for over five hundred years. Ulf the Saxon gave his name to this place, and Ulfton gradually turned into Wolfeton.

Until the early fifteenth century part of the manor had belonged to the Jurdains, who were wealthy Dorset landowners. Joan, John Jurdains' daughter and heiress, married John Mohun of Hammoon. In

Above John Trenchard, who inherited Wolfeton in 1480 and began building the present house.

Below WOLFETON HOUSE. A watercolour by John Baverstock Knight in the early 1800s.

WOLFETON HOUSE. The gatehouse towers possibly date from the late fourteenth century.

due course, Christian, the Mohun's only daughter, married Henry Trenchard of Hordle, in Hampshire. John Mohun died in 1480 and Wolfeton passed to his grandson John Trenchard, who began to build the present house. It was from here, in 1484, that John Trenchard planned the Dorset plot to put Henry Tudor on the throne. He failed. His twenty-seven manors were confiscated by Richard III and passed to Sir Morgan Kidwelly.

Fortunately for John Trenchard, in the following year the Battle of Bosworth Field turned the tables and his lands were reinstated. He died in 1495 and his sixteen-year-old son, Thomas, continued the construction work by rebuilding the south front, in 1528, and the gatehouse in 1534. An inscribed panel now reset from the destroyed south front reads 'HOC OPUS FINITU EST ANNO DNI MDXXXIIII' indicating that the house was finished in 1534. Sir Thomas died in 1550. Both he and his father accumulated most of their wealth from the great flocks of sheep that then grazed the Dorset downs.

The towers of the gatehouse are older than the rest of the house and could possibly have been in existence since the late fourteenth century, fortifying a much earlier building. From the arrow slits the archers would certainly have had an advantage over unwelcome visitors. Both towers once had lantern tops for use as dovecots, and the doors from the gatehouse to the cots still remain. There were garderobes in both towers whose waste exits are still visible just above ground level.

A house of such antiquity usually has a history to match and Wolfeton is no exception. In January 1506, Sir Thomas Trenchard, as sheriff of the county, was summoned to Weymouth. The Archduke Philip of Austria and his new wife, Joanna, daughter of King Ferdinand and Queen Isabella of Castile, were returning to Castile from the Netherlands when they were forced to put into

WOLFETON HOUSE. The Tudor south front in the eighteenth century, showing the eastern end demolished in about 1822. In 1862, Mr W.H.P. Weston rebuilt the top stage of the south-east tower.

Weymouth harbour in a storm. Sir Thomas escorted them to Wolfeton for shelter. Unfortunately he could not speak Spanish and his guests knew no English. To the rescue came his kinsman, John Russell of Berwick, near Bridport, who had travelled extensively and could speak fluent Spanish. When Henry VIII invited the royal couple to Windsor, John Russell accompanied them, so beginning a remarkable career which saw him rise through the ranks serving four sovereigns before his death in 1555. In appreciation of his service he was awarded the lands of Woburn Abbey and the title of Earl of Bedford. His descendant, the 5th earl, was created Duke of Bedford in 1694.

For Sir Thomas Trenchard's kindness, the Archduke and his wife presented him with a portrait medallion of themselves and two rare Chinese bowls, one of which is now in the Victoria and Albert Museum. In some quarters it is believed that the royal couple also presented to Sir Thomas the carved doorcase and chimneypiece located in the parlour.

Originally the house encircled a quadrangle. The gatehouse was on the eastern side and a chapel on the northern side. Early in the nineteenth century, the chapel fell into ruin and was pulled down, along with other buildings on the north side. On the south front are two distinct periods of architecture. The Tudor building at the eastern end was built by Sir Thomas Trenchard in 1528. The hood-moulds of the windows are ornamented with richly carved fruits and foliage. To the left of these windows rises an octagonal tower used as a garderobe, its conical roof topped by an unrecognisable animal playing a stringed instrument, perhaps a viol. The western end is of the Elizabethan and Jacobean period from the time of Sir George Trenchard, who inherited the house in 1570 and was responsible for the beautiful interior decoration in the Jacobean era.

The interior of the house is resplendent with traceried ceilings and sumptuous wood carvings. The door surround in the parlour is particularly magnificent. Here are the carved figures of a king and queen framed by Corinthian columns, while on the side of the entrance hall are carvings of ancient British warriors. Inside the parlour, the Jacobean chimneypiece, again framed with Corinthian columns has, among other things, two recessed panels holding the figures of Hope and Justice. Tudor panels carved with signs of the Zodiac and Labours of the Month were inserted into the chimneypiece in the nineteenth century. These sixteenth century panels originally formed a frieze in a room known as Mr. Trenchard's Smoking Room, which was demolished in 1822. The richly carved ceiling of the parlour is original, displaying figures of animals and foliage.

Passing through into the dining room, there stands another fine fireplace, smaller this time, made of plaster but painted dark brown with carvings illustrating the contest of the goddesses, with Paris awarding the apple near the city of Troy. An oak shelf below shows the date 1652. The ceiling is encrusted with foliage, masks and dolphins. Of great interest, too, is the carved figure of a chained ape with two bowls of fruit believed to date from around 1490.

WOLFETON HOUSE. The carved figure of a king. Fourteen figures of English kings once decorated the chimney piece in the Great Hall. In November 1640, on the first day of the Long Parliament, the sceptre fell from the hand of Charles I, an unhappy omen for the ill-fated king.

WOLFETON HOUSE. The magnificent doorway in the parlour with the carved figures of a king and queen framing the panel above the door.

The entrance hall is lined with beautifully restored sixteenth and seventeenth century panelling, possibly saved from another part of the house. On the left of the passage is the Great Hall, re-panelled around 1862, though some early sixteenth century panels remain depicting monkeys in human dress, also a satyr fighting a centaur. From the passage, the splendid stone staircase, built in 1580, and restored in the nineteenth century, leads up to the Great Chamber, once used as the dining hall. This was confirmed by the quantity of bones and walnut shells found under the floorboards. Around 1820 the chamber was divided into five small rooms but has now been restored to its original size. On the

WOLFETON HOUSE. The octagonal garderobe tower in the centre is part of the building of 1528. Everything to its left was built by Sir George Trenchard in the late Elizabethan and early Jacobean periods.

Jacobean stone fireplace, which rises to the ceiling, are carved figures of Faith and Hope and the heads of men and women, some bearing a likeness to North American Indians, perhaps in recognition of the travels of Sir Walter Raleigh, a frequent visitor to the house who often caused consternation with his outspoken atheistic views. There is an almost identical fireplace at Montacute. Both are dated 1600.

Sir George Trenchard, Sir Thomas's great grandson, inherited the house in 1557. Knighted by Elizabeth I, he was Deputy Lieutenant of the county throughout her reign. He was even appointed Governor of Sandsfoot Castle, which was in a dilapidated state at the approach of the Armada. The Queen was always reluctant to spend money, so he was forced to pay for the repairs himself. Sir George was held in high esteem, both in the county and by the Privy Council. He was duty bound to apprehend Catholic priests during the religious struggles of the sixteenth century, yet his sense of fairness always prevailed. In the case of the priest

John Cornelius, who was caught at Chideock Castle, home of Lady Dorothy Arundell, Sir George took him to Wolfeton and treated him kindly. Sadly, if inevitably, the priest was hanged, drawn and quartered in Dorchester in 1594.

Sir George increased his family fortune by adding Burton manor to his already considerable estate. In the late 1570s, he built the elegant south front onto Wolfeton, as well as the Riding House in 1610, which is similar in design and contemporary with Prince Henry's Riding House at St James's Palace.

Sir George received two unusual gifts from the Corporation of Lyme. The first, in 1593, was a box of marmalade and six oranges at a cost to the Corporation of seven shillings. The second, two years later, was recorded by the Mayor of Lyme as: 'Given to Sir George Trenchard a fair box of marmalade gilted, a barrel of conserves oranges and lemons and potatoes, 22s 10d'.

Sir George's long reign at Wolfeton finally came to an end in 1630. His son, Sir Thomas was an M.P. and a staunch Parliamentarian, who assisted in the siege of Corfe Castle in 1643. Two strange stories date from this time. One day Sir Thomas had invited a Judge of the Assize to dine at Wolveton. No sooner were the guests seated than the judge fled

WOLFETON HOUSE. Carvings of the signs of the Zodiac, now in the gatehouse chapel.

from the room and left the house. On his way back to Dorchester, in his carriage, he related how he had seen, behind Lady Trenchard's chair, the figure of her ladyship with her throat cut and her head under her arm. Before they had reached the town a messenger overtook them with the news that Lady Trenchard had committed suicide. The second story is also set in the dining room where, over the chimneypiece, there were once fourteen carved figures of English kings. On November 3rd 1640 the day on which the Long Parliament sat for the first time, the sceptre fell from the hand of Charles I, startling those dining in the room, who saw its fall as an ill omen for the king. And so it proved, for in January 1649 he was executed in London.

Sir Thomas died in 1657. His great grandson, Colonel Thomas Trenchard, had an only daughter, Mary, who married her cousin George Trenchard, M.P. of Lytchett Matravers. Wolfeton became increasingly neglected in favour of the family's now largely demolished manor house at Lytchett Matravers. Typical of this change in Wolfeton's fortunes was the fate of the armorial glass, described as the finest in the county, listing seven generations of the Trenchards from 1475-1657. It was completely destroyed due to careless packing when being removed from the house and transported to Lytchett in 1798.

In 1822, the back part of Wolfeton, to the north, was demolished. The Trenchards then sold Wolfeton to their cousins, the Hennings of Dorchester. However, before the Trenchards finally left the house, one of them waged a bet that he could drive a horse and carriage up the Great Staircase. Amazingly he won the bet. At times, it is said, the sound of ghostly hooves and carriage wheels can still be heard. In 1862 yet another relative, Mr. W.H.P. Weston purchased Wolfeton. He worked tirelessly to save the house from ruin. He heightened the octagonal south-east tower, adding a battlemented top as well as building another on the north side to match. He added the north porch and the walls connecting the house to the gatehouse and extensively renovated the interior.

In 1874 Mr. and Mrs. Wynne Alfred Bankes of the Kingston Lacy family became the new owners of the house and they continued the work of restoration until, in 1947, it passed to their granddaughter, Countess Zamoyska. It was divided into flats for a time until, fortunately, in the 1960s it was rescued by the present owners, Captain and Mrs. Nigel Thimbleby. Captain Thimbleby is connected to both the Mohun and Trenchard families, further extending the Wolfeton connection with these great families. Over the last forty years he and his wife have worked ceaselessly to maintain and enhance this important house. The original garden lay between two Tudor walls, one of which still remains, while on a higher level lies the original bowling green, completing the picture of a Tudor garden. Wolfeton today can be justly described as a noble house.

Woodsford Castle

WOODSFORD CASTLE is an unusual and impressive building but anyone expecting to see walls, towers and battlements is doomed to disappointment. Once it had all three, but over the centuries they gradually disappeared and the castle became a large farmhouse. Even in its heyday it seems to have fallen somewhere between being a fortified manor house and a small castle. Today it consists of a long, narrow, rectangular building with a square tower at the north-east corner and a seventeenth century extension at the north-west corner. This structure was probably always the main residential part of the castle, forming the eastern side of a walled quadrangle and the overall impression is of height and solidity. There are traces of two other towers on the eastern side of the castle, one in the centre and one at the southern end. The roof is now thatched and, at 330 square yards, is believed to be the largest area of thatch on an inhabited house in the country.

Woodsford Castle is tucked away on a narrow back road to the east of Dorchester, which passes a few farms and cottages on its way to the main road leading from Warmwell to Bere Regis. However, when the castle was built, it was near a ford across the River Frome and the track leading to the crossing ran alongside it. The ford was not important enough in its own right to require a defensive castle, but in the fourteenth century the surrounding area was subject to French coastal raids – most famously at Ringstead where the church was burnt down whilst its priest stood at the altar.

There is no information on who may have owned Woodsford before the Conquest, but in 1086, as recorded in the Domesday Book, it was held by William Belet, one of the King's Sergeants (a Sergeant was a man at arms who attended a knight or served in the knight's place). William was listed as a tenant-in-chief in Hampshire, which means that he held his land there directly from the king. In Dorset he had eleven hides and five virgates of land (approximately 1200 acres), which included Woodsford. The average knight's fee in Dorset was only one and a half hides, so it seems that William was richly rewarded for his services and it is likely that he was part of the Conqueror's personal retinue. Descendants of William continued to be influential landowners in Dorset and held Woodsford for almost two hundred years.

By 1320 it was the property of the de Whitefield family, who had probably bought the manor from William Belet in the previous century. In 1317, John Belet accused a group of men, including William de Whitefield, of stealing goods and chattels from his estates at Wyrdesford Belet. Ten years later William de Whitefield accused Belet of leading a gang who

WOODSFORD CASTLE. The castle in the nineteenth century, after its restoration by Lord Ilchester and when let to 'gentleman' farmers.

WOODSFORD CASTLE. The north side of the castle.

stole 100 oxen and 1000 sheep and felled trees and fished ponds on his estates. Within three years the two men had joined forces and were jointly accused of robbing Bindon Abbey of 100 oxen and 7000 sheep, as well as seals, documents and deeds.

In 1335 William de Whitefield was given permission by the king to fortify his manor house at Woodsford, partly because of the continued threat from the French, but also because robbery and lawlessness were then common throughout Dorset, as in the rest of the country. In 1367 Woodsford gained an illustrious new owner, Sir Guy de Brian, a famous soldier, and a personal friend of Edward III. He came from a modest background, his family being minor aristocracy with estates in South Devon and Pembrokeshire and he had begun his career in a fairly humble position in the royal household. He rose to hold many important offices, including Steward of the Royal Household, Keeper of the Great Seal, Standard Bearer to the King, Admiral of the West and Knight of the Garter. His name appears repeatedly in the State Papers of Edward III and his grandson, Richard II. The historian R.G.F. Stanes describes him as, 'a typical product of the century he so nearly spanned, a soldier and able administrator, a courtier, using his position to build up a considerable property and fortune, he must have been a brave and at the same time charming man to have won his way so completely into King Edward's favour, no mean judge of men. At the same time a man of integrity and good counsel to have been so well liked and trusted not only by his fellow nobility but by the commons of the realm'.

In 1335 de Brian was made Keeper of the Forest of Bere, then a royal hunting ground surrounding Bere Regis. The appointment may have had some bearing on his choice of Woodsford as the site for 'a little castle of his own' and he gradually bought considerable estates in Dorset. On acquiring Woodsford in 1367, he began to alter and enlarge it to suit his own requirements. The result was a walled quadrangle, probably with a gatehouse on the west and another gate on the north, towers at the outer corners and smaller towers and turrets in between.

There was a residential range on the east side, consisting internally of a main dwelling at either end, each with its own kitchen and two smaller sets of rooms in between, and perhaps also a Great Hall. This range, although much altered, is virtually all that survives from this period and constitutes the basis of Woodsford Castle as it is today. The beautiful chapel piscina, various window openings, doorways and fireplaces, particularly the huge one in the kitchen, and, more humbly, the garderobes in the north-east tower, all date from Sir Guy's time. Although it is unlikely that he lived there for any length of time, he must certainly have stayed there, raising the possibility that little Woodsford was once host to those involved in the great affairs of state in the fourteenth century.

Sir Guy lived to an extraordinary age for his time, when he died in August 1390 he was about eighty-three. Woodsford Castle is the only building still standing which can be reliably linked to him. This, together with his splendid tomb in Tewkesbury Abbey and his stall-plate in St George's Chapel Windsor as one of the earliest Knights of the Garter, commemorates a man of outstanding talent and one of the dominant figures of the mid fourteenth century.

Two of Sir Guy's three sons predeceased him and

WOODSFORD CASTLE. The south front of the castle, originally one side of an enclosed courtyard.

the third died in 1395 but his eldest son had two daughters who inherited the de Brian estates. Elizabeth, who married Richard Lovell, inherited half of the estate, including Woodsford, and later also inherited her sister's half, thus reuniting the estate under one owner. Elizabeth only had one child, a daughter, Matilda, who married Sir Richard Stafford, a relation of the Duke of Buckingham, but once again the outcome of this marriage was an only daughter, Avice. She married Sir James Ormond, who was created Earl of Wiltshire by Henry VI and had a reputation for being particularly grasping and ambitious.

Ormond changed the terms of the inheritance so that if Avice should die childless he would inherit the de Brian estate, of which Woodsford was only a small part, rather than her Stafford relatives who were the rightful heirs. Avice did indeed die childless but Ormond did not benefit from her inheritance as he was executed after the Battle of Towton in 1461 for supporting Henry VI.

Thereafter the ownership of the estate becomes extremely complicated with claims and counter claims between the Earl of Northumberland and the Earl of Ormond, brother of the executed James. However, by then Woodsford had been occupied for at least twenty years by the Strangways as heirs of Humphrey Stafford and continued to be so. This seems to have been the result of a transfer of the ownership of Woodsford to the Staffords by Elizabeth Lovell, perhaps at the time of her daughter's marriage. Whatever the details, Woodsford remained the property of the

Strangways until it was sold to the Landmark Trust in 1977.

Thomas Strangways came originally from Lancashire, arriving in Dorset in the household of the Marquess of Dorset. In 1460 he married Alianor, heiress of Humphrey Stafford thus establishing himself as a landowner in the county. During the 1530's, what was by then known as Woodsford Strangways, was settled on Thomas Symonds, who was, according to Hutchins, the illegitimate son of Giles Strangways, who rebuilt Melbury in the 1530's. The family prospered and bought more land in the area. By 1596 Thomas was living in Gloucestershire at another of their properties. It seems that the castle was abandoned, although the farm was still let, and in 1630 Coker describes it as 'almost ruinated'. He also repeats a tradition that the castle was 'beseiged and beaten down by ordnance' but there seems to be no evidence either for or against this and it is far more likely that simple neglect was responsible for its condition.

Woodsford was still a working farm producing an income and in 1649 it was settled on two daughters of another Sir John Strangways. In about 1660 the main surviving range of the castle was put in order and the farm again let to tenants. It was at this time that it lost its battlements and gained its massive thatched roof.

In 1850-53 restoration work was again carried out on behalf of Lord Ilchester, who employed as his architect, John Hicks of Dorchester. Hicks' main claim to fame is that Thomas Hardy was his pupil. Hardy himself said that he owed his place in Hicks' office to Woodsford Castle, where his father was employed as a builder. Hicks suggested that Thomas help with a survey of the castle as a test of his abilities and on the strength of it, in 1856 when he was sixteen, he was taken on for a three year pupilage. Hicks' work was skilfully done. He removed all additions and lean-tos on the east and north sides and reopened and restored medieval doors and windows on the west front and the north end. He also returned the 'Queen's Room' and the guard room to their full height by removing the seventeenth century floor.

In the wake of the improvements, Woodsford was let to a succession of tenants who might be called gentlemen farmers. Men like Thomas Lee, who took the lease in 1898 and remained there until 1934, farming some 2000 acres. During this time Thomas Hardy was a regular visitor. In the 1930's much of the land was separated from the house, which was then let to Ralph Bond of Tyneham, who lived there until 1938. Tenants continued to come and go until in 1967, Mr. & Mrs. George Sherwood, the last tenants, ran a pig farm on the remaining fields attached to the house. They remained until 1987, although in 1977 the Landmark Trust purchased the castle.

At that time the enormous thatched roof was in appalling condition and in danger of collapse. Renewing it was a huge undertaking and this may well have encouraged the Strangways estate to sell. Essential repairs, including the roof, were undertaken immediately, but it was not until the Sherwoods left in 1987 that the alterations and restoration necessary to allow it to be let as a holiday property began. The steps to the main west door were rebuilt and the lower door beside it blocked. The 'King's Room' was restored to its full height with a new oak ceiling; and a new stone floor was laid in the 'Queen's Room', chapel and chapel lobby. A new kitchen and bathrooms were created and landscaping and tree planting carried out. The majority of the restoration work was carried out by two local craftsmen, Leonard Hardy and, latterly, Andrew Coward and was completed in June 1992.

The castle is now let as a holiday property by the Landmark Trust and the income generated helps to preserve it and other notable historic buildings for future generations. Once a year it is open to the public.

Woolland Manor

DESCEND FROM Bulbarrow down Woolland Hill towards the tiny hamlet of Woolland and the Manor House lies tucked into the side of the valley at the very beginning of the village. It is almost hidden from view and is dominated by the little church and venerable yew tree on the slope facing it. The yew is massive and must be one of the most ancient in the country: a certificate inside the church claims it is 2,000 years old!

The house is of two storeys, built of warm, honey-coloured stone with tiled roofs. The old part of the house is a straight north/south range, which was once part of a larger L-shaped house, probably built

WOOLLAND MANOR. The late sixteenth or early seventeenth century north east front.

The memorial brass to Mary Argenton in Woolland Church.

in the late sixteenth or early seventeenth century. There is a nineteenth century addition to the west and south and a twentieth century addition at the rear. The central porch and main door came from the old church, built in 1743, which was demolished and rebuilt in the mid nineteenth century. Behind the house, facing west, is a garden enclosed by old stone walls, which has a deep sense of peace. Perhaps its long association with Milton Abbey contributes to the atmosphere still sensed there.

The earliest mention of Woolland seems to be in 939, when King Athelstan signed a charter giving five hides of land in Wonlonde to the Abbey of Middleton. This was duly noted in the Domesday Book and confirmed by King Henry I. It remained the property of the Abbey until, in 1540, Henry VIII granted the manor and grange to William Thornhull. The Thornhull family was one of the oldest in the county and was said to have arrived with William the Conqueror. It is probable that either William Thornhull or his son Robert built the house, although it is likely that there was an older dwelling on the site.

Robert died in 1573 leaving the manor to his wife Mary for her lifetime and then jointly to his two sons, Thomas and Jerom. Mary remarried and became Mary Argenton and when she died in 1616 a brass memorial tablet was erected in the church, which still survives in spite of the church being twice rebuilt. This refers to her as 'our landladie loved of all' and praises her generous hospitality, blameless life and religious observance before reminding the reader that she was first Williams then Thornhull and only finally Argenton. Local folklore relates that at one time two brothers inherited Woolland between them and, being unable to agree which one should live in the house, decided to take it in turn. This arrangement apparently led to endless recriminations at every changeover. Could this possibly be Thomas and Jerom?

In 1731 Henry Thornhull sold the manor to John Gannet of Blandford. It must therefore have been John Gannet who was responsible for the first rebuilding of the church in 1743, 'it being ancient and ruinous'. He had five daughters but no sons and Woolland was bequeathed to John Feaver, his grandson by his eldest daughter Mary. John married Catherine Aust and in 1772 he built a new house to the east of the church. The main part of the old house was then pulled down and the remainder used as a farmhouse.

John died in 1788 at the early age of thirty-four but his wife survived him until 1839. The estate was then inherited by their daughter, Catherine, whose second husband, Colonel George Colby Loftus 'improved and embellished' John Feaver's new house, impoverishing himself in the process, and so in 1852 the property was sold to Mrs. Williams, who handed it over to her son, Montague. The old manor house was refurbished and turned into a rectory, known as 'The Parsonage', and in 1856 Montague Williams had the church demolished and rebuilt, entirely at his

WOOLLAND MANOR The central porch and door came from the eighteenth century church, which was demolished and rebuilt in Victorian times.

own expense, to a design by Gilbert Scott.

Montague Williams died in 1890 and was succeeded by his son, whose large family included eight sons, all but one of whom served in the First World War. The eldest son, Charles was killed at Arras. One daughter, Agnes, remained single and lived in the old manor house throughout the Second World War until 1958 when she moved to Blandford, where she lived until her death in the 1990s. The 'new' house was demolished in 1963, leaving only the stables and some ancillary buildings, which were lived in until her death by the artist, Dame Elisabeth Frink.

By 1965 the old manor house was in a state of considerable disrepair, having been empty for seven years, and John Scott Williams sold it to Mr. and Mrs. Verrinder, who carried out much needed repair and restoration work. Thirty-one years later, after her husband's death, Mrs. Verrinder sold the Manor House to Mr. and Mrs. Andrew Horsey, who have completed the restoration of the house and laid out a beautiful garden that mirrors the intimacy of the house and its setting.

Wraxall Manor

A DELIGHTFUL MEDLEY of fully-grown trees lines the road out of Higher Wraxall, more reminiscent of a private driveway than a country lane. The house soon appears on the left surrounded by farm buildings, and then we catch a view of the front with its four gables, each with windows of four transomed lights. Interestingly, each gable is crowned with a chimneystack. The centre porch has an upper storey with a three light window and a pinnacle on the gable. Altogether this symmetry presents a pleasing picture. Built early in the seventeenth century, probably by William Laurence, the interior has been greatly altered through the centuries, but the area of the hall and staircase still retains its former grandeur, with the wide sweeping staircase leading to the upper landing. Several of the original stone fireplaces are still in situ, and a bedroom retains some handsome eighteenth century panelling.

Originally the house was in two blocks, joined together in more recent times. The loggia on the south west side of the main block was constructed from ceiling beams taken from other parts of the house. The block towards the south west, known as the chapel, has a three light window which could certainly date from the fifteenth century.

At Domesday the land was held by Roger de Arundel and known as Brocheshale. In the thirteenth century it passed to William de Deneys and his descendants, then through the Fitzpain family until, around 1483, the manor passed to Sir William St Maure, whose descendant, Joan, in the sixteenth century divided the manor between her nephews, John Stawel and Edward Bampfield. It remained divided until the early 1800s.

WRAXALL MANOR. Built around 1620 by William Laurence.

WRAXALL MANOR. Its symmetry is enhanced by the chimneystacks on each gable.

Sir John Stawel was a Royalist. From 1645-52 his rents from the manor were confiscated and, in 1652, his part of the estate was purchased by the Parliamentarian, William Laurence, who was born on the estate in 1611 when his father was lessee of a farm there. From Trinity College, Oxford, William was called to the bar at Middle Temple and became an eminent lawyer. In 1649 he married Martha Sydenham of Wynford Eagle. He was appointed as a judge in Scotland in 1653 and three years later, 1656, he stood for parliament and was elected M.P. for the Isle of Wight.

At the Restoration in 1660, William returned to his law practice and vowed allegiance to Charles II. His married life, though, was less than harmonious. His wife, 'a red haired buxom woman', provoked him into writing *Marriage by the Morall Law of God vindicated against all Ceremonial Laws of Popes and Bishops destructive to Filiation, Aliment, and Succession, and the Government of Familyes and Kingdomes*.

It has been suggested that he wrote the book 'upon a discontent arising from his wife, whom he esteemed dishonest to him'. In the following year he wrote another book in which he argued in support of the succession of the Duke of Monmouth. He died in the same year, 1681, and was buried in Wraxall church. He wrote his own epitaph in a descriptive poetic style, which alone makes a visit to the church worth while.

'Welcome dere death let sweetest sleep here take me
In thy cool shades and never more awake mee
Like a rich cortege draw thy darkness round
Like a closed Chamber make my grave profound
In it I'le couch secure no dreames affrights
A silent lodger here no cares dare bite'

Sometime after the Restoration William returned to the Stawel family their half of the estate, but in about 1688 the then Lord John Stawel ran into debt and his portion was sold yet again, this time to Francis Bennet of Merrifield. Within a hundred years it returned once more to the Stawel family, and Baroness Stawel, who died in 1780, passed it to her son Henry. In 1816 he bought the Bampfield's half, finally uniting the estate after three hundred years.

In 1904, Mr. and Mrs. William Busk purchased the house from John Lord Sherborn adding the stables and other outbuildings. Between 1934 and 1937 it belonged to Mr. and Mrs. Ruskin, who were Americans and joint masters of The Cattistock. During the Second World War the army requisitioned the house and King George VI visited the troops billeted there just before D-Day in 1944. At that time Mrs. Le Poer Trench was the owner. From 1947-85 it belonged to Mrs. E. L. Inchbald and Colonel D. S. Branson. Mrs. Inchbald's daughter Gillian married Sir Stephen Hammick, who was High Sheriff in 1981, and together they ran Lower Wraxall Farm. It was afterwards purchased by Mr. and Mrs. Stuart Boyd.

Wynford Eagle Manor

WYNFORD EAGLE MANOR is best approached along a narrow country lane leading south from Maiden Newton along the valley created by a small tributary of the River Frome. About three miles from the town, where the road forks, is the little cluster of cottages and farm buildings, which together with the church of St Lawrence and the manor house, form the tiny hamlet. One fork passes the house and church and eventually leads to Eggardon Hill, whilst the other continues to the equally tiny hamlet of West Compton and on up to the old Roman road along the Ridgeway.

The suffix Eagle became attached to the earlier name of Wenfrot in Norman times, when it became part of the huge estates later known as 'The Honour of the Eagle', granted to Gilbert de Aquila, who held Pevensey Castle for William the Conqueror. Mounted in the outer wall of the church, beside the door, is a small Ham stone tympanum, carved with two wyverns, the emblem of the ancient Royal House of Wessex, and inscribed with the legend 'MAHALD DE L'EGELE' and 'ALVI ME FECIT', which translates as 'Maud of the Eagle' and 'Alvi made me'. The interesting conjunction of the Norman title and the Saxon emblem on what was possibly the door lintel of the original Norman church, suggests a possible illustrious Saxon ancestry for Maud.

The house is built of warm, yellow, local stone with tiled roofs, although there are indications that it may originally have been thatched. It is an imposing building, whose main west front has a central three-storey porch with symmetrical gables on either side. Surmounting the porch is a stone eagle, a Victorian successor to the original, whose partial remains, much eroded and sadly headless, were found quite recently in the garden.

Lord Wynford, the present owner, says that in the course of restoration work inside the house it became apparent that the layouts of the rooms on either side of the porch were symmetrical. Several original fireplaces have been uncovered. Beside one of these, in a bedroom, is a square wall niche designed for drying wigs. A blocked doorway has also been discovered at the north end of the room to the left of the porch. This seems to connect at right angles with another blocked doorway, the lintel of which can be seen in the middle of the exterior north wall. Heavy-duty hinge brackets in the door-jamb suggest a strong external door, so perhaps originally there was a porch or lobby of some kind here.

William Sydenham's great grandfather, Thomas, had bought the estate in 1544 and in 1630 William built the main part of the present house, which still contains much beautiful seventeenth century panelling. At the eastern end is a smaller, earlier,

WYNFORD EAGLE MANOR. The house in the early nineteenth century.

building now attached to the main house. The Sydenhams were strong supporters of Parliament and the style of the house, a handsome, substantial, family home with no unnecessary ostentation, seems to reflect their outlook.

During the reign of Henry I, Gilbert De Aquila's estates reverted to the king and thereafter were granted by the Crown to a succession of nobles, until, in 1544 the then owner, Lord Zouch and St Maur sold his estates, including Wynford Eagle, to Thomas Sydenham, who came from Dulverton in Somerset. The Sydenham family was to be deeply involved in the cataclysmic events of the seventeenth century, both militarily and politically.

William Sydenham inherited the estate from his grandfather in 1607 at the age of about fourteen, his own father having died before he was a year old. In 1611 he married Mary Jeffrey of Catherston and they had seven sons, five of whom survived to adulthood, and three daughters. When William was building his fine new house at Wynford Eagle during the 1630s, he can have had no premonition of the heroism, tragedy, fame and disgrace, which the future held for his family. All the men took up arms for Parliament in the Civil War and were involved in hostilities across the length and breadth of Dorset and further afield for the duration.

Tragically, the first casualty of the fighting was William's wife, who was killed in front of the house in August 1644 by a Major Williams, whilst attempting to deny entry to a raiding party of Royalist soldiers. At the time three of her sons were involved in the successful defence of Dorchester against a Royalist attack, so perhaps the raid on Wynford Eagle was retaliatory. Her death was avenged by her second son, Francis in November of the same year. He recognised the murderer in a troop of Royalists whom he had routed from an attack on Poole and pursued as far as Dorchester. There he rode up to Williams and shot him dead. Francis went on to serve with great distinction in the Parliamentary forces until he was killed in action in 1645, serving under his brother William, who was then military governor of Weymouth and Melcombe Regis.

William had a distinguished career in the army and politics. In the summer of 1643 he was part of the besieging force attempting to take Corfe Castle. When the commander of the force, Sir Walter Erle, fled in the face of a large approaching Royalist relief force, Captain Sydenham was left to extricate his men from almost undoubted slaughter. He fought a skilful rearguard action all the way to Swanage and then evacuated his men by boat back to the Parliamentary stronghold of Poole.

In 1644 he was made governor of Weymouth and Melcombe Regis, where there was much bitter fighting. In 1649 he was appointed Governor of the Isle of Wight, in 1653 was a member of Cromwell's Council of State and the following year was also appointed Commissioner of the Treasury. These two appointments earned him the sum of £2000 per annum, a princely salary in those days. A contemporary wrote of him, 'He was one of the most brilliant men of the day and had a paramount influence in the Councils of the Parliaments only second to that of Oliver Cromwell.'

At the Restoration Sydenham was listed as one of the twelve most dangerous men in the Kingdom and was permanently barred from office. It was probably only the fact that he had been opposed to the execution of Charles I that saved his property and possibly his life. In failing health, he returned to Wynford Eagle where he died in August 1661, aged 46, leaving a wife and five children. He had lost three of his four brothers to the Civil War, leaving only Thomas, who had been wounded but survived and returned to his studies at Oxford. Only two months later, at the beginning of November, his father followed him to the grave, leaving William's twenty-one year old son, also William, to inherit Wynford Eagle.

The surviving brother,Thomas became an eminent physician, whom later generations called 'the father of modern medicine'. His philosophy was that 'the art of medicine is to be properly learned only from its practice'. This principle of observation and study, revolutionary at the time, led to the first clinical descriptions of many diseases, including scarlet fever, pleurisy and gout; the latter being of

Above WYNFORD EAGLE MANOR. The west front, showing the three storey porch and matching gables.

Right Thomas Sydenham (1624-1689), 'the father of modern medicine.'

particular interest to him as he was a lifelong sufferer. A colleague described him as 'the prince of practical medicine, whose character is as beautiful and as genuinely English as his name'. He died in 1689 without receiving any honours from either the Royal Society or the Royal College of Physicians, but his marble bust now graces the front lobby of The Royal College of Physicians.

In 1662 William married Martha Michel of Kingston Russell and they had a family of two sons and two daughters. William achieved high office, becoming Squire of the Body to King William III, but his inheritance had been greatly reduced as much of the family wealth had been expended in the Civil War and by the early 1690s he was deeply in debt. By this time both his sons had died and he had been mortgaging the estates for several years.

In 1699 William decided to run a private lottery, then quite a fashion, in the hope of solving his financial problems. The lottery was known as a land lottery and the prizes were parts of the Wynford Eagle estate. Winners could take the cash equivalent or the annual income from the land, but the main prize was the manor house itself. Two hundred thousand tickets at 5s each were to be sold, which would raise £50,000, £4,000 of which was to be deducted for expenses and prizes to the value of £20,000 awarded, leaving William with a profit of about £26,000 if all the tickets were sold.

Earlier that year a young woman called Ann Michel, a distant relative, had come to live at Wynford Eagle as companion cum servant to Martha, William's wife. She bought the winning ticket and contemporary accounts suggested that William had arranged a fraud so that she would win and then return the property to him for a consideration. Quite how this would be possible is difficult to see, as the draw was held in public at the Mercer's Hall in London, supervised by independent trustees and with the tickets and prizes actually drawn by Blue-Coat boys from Christ's Hospital.

Ann married William's brother-in-law, Doyly Michel (immediately after the lottery according to contemporary reports, although there seems to be no documentary evidence for this) and William refused to hand over the deeds of the house to her. William was never charged with fraud, only with failing to hand over the main prize, the other prize winners having apparently received their dues, and it was for this offence that he and his two daughters were committed to Dorchester prison in 1709. In that year private lotteries were abolished in England. His daughters were later released but William died in gaol in 1718, a sad end to a distinguished family.

When Doyley Michel finally gained possession of the estate he almost immediately sold it to George Richards of Long Bredy. The truth of the affair has never really been established, but various members of the Michel family were involved as mortgagees of the estate and it all seems to have been a very murky business.

In the early nineteenth century Wynford Eagle was bought by William Draper Best, later to become 1st Baron Wynford. He was the son of Thomas Best of Hazelbury Plucknett and was destined for a distinguished career in the law and politics. In 1812 he was MP for Bridport and by 1816 he was Attorney General to the Prince of Wales. In 1824 he was appointed Chief Justice of the Court of Common Pleas and in the same year was admitted to the Privy Council. He was created Baron in 1829 on his retirement from the Bench, taking Wynford as his title, and died in 1845 aged 78.

Since that time the manor and farm have remained in the Wynford family, many of whom have given distinguished service to their country in the armed forces. The present Lord Wynford's father, the 8th Baron, made his career in the Army, being commissioned into the Royal Welsh Fusiliers in 1937. In the Second World War he was severely wounded, losing an arm during the Italian campaign. At the end of the war he was awarded the Croix de Guerre with Silver Star for service with the Free French in North Africa. On his retirement from the Army in 1960 he returned to Dorset and ran the family estate. Despite the loss of his arm, he remained a crack shot. He became Deputy Lieutenant for Dorset and was much involved with the Country Landowners Association. He died in 2002.

During most of the years of the Wynford's ownership of the manor, the house and farm have been let to tenants, the family home being Wynford House a little further up the valley. In the mid 1970s the farm became vacant and in 1981 the present Lord Wynford moved into the Manor House with his family and now runs the farm.

Further Reading

Bailey, C.J., *The Bride Valley,* Dorset County Museum 1982.

Bailey, M., *The English Manor 1200-1500*, Manchester University Press 2002.

Bettey, J.H., *Dorset,* David & Charles 1974.

Bettey, J.H., *Man and the Land, Dorset Farming 1846-1996,* Dorset County Museum.

Cecil, D., *Some Dorset Country Houses*, Dovecote Press 1985.

Country Life Magazine, various articles.

Cullingford, C.N., *A History Of Dorset,* Phillimore, 1980.

Davis, T., *Wareham – Gateway to Purbeck.*

Delderfield, E.R., *West Country Historic Houses,* vol.2, David & Charles 1970.

Gardiner, D., *Companion into Dorset,* Methuen, 1937.

Goodwin, T., *Dorset in the Civil War,* Dorset Books 1996.

Heath, S. and Prideaux, W. de C., *Some Dorset Manor Houses,* Bemrose & Sons 1907.

Henderson, P., *The Tudor House and Garden,* Yale University Press.

Hine, R., *History of Beaminster*, 1914.

Hoskins, W.G., *The Making of the English Landscape,* Penguin.

Hutchins, J., *History and Antiquities of Dorset,* 3rd edition, Nichols & Sons 1861.

Hyland, P., *Purbeck, The Ingrained Island*, Dovecote Press 1978.

Kaufmann, H.A., *The Conscientious Cavalier,* Cape 1962.

Lewer, D. and Small, D., *Swanage Past,* Phillimore 1994.

Lloyd, R., *Dorset Elizabethans*, John Murray 1967.

Miller, A., *The Monasteries of Dorset,* Albemarle Books 1999.

Newman, J. and Pevsner, N., *The Buildings of England, Dorset,* Penguin.

Ollard, R., *Dorset,* Dovecote Press 1995.

Oswald, A., *Country Houses of Dorset,* Country Life 1959.

Pafford, J., *John Clavell 1601-43*, Leopard's Head Press 1993.

Proceedings of the Dorset Natural History and Archaeological Society, various articles.

Robinson, C.E., *Picturesque Rambles in the Isle of Purbeck*, London 1882.

Ryder, R.D., *The Calcrafts of Rempstone Hall*, Halsgrove 2005.

Somerset and Dorset Notes and Queries, various articles.

Speed, P., *Dorset, A County History*, Countryside Books 1994.

Taylor, C., *Dorset, (Making of the English Landscape)* Dovecote Press 2004.

The Royal Commission on Historic Monuments: *County of Dorset.*

White, J.D., *Reminiscences of English Country Life,* 1928.

Wood, M., *The English Medieval House,* Bracken Books 1965.

Acknowledgements

FIRST AND FOREMOST, we would like to thank all the owners of the houses who have welcomed us into their homes and been so generous with their time and knowledge. Without their support and encouragement this book would have been much the poorer.

We would like to remind readers that with a few exceptions the houses included in this book are private homes and not accessible to the public. Some do occasionally open their doors, and many open their gardens to help raise for charity.

Our thanks are also due to the patient and helpful staff of the Dorset County Library, Dorchester, the Dorset County Museum, in particular, Judy Lindsay, Gwen Yarker and Sue Taylor, the Dorset History Centre, and David Burnett for his guidance and help to two novice authors.

The following people were kind enough to loan, or allow us access to, documents, pictures, photographs or books in their possession and so our special thanks go to Mrs. J. Bowerman, Mr. and Mrs. S. Boyd, Mr. and Mrs. D. Coombes, Mr. and Mrs. M. Cree, Mrs. W. Crutchley, Mr. and Mrs. D. Edwards, Mr. and Mrs. R. Fielding, Sir John and Lady Grey-Egerton, Mr. and Mrs. A. Hichens, Mr. and Mrs. J. Isaac, Mrs. P. Jaffé, Mr. J. Lane, Mr. and Mrs. J. Kitchener Fellowes, Mr. and Mrs. G. Marking, Mr. and Mrs. O.B. Paine, Mr. H. Ross Skinner, Lady Salisbury, Mr. and Mrs. J. Shackleton, Lady Shaftesbury, Mrs. J. Silavs, Mrs. J. Smith, Miss M. Spencer-Watson, Mr. and Mrs. A. Thompson, Mrs. P. Thorniley, Mr. P. Ventham, Mrs. Verrinder, Mr. and Mrs. N. Viney, Mr. and Mrs. I. Wainwright, Mr A. Walbridge, Sir Philip and Lady Williams, Mr. R. Williams, Lt. Colonel J. Woodhouse.

We would also like to thank the following for allowing us to use illustrations in their possession or for which they hold the copyright: Merle and Alan Graham: page 1, 2/3, 9, 15, 17, 23 bottom, 28 both, 29, 31, 32 left, 34, 35 top, 36, 37, 39, 41, 45 top, 46/47, 48, 50, 51, 53 both, 55, 56, 57, 59, 61, 68, 71, 72, 73, 75, 76, 77 both, 78, 79 lower right, 80, 82 both, 85, 86, 87 both, 88 bottom, 91, 92, 93, 95, 96, 97, 98 top, 99 top, 100, 102, 105, 106, 108/109, 111, 113, 115, 116, 117, 118, 119, 120/121, 124 left, 125, 126, 131, 132 both, 133, 134, 135, 137, 140, 141, 148, 149 both, 151, 152, 155, 159 both, 165, 169, 171, 177, 179, 180, 181, 182, 183, 185, 187, 191, 194, 204, 205 both, 207, 208 bottom, 209, 210, 211, 212, 215, 218 top, 219, 221, 224, 227, 229, 230, 232, 235, 236/237, 238, 241, 244, 246, 248, 249, 251, 249, 251, 253, 254, 255, 257 both, 259, 261 both, 262/263, 264 both, 269, 271, 272, 273, 276 top; David Bailey: page 162 top; The British Library: page 186; *Country Life*: page 200 top left & top right; Dorset County Museum: page 18, 20, 24 both, 33, 35 bottom, 42, 45, 70, 79 left, 104, 127, 143, 193 left, 213, 228, 233, 256, 258 bottom, 265, 274, 276 bottom; page 99 bottom by permission of The Linnean Society of London; The National Maritime Museum: page 122; The National Portrait Gallery, London: page 145 both; Una Russell: page 10, 23 top, 25 both, 43, 88 top, 89, 90, 128, 129, 130, 243, 245, 255, 266, 267; Savilles (Jon Stone): page 172/173, 175; The Dovecote Press collection: page 4, 8, 11, 12, 19, 27, 32, 40, 52, 58 both, 62 both, 63, 64 both, 65, 66, 67, 79 right top, 81, 84, 94, 98, 101, 110, 123, 124 right, 136, 139, 147 both, 150, 156, 157, 160, 161, 162 bottom, 163, 164, 167, 188, 189 both, 190, 192, 193, 196, 197, 198, 199, 200 bottom, 201, 206, 208 top, 217 both, 218 bottom, 231, 250, 252, 258 top. We are also grateful to Christopher Chaplin for drawing the map on page 13.

Index